WJEC Psychology

for A2

Andy Favager and Dot Blakemore

Edited by John Griffin

HODDER
EDUCATION
AN HACHETTE UK COMPANY

Orders: please contact Bookpoint Ltd, 130 Milton Park, Abingdon, Oxon OX14 4SB. Telephone: (44) 01235 827720. Fax: (44) 01235 400454. Lines are open from 9.00–5.00, Monday to Saturday, with a 24 hour message answering service. You can also order through our website www.hoddereducation.co.uk

If you have any comments to make about this, or any of our other titles, please send them to educationenquiries@hodder.co.uk

British Library Cataloguing in Publication Data
A catalogue record for this title is available from the British Library

ISBN: 978 1 444 13750 7

First Published 2011
Impression number 10 9 8 7 6 5 4 3 2 1
Year   2015, 2014, 2013, 2012, 2011

Copyright © 2011 Andy Favager and Dot Blakemore

Hachette Livre UK's policy is to use papers that are natural, renewable and recyclable products and made fromwood grown in sustainable forests. The logging and manufacturing processes are expected to conform to the environmental regulations of the country of origin.

Cover photo © Troyka – Fotolia.com
Illustrations by Barking Dog Art
Typeset by Fakenham Prepress Solutions, Fakenham, Norfolk NR21 8NN
Printed in Italy for Hodder Education, An Hachette UK Company, 338 Euston Road, London NW1 3BH

Contents

Introduction

This book has been written for students following the WJEC A2 Psychology specification.

WJEC A2 Exams

At A2 there are two exams:

PY 3 Research Methods and Issues in Research

This is a 1½ hour written paper, worth 80 marks (40% of the A2 marks, 20% of the whole A Level). It is made up of three sections; A and B contain compulsory questions and in Section C you answer two questions from a choice of three.

PY 4 Controversies, Topics and Applications

This is a 2½ hour written paper, worth 100 marks (60% of the A2 marks, 30% of the whole A Level).

PY 4 contains three sections. In Section A you will answer one question from a choice of two about controversies and issues in psychology. In Section B and Section C you must answer one question from each section and one additional question. Section B tests your ability to describe, analyse and evaluate topics within psychology. In Section C you must focus on applications of psychological research. The areas of the specification relating to each Section of the PY 4 exam are shown in Table 0.1.

Table 0.1 Areas covered by the sections of the PY 4 exam

CONTROVERSIES (SECTION A)	TOPICS (SECTION B)	APPLICATIONS (SECTION C)
• The status of psychology as a science	• Memory	• Health psychology
• The balance of scientific benefits measured against ethical costs in psychology	• Relationships	• Educational psychology
• The balance of genetic and environmental influences on human behaviour	• Intelligence	• Forensic psychology
• Issues of cultural bias in psychology	• Adolescence and adulthood	• Sport psychology
• Issues of gender bias in psychology	• Levels of consciousness	• Abnormal psychology
• The question of free will and determinism in respect of human behaviour		

Assessment objectives

The exam questions are designed to test your skills, in particular those identified in the assessment objectives:

- Assessment objective 1 (AO1): this tests how well you understand and can describe theories, studies, concepts and research methods and how effectively you can communicate this knowledge.

- Assessment objective 2 (AO2): this tests how well you can analyse and evaluate psychology principles, perspectives and applications in relation to research issues, debates and controversies.

- Assessment objective 3 (AO3): this measures your understanding of how science works; the issues involved in designing, conducting and reporting psychological investigations reflecting on issues such as ethics, reliability and validity.

Table 0.2 shows the weighting of the assessment objectives across the WJEC psychology specification.

Table 0.2 Weighting of assessment objectives

UNIT	% OF TOTAL MARKS	AO1 %	AO2 %	AO3 %
PY 1	20	8	8	4
PY 2	30	12	12	6
PY 3	20	4.5	6.1	13.6
PY 4	30	10	15.8	4.5
Total	100	32.7	40	27.3

Walk through

The book is made up of 18 chapters, one to seven cover the material you will need to cover for the PY 3 exam, and eight to eighteen cover PY 4. There are regular features throughout the book designed to help you get the most out of your studies:

Objectives

Found at the beginning of each chapter, these outline the part of the specification that will be covered.

Key terms

Clear explanation of important terms and phrases associated with each topic.

Remember!

This feature helps to highlight key points in the text.

Key example

These supplement your learning by providing examples of research studies, or even real life cases, linked to the material you are learning.

Over to you

These are questions and activities designed to help you think more deeply about the material you are studying.

Exam focus

This will give you a detailed look at the structure of the different parts of the exam, as well as providing exam hints and tips and, in the later chapters, exam-style questions.

Evaluation

Preparing you with the information you will need to be able to evaluate key psychological concepts and issues.

Summary

Each chapter ends with an overview of the material in the form of a concept map, this should allow you to see at a glance all the material you have covered.

Picture Credits

The authors and publishers would like to thank the following for the use of photographs in this volume:

Figure 2.2 © PATRICE LATRON / LOOK AT SCIENCES / SCIENCE PHOTO LIBRARY; Figure 2.6 © Jose Manuel Gelpi – Fotolia; Figure 3.4 © Jakub Jirsák – Fotolia; Figure 3.5 © Medical-on-Line / Alamy; Figure 3.6 © Rex Features; Figure 4.1 © Paco Ayala – Fotolia; Figure 4.2 © Junial Enterprises – Fotolia; Figure 7.4 © Rajko Trostorf – Fotolia; Figure 7.5 © Michael Kemp / Alamy; Figure 8.1 © Alexander Raths – Fotolia; Figure 8.2 © Ethno Images, Inc. / Alamy; Figure 8.3 © Stuart Monk – Fotolia; Figure 8.5 © AP / Press Association Images; Figure 9.4 © Ken Tannenbaum NYC 2001 – Fotolia; Figure 9.5 © Rafal Olechowski – Fotolia; Figure 9.6 © Janeczek Piotr – Fotolia; Figure 9.7 © JOHN DEE / Rex Features; Figure 10.3 © Omtapas / Alamy; Figure 10.4 © ParisPhoto – Fotolia; Figure 11.1 © Brebca – Fotolia; Figure 11.03a and b © EDELMANN / SCIENCE PHOTO LIBRARY; Figure 12.2 © iofoto – Fotolia; Figure 12.4 © Freefly – Fotolia; Figure 13.1 © Universal Images / SuperStock; Figure 14.1 © NATIONAL CANCER INSTITUTE / SCIENCE PHOTO LIBRARY; Figure 14.3 © WILL & DENI MCINTYRE / SCIENCE PHOTO LIBRARY; Figure 14.4 © Kovalenko Inna – Fotolia; Figure 15.1 © Juice Images / Alamy; Figure 15.3 © Jennie Hart / Alamy; Figure 15.4 © iofoto – Fotolia; Figure 16.1 © Loren Rodgers – Fotolia; Figure 16.4 © Wellcome Library, London. Wellcome Images; Figure 16.6 © INSTITUT PAOLI-CALMETTES, ISM / SCIENCE PHOTO LIBRARY; Figure 17.1 © Orlando Florin Rosu – Fotolia; Figure 17.3 © Michael Schwarz – Fotolia; Figure 18.2 © Peter Widmann / Alamy; Figure 18.4 © DR. MONTY

BUCHSBAUM, PETER ARNOLD INC. / SCIENCE PHOTO LIBRARY;
Figure 18.5 © sharky1 – Fotolia

1 Introduction to research methods

INTRODUCTION

This chapter discusses how psychologists go about collecting research. It discusses how an idea or question can be posed and, from this, how a research hypothesis can be constructed. The chapter also describes the components that make up any hypothesis and the different types of hypotheses that exist. It also explains the different types of variables that exist, such as extraneous and confounding variables. The chapter then discusses the different kinds of data that can be produced by different research methods, such as quantitative and qualitative data.

The following six chapters cover PY 3, but they clearly build on the information for PY 2 to allow students to further develop their knowledge and application of research methods. At the end of chapter 6, on page 62, you will find an Exam Focus section explaining the structure of the PY 3 exam and giving you some tips about how to tackle it.

OBJECTIVES

The specification requires you to have an awareness of the following:

● Aims and hypotheses (directional, non-directional and null hypotheses).

Methods of investigation

Psychology is the study of the human mind and behaviour. When carrying out research in this area, the psychologist has a range of research methods to choose from:

- laboratory experiments
- field experiments
- natural experiments
- correlations
- observations
- interviews
- questionnaires
- case studies.

Starting your research

Before considering research methods, the researcher must identify the subject area he or she is interested in studying. The researcher gathers data on this chosen area and then narrows the focus of the research to a subtopic or a specific area or idea that he or she is drawn to. For example, the researcher may be interested in the subject of eating disorders. This is a large subject and the researcher may begin researching different disorders, which might lead to a subtopic (e.g. anorexia), a specific area (e.g. biological explanations) or a specific idea (e.g. the role of the media in the increased number of people with anorexia).

This primary research would then lead to the development of a question. The researcher must develop a question for research and also think about the specific aims of the research. What is it trying to prove, and why? Will it benefit society? It is often useful to find out how much research has been done on the chosen topic, because this groundwork can then be used to back up any subsequent research findings. Questions for research could include the effect society has on causing eating disorders. Do more boys than girls have phobias? Are boys more aggressive than girls? Is there a relationship between the weather and people's moods? The choices are endless.

The research question will then lead to a prediction (a hypothesis) that the researcher believes he or she can prove. A hypothesis is a testable research statement that the researcher believes might be true. So the aim of the first part of this planning is to come up with a **hypothesis**.

1. Subject area

2. Subtopic/idea/specific area

3. Question

4. Hypothesis

This testable statement must be clearly expressed – for example, loud noise affects how much information a student can memorise, or noise has a significant effect on how much information a student can memorise.

Key term

Hypothesis – a statement made at the beginning of an investigation that serves as a prediction or an explanation of events. It must be tested and then supported or rejected.

Hypotheses and variables

Most hypotheses have an **independent variable** (IV) and a **dependent variable** (DV) – for example, men have more phobias than women (IV = gender, DV = phobias). The IV is manipulated to see its effect on the DV, which is measured – for example, the effect of noise (IV) on how much information a student can memorise (DV), or the effect of drinking protein drinks (IV) on an athlete's performance when lifting weights (DV). Not every hypothesis has an IV or a DV. For example, in a correlational hypothesis such as 'is there a relationship between age and memory', there is no IV or DV just covariants.

There are two types of hypotheses that you can choose from: **directional** or **non-directional**. A directional hypothesis (also known as a one-tailed hypothesis) predicts the direction in which results are expected to occur. For example, the prediction that boys are stronger than girls only goes one way. A non-directional hypothesis (also known as a two-tailed hypothesis) does not predict the direction the results will go. For example, the prediction that there is a significant difference in strength between boys and girls could go either way.

To take another pair of examples, the hypothesis that men have more phobias than women is directional – the results can only go one way.

There is only one possible outcome.

The hypothesis that gender has an effect on the number of phobias people have, on the other hand, is non-directional – the results can go both ways (e.g. men might have more phobias or women might have more phobias).

There are two possible outcomes.

Once the researcher has stated his or her hypothesis, this is called the **research hypothesis**. The researcher also states the null hypothesis. In the last example above, the null hypothesis would be that gender does not have an effect on the number of phobias a person has.

So there are two hypotheses researchers may determine: either the **null hypothesis** or the **alternative hypothesis** (also known as the experimental hypothesis). Let us use the example hypothesis that noise has a significant effect on how much information a student can memorise. The null

Figure 1.1 Does gender have an effect on the number of phobias people have?

Remember

In fact, it is the null hypothesis that the researcher attempts to investigate, so that he or she can remain objective. When the researcher cannot prove the null hypothesis, then he or she has proved the research hypothesis. When the research hypothesis is proved, it is called the experimental/alternative hypothesis.

Figure 1.2 Both men and women can have phobias

> ### Remember
>
> Once all results from a study are collected they can be subjected to descriptive and inferential analysis. (The results can be shown following statistical analysis, and it can be decided whether to reject or retain the null hypothesis.)

> ### Remember
>
> It is generally the DV that is being measured. This clearly needs to be defined in order to measure it. However, some researchers argue that it is important to define any variable within a study, including the IV.

> ### Remember
>
> Research is often referred to as 'empirical'. This is the experimental collection of data from a representative sample of the population. 'Empirical' tends to be linked to 'experimental', but it can also be applied to data collected through other methods, such as observation. Most experimental methods will have a hypothesis that the researcher will try to prove or disprove, but other non-experimental methods may also begin with a hypothesis (e.g. correlations and observations), while other methods, such as interviews and questionnaires, may just be used to collect an amount of data on a specific topic.

would predict that the results obtained from an investigation are due to chance alone (e.g. loud noise does not have a significant effect on how much information a student can memorise). So the results found may have been caused by a coincidence or random differences between the participants. The task of the researcher is to decide whether to retain or reject the null. The researcher is trying to disprove his or her theory, and when they cannot do so there is only one explanation for the result – the independent variable (e.g. the noise) is responsible for the outcome. The researcher will have proved the theory and can retain the alternative (or experimental) hypothesis and reject the null hypothesis.

Any hypothesis must be stated in precise terms and it must be clearly operationalised – that is, what does the IV mean and what does the DV mean? We need to be able to clearly define the DV in order to measure it. We also need to define the IV clearly so that it can be manipulated. This is because certain terms within psychology are abstract (e.g. 'self-esteem' and 'stress') and are difficult to define. However, with a simple hypothesis such as 'women have lower self-esteem than men' it is obvious to most researchers what is being tested, although some academics still maintain that such a hypothesis needs to be operationalised. What is probably more important is *how* the researcher is going to test the hypothesis.

Most experimental methods and some non–experimental methods rely on control in their attempts to prove/disprove their hypothesis and to demonstrate good validity (accuracy) with their results. This control is exerted by controlling any variables that may affect the results. When these variables cannot be controlled they are called confounding variables.

Variables are divided into three areas:

- the independent variable – what the experimenter is manipulating

> ### Key term
>
> **Operationalisation** – This means how the concept is defined so that it is clearly measurable. For example, in research on an abstract feeling such as anger, it is difficult for outside observers to directly measure the presence and depth of the emotion. It may seem easier to ask the participants themselves how angry they are, but this may not reflect the true nature of their feeling. One person may say they are 'extremely angry' and yet they may only be slightly annoyed, whereas another person may say they are 'slightly annoyed' and be very angry.

- the dependent variable – what the experimenter is measuring after manipulating the independent variable to see its effect on the dependent variable

- extraneous variables.

Extraneous variables are any other variables that might affect the dependent variable. In the case of an experiment, it might be the temperature in the room or the noise in the room. The experimenter would try to control as many of these variables as possible and keep them constant (e.g. constant temperature at all times during the experiment). Controlling these variables becomes harder when the research is non-experimental or carried out outside the lab setting. Unfortunately, even in a lab setting some extraneous variables may not have been controlled and these can affect the results. These variables are known as **confounding variables**.

Confounding variables may influence the behaviour being measured. Let us take the example of a study to test the effect of protein drinks on strength. One group is given the protein drink while another group is not; the strength of both groups is then tested. The group given the protein drink is found to be stronger, therefore proving the hypothesis. Unfortunately, later research finds that all the subjects in the first group, who were given the protein drink, were male, and all those in the second group were female. The results could therefore be put down to gender rather than the drink, so in this case the confounding variable was the gender of the subjects.

> ## Over to you
>
> How would you operationalise (that is measure) anger?

> ### Key term
>
> **Extraneous variables** – any variable other than the IV (being manipulated) that could affect the DV (being measured).

> ### Key term
>
> **Confounding variables** – extraneous variables that have not been controlled and have had an effect on the behaviour being measured.

> ## Key example
>
> The researcher is interested in phobias and their causes. The researcher studies a range of phobias and focuses on specific phobias, such as arachnophobia (fear of spiders). There seems to be a range of explanations for phobias and the researcher decides on the behavioural approach, which states that phobias are learnt. The researcher decides to carry out a correlation to see if there is a relationship between specific phobias and childhood experiences.

Qualitative and quantitative data

So once the researcher has an idea or a hypothesis, he or she has to decide on which research method to choose. Today's psychologist has a range of research methods to choose from, each with its good and bad points. Some methods have good control and allow the researcher to prove or disprove the chosen hypothesis, while other methods have poor control but are better for recording natural behaviour (they have good ecological validity). The research method chosen will therefore depend on the hypothesis and/or the topic being studied. One last point to note is that as we go through the research methods, we will see that some produce **quantitative data** while others produce **qualitative data**.

Key terms

Qualitative data – research findings that are in written or spoken form, generally gained from questionnaires, interviews, observations and case studies. These kinds of data provide rich, detailed information. Many psychologists prefer these data over numbers, which can simply dehumanise research. For example, if a participant has a self-esteem score of 36 out of 100, what does this really tell us? Qualitative data can give us more of an explanation about a person's self-esteem though it can be difficult to analyse; one way of doing so involves turning it into quantitative data, using content analysis, for example.

Quantitative data – data that are numerical in form and are generally gained from experimental and correlational methods. The data are then analysed using descriptive statistics (e.g. the mean) and inferential statistics to see if the results are significant (see page 56). Although less detailed than qualitative data, quantitative data are much easier to analyse and patterns in the data can be identified.

Summary

Methods of investigation

The type of research method you choose depends on your hypothesis. Some methods will have better control than others.

Starting your research

The researcher must choose a subject area he or she is interested in. This can then be narrowed down to a specific subtopic or idea. The researcher must then decide on a question that he or she wants to answer within this area.

Qualitative and quantitative data

Some research methods produce qualitative data, others produce quantitative data. Qualitative data are usually in written or spoken form, generally gained from questionnaires, interviews, observations and case studies. Quantitative data are numerical in form, generally gained from experimental and correlational methods. Quantitative data are much easier to analyse, but are less detailed than qualitative data.

Introduction to research methods

Hypotheses

Once the researcher has decided on a question to answer, he or she must make a prediction. This is the experimental hypothesis: a testable statement that the researcher believes to be true. For example, bullying reduces self-esteem. There also has to be a null hypothesis: in this case, bullying will not affect self-esteem. The researcher must set out to contest the experimental hypothesis.

Extraneous variables

Variables other than the IV and DV, extraneous variables, must be controlled to ensure that they do not affect the outcome of the experiment.

Variables

Every hypothesis must have an independent and a dependent variable. The independent variable is an aspect of the experiment situation that can be manipulated by the researcher to see whether it has an impact on the dependent variable. For example, what impact does light level (the independent variable) have on plant growth (the dependent variable)?

Directional and non-directional hypotheses

A directional hypothesis will predict the direction in which results are expected to occur. For example, bullying will negatively affect self-esteem. A non-directional hypothesis does not predict the direction. For example, bullying will affect self-esteem.

2 Experimental methods

When studying human behaviour, it is often very hard to show cause and effect, but the use of the experimental method allows for this. The use of experimental methods also gives more credence to results and data gained, especially quantitative data, which can be subjected to statistical analysis, allowing hypotheses to be accepted or rejected.

This chapter describes three main experimental methods: the lab experiment, the field experiment and the natural experiment, explaining the advantages and disadvantages of each one, as well as describing and explaining the different terminology associated with experimental methods. This chapter also explains the three different experimental designs that can be used when carrying out an experiment, along with their advantages and disadvantages.

INTRODUCTION

As psychology is developing and advancing all the time, it is making more and more use of a wider range of different research methods. Research methods are the means by which researchers/psychologists can study topics, collect data and prove specific hypotheses. The research methods listed in the following chapters are by no means a full and comprehensive list, but rather they are the main methods used by many psychologists in their research.

This chapter tends to cover the methods that are considered the most scientific in nature, such as the experiment. These methods tend to have good control and therefore allow for cause and effect to be stated. The use of experimental methods, especially the lab experiment, allow the psychologist to collect data in a controlled environment.

OBJECTIVES

The specification requires you to have an awareness of the following:

● Design issues relating to specific research methods and their relative strengths and weaknesses.

Features of experiments

One of the most popular research methods used by psychologists is the experiment. Many psychologists favour this as it is the method that allows for the most control, and therefore shows cause and effect. There are three types of experimental design: **naturalistic, laboratory** and **field**.

Most experiments have three main key features, which include the following:

1 An independent variable is manipulated by the researcher to make a change in the dependent variable (e.g. the effect of noise (IV) on memory (DV)).

2 All other variables which might affect the results are fixed or eliminated (e.g. heat, light, temperature).

3 Participants are allotted to the experimental conditions using the random sampling method.

Remember

Although laboratory experiments generally have all these attributes, other types of experiment may not have all three features and therefore are often considered not to be true experiments, although they still have more control than most other research methods. These experiments are referred to as quasi-experiments; these are similar to true experiments but do not have all the three variables above. With a natural experiment, you carry out research on a naturally occurring event (e.g. the effect of divorce on children) and therefore you cannot allocate participants randomly to the experimental condition as it has occurred naturally. With a field experiment you do not have control over all other variables that might affect the dependent variable because the experiment tales place in a natural setting.

Figure 2.1 An IV is manipulated to study the effect on a DV, such as the effect of noise on memory

The laboratory experiment

This gives the researcher complete control over the experiment and all the variables (or as many as possible); it provides the researcher with the highest level of constraint. A laboratory experiment takes place in a controlled environment where as many variables as possible are controlled. Examples of these variables might include light, temperature and noise – anything that might distract the participants. Examples of laboratory experiments can include studies such as Sherif's (1935) and Asch's (1951) on majority influence.

Figure 2.2 A laboratory is a sterile, controlled environment

Key example

Research study: laboratory experiment

Asch (1951): Effects of group pressure upon the modification and distortion of judgment

Asch (1951) carried out an experiment to investigate whether people would conform in highly unambiguous situations. Asch's study used seven participants, six of whom were confederates. The participants were told to look at a sequence of three lines, A, B and C, and state which line matched the stimulus line X in each case. The line that matched line X was always obvious, but the six confederates were told to say the wrong line. The experimenter wanted to see if the one true participant would change his mind and go along with the group's answer.

Key terms

Laboratory experiment – a study that takes place in an artificial environment where variables being altered and measured are controlled and as many extraneous variables as possible are held constant or eliminated.
Mundane realism – when the artificial situation or activity is made to resemble a real-life situation, giving any study more ecological validity.
Demand characteristics – this is when participants attempt to work out the hypothesis being tested and provide results that they think are expected. The participant looks for cues from the researcher (e.g. tone of voice or body language) or from the questions asked.

Advantages of the laboratory experiment

- A lab experiment can drive the speed of any research; the researcher does not have to wait for an event to happen – he or she can make it happen in a lab.

- Behaviour can be measured with greater precision in the lab than could ever be possible in the outside world.

- All the variables within the lab can be controlled to a certain degree and therefore cause-and-effect relationships can be established.

- Because a lot of extraneous variables can be controlled, the lab experiment has good internal validity (accuracy) and the experimenter can state that the IV had an effect on the DV.

- Because of the good control, a lab experiment has good reliability (consistency) – that is, it can be repeated with the same participants and the same results should occur.

- Experiments can also produce a lot of quantitative data that can be analysed, indicating patterns and trends.

Disadvantages of the laboratory experiment

As the laboratory is an artificial environment, it has no ecological validity (i.e. behaviour observed in a lab may not be generalised to the outside world). Any results gained from a lab experiment are therefore thought to lack relevance to real life. For example, Asch's (1951) study on conformity lacks ecological validity, because in real life you not do sit with a group of people and answer questions about the length of lines on a board. (It also lacks **mundane realism**.)

The lab also puts demands on the subject or subjects, who may act differently in the lab. They might act in the way they think the experimenter expects, for example. This is known as **demand characteristics** and would bias any results. The participants may say things or behave in a way that they think is expected of them.

For example, you are a male participant in a room with an equal number of men and women; you are all shown an action film and then a romantic film and then asked to fill in a questionnaire about which one you preferred. You may actually have preferred the romantic film, but you think that the study is about different

films men and women prefer, so you answer that you preferred the action movie. The results are therefore incorrect. You have not answered the actual question, but given the answer that you think is expected.

The participant may also feel pressured by being in the experiment and concerned that he or she is being judged in some way; this is known as **evaluation apprehension**. The participant may behave in an unnatural way and change his or her behaviour in order to be judged in a positive way.

For example, in an experiment that measures aggression, the participant may not want to be considered aggressive and may therefore change his or her behaviour so as to be viewed in an approving way.

The individual experimenter may also consciously or unconsciously affect the results – for example, the experimenter's personality may have an effect on how the participants behave within the lab setting. This is known as **experimenter effects**.

For example, the experimenter asks participants to fill in a questionnaire on the computer while watching images that flash up on the screen. One participant puts up his hand and says he does not understand what he has to do. The experimenter replies by asking the participant if he is stupid and why he cannot understand basic instructions. By being rude to the participant, the experimenter may create an atmosphere in the lab which influences the behaviour of a specific participant or all the participants. The experimenter may also influence a participant's behaviour in other ways. It has been found that the sex, race, age and physical appearance of an experimenter can have an influence on the behaviour of participants. Many of these influences are unintentional; sometimes an experimenter can cause bias by having their own preconceived ideas about what the results will be and influencing the participants' behaviour through body language and speech (leading to demand characteristics). Consider if any of the following characteristics in an experimenter would have an effect on you if you were taking part in an experiment:

- very good-looking

- extremely overweight

- American

- Chinese

- very old (90)

- very young (20)

- very confident and sure of him- or herself

- very shy and unsure of him- or herself.

A lot of research takes place at universities and most subjects used in lab experiments are university students, which does not provide an accurate representation of the population. The experimenter also has expectations about the outcome of an experiment and may unconsciously pass these to the participants. Also, when analysing the results, the experimenter may interpret them in a way that fits what they would expect.

The lab experiment may also produce ethical issues, such as protection from harm (e.g. participants may become stressed in a lab/artificial setting). Also, many experiments involve the use of deception in order to avoid evaluation apprehension and demand characteristics. Right to withdraw may also be an issue with experiments. Even though participants are told they have a right to withdraw once they begin an experiment, they may believe (rightly or wrongly) that leaving the experiment before the end might disrupt the experimenter's research.

The field experiment

This type of experiment is carried out in a natural setting instead of the artificial setting of the laboratory. This is not regarded as a true experiment as the participants cannot be chosen for the study. Often with a field experiment participants are not aware that they are taking part in an experiment. Instead of the controlled setting of the lab, where the experimenter tests how the IV affects the DV, a field experiment takes place in a more natural setting, such as on the street or in a public park. A key variable is altered so that its effect can be measured. The experimenter creates the situation to be researched and then records participants' reactions to it. For example, the experimenter might test how age affects conformity, where someone old or young stands pointing up at the sky and the experimenter watches to see if other passers-by copy this behaviour. The DV is conformity and IV is age of person affecting the conformity.

Figure 2.3 Research can also take place in a fieldwork setting

Key term

Field experiment – an experiment that takes place in the natural environment.

Advantages of the field experiment

- This method has increased external (ecological) validity as it takes place in the natural setting.

- It is less likely to suffer from demand characteristics, evaluation apprehension or experimenter effects because participants are often unaware that they are taking part in an experiment.

- The experimenter can still control the key variable (IV), so cause–and–effect relationships are still possible.

Disadvantages of the field experiment

- There is a lot less control over the effect of extraneous variables which may cause a change in behaviour (e.g. the DV that is being measured). For example, the weather may have an effect on whether people stop to see what someone is looking up at in the example given above – they are less likely to stop if it is raining heavily.

- The lack of control over extraneous variables means that this method lacks good internal validity.

- The method lacks good reliability – because it is the natural environment, it may be harder to repeat the study and get the same results.

- You cannot control the extraneous variables, which may change from day to day (e.g. the weather, the type of people around, the specific day of the week).

- This method also raises ethical issues, such as deception and lack of informed consent, particularly because participants are often not aware that they are taking part in an experiment.

The natural experiment

Like the field experiment, the natural experiment is not regarded as a true experiment for two reasons: first, the independent variable is not under the absolute control of the experimenter, and second, there is no control over the allotment of participants to each condition of the experiment.

A natural experiment measures variables that have not been manipulated directly. The experimenter exploits a naturally occurring event, but in this case uses differences in the IV but is not controlling or manipulating these differences. One example might be to look at the stress levels of people living in New York after 9/11; the IV is the terrorist attack and the DV is the stress levels of the city dwellers. Another example might be to look at the effect divorce has on children; the IV is whether a child's parents are divorced or not, which happens naturally, and the DV is the effect this has on the child (e.g. the child's behaviour).

Figure 2.4 A natural event is beyond the control of the researcher

Advantages of the natural experiment

- This method has good ecological validity. The behaviour observed should therefore be considered natural; the researcher cannot affect the results because he or she does not intervene directly.

- Like the field experiment, this method is less likely to suffer from demand characteristics, evaluation apprehension or experimenter effects, because participants are often unaware that they are taking part in an experiment.

- There are fewer ethical issues as there is no direct manipulation of variables, which happen naturally. This allows us to study areas that would cause ethical issues if we artificially changed or manipulated them in any way, such as the effect of observed aggression on children. It would be unethical for the researcher to make children watch the aggressive behaviour of others just to measure the effect it has on them.

Disadvantages of the natural experiment

- There is no control at all. The independent variable is not controlled by the experimenter, there is no control over any confounding variables and the participants are not selected by the experimenter. Cause-and-effect relationships are therefore harder to establish.

- This method has poor internal validity. It is impossible to randomly allocate

participants to different conditions as the IV must happen naturally; therefore the participants used may affect the results of the study. For example, if the researcher is looking at the effect of divorce on young children, he or she may find that the behaviour of a group of children from divorced families is more aggressive than the behaviour of children from non-divorced families. The children from the divorced group have not been picked randomly and may naturally be more aggressive, not just because they have experienced divorce.

- Natural experiments are very unreliable because many variables can affect a participant's behaviour. This makes the natural experiment hard to replicate, giving this method poor reliability.

- Some researchers argue that this method is the least likely to cause ethical issues as the changes in the IV are not caused by the experimenter (although informed consent is still needed). However, the issue of protection from harm should be considered. Many natural experiments are based around the effects of natural disasters on people. Researchers who carry out these experiments need to be aware of the upset and stress their research may cause. For example, a researcher might be interested in the effect the 2004 tsunami had on people who survived it. The researcher might hypothesise that the stress levels of people who lived through this disaster and still live in the same area is higher than in those people who have moved away. Accumulating data on such a topic could cause upset for those involved, as it would make them remember what they went through.

Experimental design

Remember

Designs are different from research methods.

When carrying out an experiment you have a choice of three different designs to use, each with its own individual advantages and disadvantages. The three different designs are:

- independent groups design
- repeated measures design
- matched subjects design.

Independent groups design

With this design, different participants are used in each of the experimental conditions. In an experiment you can have a control condition and an experimental condition. An example of this is testing to see whether noise (IV) has an effect on memory recall (DV), the hypothesis being that noise does have an effect on a person's memory recall.

Two groups will be used. Group A will be asked to learn ten words while loud music is played – this is called the experimental condition. Group B will be asked to learn ten words with no music being played – this is the control condition. The independent variable is the noise and the dependent variable is memory recall, in this case measured by how many words are remembered. With this experimental design you can also have no control condition and more than one experimental condition – for example, testing to see whether the type of

music being played or the level of noise has an effect on memory. In this experiment, Group A has loud music played and Group B has soft music played, therefore both are experimental conditions.

In this type of experiment, subjects would be allocated randomly to each of the conditions (see random sampling on page 48) to ensure that participant variables do not differ between each group, which would lead to the results being confounded (e.g. all the subjects in one group are girls and all the others are boys). Although with random sampling you may still end up with all girls in one group and all boys in another, if this did happen then the results might be due to gender rather than noise, meaning that gender would be a confounding variable.

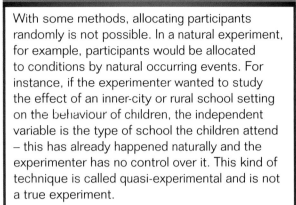

Remember

With some methods, allocating participants randomly is not possible. In a natural experiment, for example, participants would be allocated to conditions by natural occurring events. For instance, if the experimenter wanted to study the effect of an inner-city or rural school setting on the behaviour of children, the independent variable is the type of school the children attend – this has already happened naturally and the experimenter has no control over it. This kind of technique is called quasi-experimental and is not a true experiment.

Advantages of the independent groups design

This design has no problem with order effects, which occur when a subject's performance is positively or negatively affected by taking part in more than one experimental condition (e.g. in the example given above, if the participants' memories were tested more than once they might get better the second time because of practice (positive effect). But order effects could also play a negative role if the subject gets tired or bored when it comes to repeating the test.

Disadvantages of the independent groups design

The potential for error results from individual differences between the groups of participants taking part in different conditions. As in the above example, even though the participants are chosen randomly, it may be, by chance, that all the participants put into Group A may be the same gender or may naturally have better memory than the participants randomly chosen to go into Group B (see sampling on page 47). Therefore it may not be noise/music that affects a person's memory, but individual differences such as whether they simply have a good memory. Another disadvantage with this design is that more participants are needed (compared with repeated measures).

Repeated measures design (within groups or within subjects)

With this method all the participants take part in all conditions of the experiment. In the experiment above to test whether noise affects memory recall, the same participants would be used in the noise condition (experimental) and the no noise condition (control).

Key terms

Independent groups design – two or more groups are used in different conditions of the experiment.
Individual differences – the variables between participants in different experimental conditions may affect the DV instead of the IV.

Figure 2.5 A repeated measures design, with two different experiment conditions

Advantages of the repeated measures design

Individual differences between participants are removed as a potential confounding variable as the same participants are used in all conditions. Also, fewer participants are needed (compared with independent groups).

Disadvantages of the repeated measures design

The main disadvantage with this method is the issue of **order effects**. This design also takes longer to carry out than independent groups, as each condition has to be carried out one at a time.

Matched subjects (participants) design

With this design two separate groups are used – either an experimental and a control or two experimental groups, though an attempt is made to match or relate an equal number of participants in some way. The participants are matched in terms of whatever the experimenter feels might have an effect on their performance and so may counter the effect of the independent variable. For example, the age of the subjects used in the above experiment on how noise affects memory recall may affect the results; to avoid this, the subjects would be matched by age.

Figure 2.6 In a matched subjects design, members of each group are matched on as many variables as possible

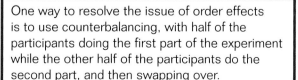

Remember

One way to resolve the issue of order effects is to use counterbalancing, with half of the participants doing the first part of the experiment while the other half of the participants do the second part, and then swapping over.

Advantages of the matched subjects design

This method aims to eliminate the disadvantages from the other two methods – for example, there is no problem with individual differences since subjects are matched and paired up; there is no problem with order effects, as the matched participants each perform in only one part of the experiment (e.g. one member of each pair tries to remember with noise (experimental) and the other member tries to remember without noise (control)).

Disadvantages of the matched subjects design

This method is very time-consuming. It is difficult to match pairs up as you need reliable and valid procedures for pre-testing participants in order to obtain matched pairs.

Another disadvantage is that if one of the participants wishes to drop out, that means the pair must drop out and another pair found.

Over to you

Imagine that you wish to test the hypothesis 'heat makes people stressed'. The experimenter is going to use the matched subjects design for this study and the researcher constructs a list of factors that they feel they need to match up their participants on. Look at the list below and think about what else you might need to match your pairs up by (i.e. what else needs controlling that may make them stressed?):

- Age
- Gender
- Personality
- Financial status

Remember

The question also has to be asked if it is possible to match people up completely. The obvious choice would be to use identical, or monozygotic (MZ), twins, but even these are not 100 per cent the same.

Summary

Experimental design

There are three types of experimental design: lab, field and natural experiments. Most experiments have three key features: an independent and dependent variable, the elimination of extraneous variables, and the selection of participants using random sampling (although remember that in natural experiments it is impossible to select at random).

The laboratory experiment

The advantage of the laboratory experiment is that the researcher is in complete control of proceedings and can eliminate extraneous variables. However, behaviour in a laboratory environment might not reflect that in the real world.

The field experiment

Field experiments have high external validity as they take place in a natural setting, but there is a lower level of control over extraneous variables.

Matched subjects design

Two different groups are used for each scenario, but an attempt is made to match the participants in each group in some way, trying to eliminate both order effects and individual difference. But it is difficult and time-consuming to match people.

Experimental methods

The natural experiment

Like field experiments, natural experiments have high external validity as they take place in a real environment; however, the researcher has no control over the variables and it is difficult to choose participants at random.

Repeated measures design

All participants take part in all the situations, removing individual differences as a confounding variable, but introducing the problem of order effects.

Independent groups design

In this design, a different group of people is used in each of the experiment conditions, eliminating order effects, but outcomes might be affected by individual differences between groups.

3 Non-experimental methods

INTRODUCTION

Non-experimental methods in psychology can still be considered scientific, but they lack the control and manipulation of the lab experiment. This is not to say that some control and manipulation cannot take place, but generally these methods use less manipulation of the specific variables. These research methods tend to produce a lot more detailed qualitative data (except for correlations). Many psychologists support the use of these methods as they allow for a more detailed description and explanation of any behaviour that is being observed. However, the nature of these methods means that the data produced are notoriously difficult to analyse and to use to show cause and effect.

The research methods this chapter covers include observations, interviews, case studies, questionnaires and correlations. This chapter also explains the advantages and disadvantages of each of these research methods, as well as describing and explaining the different terminology associated with non-experimental methods.

OBJECTIVES

The specification requires you to have an awareness of the following:

- Design issues relating to specific research methods and their relative strengths and weaknesses.

Psychological research also involves using methods that are not experimental, although they can still be referred to as scientific.

Observations

The first non-experimental method to be described is the observational method; this is where the deliberate manipulation of variables does not take place. Research methods that are rigorously controlled are criticised on the basis that they are artificial. Naturalistic observations focus on how people or non-human animals behave in the natural environment, with no effort being made to influence the behaviour being studied. However, some naturalistic observations can be laboratory-based, because some animals (e.g. white rats) behave naturally in this kind of artificial setting.

Remember

White rats were bred in laboratories, so this is their natural environment.

A distinction needs to be made here between different types of observational methods. The term **naturalistic observation** involves research methods designed to study behaviour without manipulation of any variables or interference by the experimenter/observer in any way. Another type of observation is **participant observation**, where the observer joins in with the behaviour, participates in the group being studied. In **non-participant observation** (similar to naturalistic observation) the researcher observes from outside the group and tries not to be intrusive in any way; this method may include telling the subjects they are being observed or not telling them and carrying out covert observation.

Key terms

Naturalistic observation – no interference in any way, generally used when studying non-human animals (e.g. wildlife documentaries studying the hunting patterns of lions in Africa).

Participant observation – the observer joins in with the group to be observed (e.g. observing young children playing in a nursery setting, the observer may join in and play too). This can be done in two ways. The researcher either blends in with the group and hides his or her true identity or the observer can be introduced to the group and explain the research to the participants.

Key example

Research study: naturalistic observation

Konrad Lorenz (an ethnologist) was interested in attachments. Lorenz studied certain species of birds, observing them in their natural habitat. Lorenz found that the young of these birds tended to follow the first moving object that they saw when hatching. Lorenz referred to this as 'imprinting', and stated that it occurred within a short critical period after birth and that it is irreversible. Lorenz also stated that imprinting forms a lasting bond between the caregiver and its young.

Finally, it should be noted that researchers can also use controlled observation. This is where participants are observed in an environment that is to some degree governed by the observer. This type of controlled observation can be contrasted with a naturalistic observation, where behaviour is studied within its natural context (e.g. observing squirrels foraging for food in their natural habitat). Observational research is very popular with studies on non-human animals.

With observations it must be clear what is being observed; this often means that the behaviour to be observed or measured must be clearly operationalised (see page 43). Observations also tend to include a time frame – for example, how long behaviour is going to be observed for and at what time of day. The observation is often guided by the use of specific observational categories: an event may be recorded every time it happens (event sampling) or by the frequency of it happening within specific time periods (time sampling).

Remember

An example of a controlled **observation** would be Milgram's (1963) observational study on obedience. A more up-to-date example would be the television programme *Big Brother* (a controlled observation of participants in the Big Brother house), where the environment was controlled and the behaviour was observed. Since the producers of the show tried to manipulate the participants' behaviour by setting them tasks which made them compete against each other, some researchers might argue that the Big Brother house was a kind of experiment – a field experiment or possibly even a lab experiment. But as became clear in many episodes, a lot of what happened could not have been predicted, which goes against the experimental method. This raises an issue with certain studies that have been carried out – that is, the specific method used can be open to interpretation. For example, is observing how secondary school children behave in a classroom a naturalistic observation or a lab experiment? The classroom itself is an artificial environment that is highly controlled.

Key terms

Non-participant observation – the observer studies behaviour without participating. There are two ways to do this: the observer can either be seen to observe the specific group and their behaviour or can remain hidden while studying the behaviour of the group (i.e. naturalistic).

Observation – simply observing and measuring the behaviour of animals and humans, generally in a natural setting with no interference from the researcher.

Figure 3.1 Observing and measuring behaviour usually takes place with no interference from the researcher

Advantages of the observational method

- Good observations can lead to new and appropriate hypotheses for further research. The observation may also lead the researcher to change the hypothesis or the researcher may observe some new kind of behaviour never seen before.

- It is a useful method for studying unknown or little known behaviour.

- Naturalistic observation is good with animals that do not thrive or behave normally in laboratory conditions.

Over to you

Do humans fall into this category?

- This method avoids demand characteristics. The subjects under observation will feel no pressure to impress the observer, especially if it is an undisclosed observation, which also avoids the problems of evaluation apprehension and experimenter effects.

Many psychologists feel that the observational method is the best as it has the most ecological validity, especially naturalistic observation, which observes participants/subjects in their natural environment.

Disadvantages of the observational method

- There is no control over any extraneous variables, so this method lacks good internal validity. For example, the behaviour of the subject(s) being observed may be affected by the weather on a particular day or by some previous event that has altered their mood and, consequently, their behaviour.

- The presence of the observer may affect the behaviour being observed if participants/subjects are aware or become aware of the observer. Therefore it is hard to establish any kind of cause or effect. For example, if you are walking down a busy street and you realise someone is watching you, you often change your behaviour; these changes may be only subtle, but they happen; if you are conscious about being observed you might walk slightly differently or look down at the ground more. The same might happen when studying animals, which may flee at any noise or become wary of possible predators if they are aware of being watched.

- The observer may be biased in what he or she sees or thinks he or she sees. There is very low reliability even between two observers studying the same thing (inter-observer reliability). We all see the world from our own point of view, which is affected by our individual experiences and personality. Therefore any behaviour to be observed must be clearly defined with applicable categories, so there is agreement between different observers on what they have observed (see operationalisation, page 43).

- Naturalistic observation can also be very expensive.

- The data are hard to structure.

- The lack of control means that replicating any naturalistic observation is extremely difficult.

- Lack of control also means that it is very difficult to generalise the findings: the subjects may behave in one way at a specific time and place, and behave totally differently on another occasion.

- It is almost impossible to study unusual phenomena since you never know when they are going to occur.

- There are also ethical issues to consider, especially if the observation is undisclosed, invading people's privacy. This can also lead to the issue of deception, as the subjects are unaware that they are being observed.

- Observations might lead to the ethical issue of harm, as people who are observed without their knowledge may get upset and stressed about what they were doing. When observing animals in their natural environment, the researcher might disturb them during critical periods, such as when they are mating or looking after their young.

Correlation studies

The correlational method is used when the researcher wants to look at the relationships between two different variables. For example, we already know in life that certain correlations (relationships) exist. We know that there is a **correlation** between smoking and lung cancer, and between obesity and fatty foods. But with a correlation we cannot clearly state the cause and effect. The term 'correlation' refers to a descriptive statistical technique that attempts to measure the relationship between two or more variables – the amount to which high values on one variable are related to high values on another variable (positive correlation), or the amount to which high values on one variable are related with low values on another variable (negative correlation).

Correlation analysis is often used to measure the extent of a relationship between variables that are thought likely to co-vary. This method can also help establish the reliability and validity of specific psychological measuring instruments, such as psychometric tests of intelligence and personality. In psychology we attempt to measure a lot of abstract terms, so it can help if the results of two different tests measuring the same variable correlate positively. Would you expect someone who does well in their A level exams to also do well in a pub quiz? Both measure intelligence, don't they? Would they correlate? Or do they measure different kinds of intelligence? The correlation method would show us if there was a relationship between these two measurements or not.

Figure 3.2 A correlation study looks at how one variable is related to another

Remember

With this particular method, a statistical test is carried out (Spearman's rank order correlation coefficient – see page 56) and a correlation coefficient is calculated which has value between +1 (a perfect positive correlation) and –1 (a perfect negative correlation). For example, we know that smoking and cancer have a strong positive correlation – the more you smoke (increase in one variable), the more your chance increases of developing lung cancer (increase in second variable); and we know that there is a strong negative correlation between old age and exercise – the older you get (increase in one variable), the less exercise you do (decrease in second variable). (Although we know there are some exceptions to that.) The closer to –1 or +1 you are, the stronger the correlation is. This method is classed as a non-experimental method, but it can also be used to support experimental methods.

Remember

A correlational hypothesis does not have an IV or a DV; it just has two or more variables that co-vary. The key word that identifies a correlational hypothesis is 'relationship'.

Over to you

Look at the possible correlations below and decide if they are positive or negative correlations.

1 Heart disease and junk food.
2 Old age and sexual activity.
3 Height and weight.
4 Number of psychology lessons and student happiness.

Key term

Correlation study – a study that attempts to see how one variable is related to another.

Advantages of correlation studies

- They can provide useful information about the strength of the relationship between different variables and also provide good evidence to show when no relationship between variables exists.

- Correlations are also useful when the researcher is trying to unravel complex relationships; findings from correlational research can lead to using other methods to establish possible cause or effect. If we know a strong relationship exists, we can look at specific causes using more scientific methods.

Disadvantages of correlation studies

It is impossible to establish cause and effect. Correlations only tell us the degree of the interrelationship between specific variables; they do not tell us what causes the relationship – one variable could be the cause and the other the effect, or there could be a third or fourth variable that has caused the relationship. Take, for instance, the example already used about smoking and cancer. We know that smoking is positively correlated with an increased chance of developing lung cancer, but we cannot state with 100 per cent certainty that one will cause the other. Not everyone who smokes develops lung cancer, and not everyone who has lung cancer has smoked. Another example is obesity and fatty foods. Not everyone who eats junk food is fat, and not everyone who is fat has eaten junk food.

Interviews

Compared to the other research methods already discussed, this method can and often does involve more personal interaction between the researcher and the participants. This is an important tool for the research psychologist and frequently involves face-to-face interaction. Interviews can vary in their nature and are often used when specific research topics need to be studied. For example, if you are interested in what young girls feel causes eating disorders such as anorexia, the interview method would probably be the best one to use.

Interviews can be either structured or unstructured or a combination of both, and can contain **open** and **closed questions** or a combination of both. Often an interview needs to be piloted before being carried out, in order to establish that all the questions asked are understood (for pilot studies see page 44 on overcoming confounding variables).

Usually, with a structured interview, the researcher is aiming to produce quantitative data – for example, 'How do you rate your stress level from 1 to 5, where 5 is the highest?' But structured interviews can also produce qualitative data, although this still often involves using questions which are decided in advance, thus guiding the interviewee's responses. Often the questions will be in the same order for each interviewee, which makes the analysis easier.

The other type of interview is the unstructured interview, which is less rigid and more natural. Generally, this type of interview will use open questions to give

interviewees free rein to talk about themselves or relevant topics. This method allows the interviewees to answer the questions and then add to their answers if they feel they wish or need to. An example of an unstructured question might be, 'How do you feel?' The answers can be wide and varying and provide qualitative data.

Advantages of the interview

Key term

Interview – a way of asking questions by face-to-face interaction; questions are usually asked verbally and can be open or closed.

- An unstructured **interview** can obtain good qualitative data about a specific topic, with rich, detailed information. A good interviewer can put the interviewee at ease and get good, full answers, especially in an unstructured interview using open questions. If carried out sensitively, the interviewer can collect knowledge about aspects of behaviour which are often private to the participants concerned.

- The unstructured interview can explore other relevant areas and add or change questions to be asked, depending on the interviewee's answers.

- The structured interview can also gain good qualitative data, but with this method there is less chance of deviating from the chosen topic, thus keeping the answers of the interviewee more focused. This can make data analysis easier and there is less risk of interview bias.

Figure 3.3 The interview method involves personal participation between the researcher and participants

Disadvantages of the interview

- A structured interview may not produce qualitative data; it may only produce one-word or fixed answers which do not provide enough information about the topic being studied.

- Although structured and unstructured interviews can provide qualitative data, this kind of data is notoriously hard to analyse.

- Any information obtained from an interview is open to bias from the interviewer when being interpreted. The interviewer may interpret the information in the way he or she thinks fits best with his or her own preconceived ideas about a topic or subject.

- The interviewer may conduct the interview in a biased way, using leading questions to get the results he or she expects or wants.

- This method can lack reliability, particularly the unstructured interview.

- Any interview method may suffer similar problems to experiments, such as demand characteristics, evaluation apprehension and experimenter effects. This can then call into question the validity of the answers given in the interview. The interview method may suffer from this more because most interviews take place on a one-to-one basis, where the interviewee feels more pressure.

Key term

Social desirability bias – participants change their normal behaviour in order to be viewed in a more favourable light.

- Demand characteristics can lead to **social desirability bias**, with the interviewee giving answers that are considered socially acceptable – these may not necessarily be truthful answers.

- With evaluation apprehension, the interviewee may be very nervous about the interview and feel that he or she is being evaluated. Many people feel nervous in interviews, and the behaviour they demonstrate and the answers they give are often not what they would do in less artificial circumstances.

- The issue of evaluation apprehension may also lead to ethical issues, with the interviewee feeling under stress or pressured to answer certain questions. Also many interviews may use deception to get round the issue of social desirability bias, and this might mean keeping the true purpose of the interview hidden. This raises the issues of deception and lack of informed consent.

Over to you

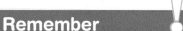

How would you answer if you were asked if you are a liar? Many of us would deny this and give an answer that would portray us in a favourable light. The truth is that we all lie sometimes; it is a defence mechanism that protects us and others from hurting people's feelings.

Over to you

How would the interviewer affect your answers if they:

- Dressed very scruffily?

- Behaved in a very rude way?

- Were very attractive?

- Had trouble saying the questions?

- Constantly stared at you throughout the interview?

Have you been in an interview situation? How did you feel physically and mentally?

Remember !

Interviewer effects exist in the same way as experimenter effects, with the interviewer's appearance, behaviour and personality affecting the outcome of the interview.

Remember !

The semi-structured interview is often the best approach, as it incorporates some of the structured approach with prepared questions but is also adaptable, allowing the participant to expand the answers he or she gives.

Remember !

Questionnaires are similar to surveys, which can also be used to collect quantitative data on, say, the incomes of MPs, or qualitative data on people's opinions of the government.

Questionnaires

Questionnaires (surveys) are another way of collecting written information, although this method is less formal and personal than the interview method. Questionnaires are similar to interviews and you can have open and closed questionnaires. The closed questions produce data that are quantitative (e.g. Do you think abortion should be abolished?, with the participant rating on scale from 1 to 5 how much they agree with this statement, with 1 being agree and 5 being disagree). The closed questions could also require simple one-word answers such as yes/no. The open questions would produce qualitative data (e.g. Explain why you think abortion should or should not be abolished). This kind of question allows the respondent to give a more detailed answer.

Questionnaires can be written, or can be carried out face to face or over the phone, but most questionnaires are written and can be carried out in a controlled environment, to prevent any confounding variables.

Unlike interviews, questionnaires have a wide range of purposes. They can be used to:

1 Measure a specific behaviour – for example, read the following statement and mark how aggressive this makes you feel on a scale of 1 to 5. 'You are waiting in a queue and someone pushes in front of you'. 1 = annoyed, 5 = very angry.

2 Measure attitudes using attitude scales, which are intended to measure a relatively permanent and habitual position of the individual on a particular issue – for example, mark on a scale of 1 to 5 how much you agree or disagree with the following statement: 'The best movie ever made was *The Shawshank Redemption.*'

3 Measure personality types – for example, 'Are you introvert or extrovert?'

4 Obtain current views on a particular issue – for example, underage drinking.

5 Obtain information about regular behaviour – for example, eating habits and typical leisure activities.

(Note: the first three questions would collect data that could be classed as quantitative data; the last two questions would collect qualitative data.)

Advantages of questionnaires

- This depends on the type of question asked on the questionnaire. Although questionnaires suffer from the same problems as interviews, this may be to a lesser degree.

- Participants may not feel as pressured to answer and take more time over some of the questions.

- If the questionnaire is kept confidential, participants may feel at ease to answer truthfully.

- If closed questions are used, this allows the data to be analysed more easily (e.g. in the form of quantitative analysis); if open questions are asked, this can provide rich, detailed information.

- Most questionnaires are a quick and cheap way of collecting a large amount of data. If a large number of participants are tested, the results can be generalised to the overall population.

Over to you

If you fill in a questionnaire on the bus on the way home, would anything distract you from filling it in correctly?

Key term

Questionnaire – a way of gaining information about a particular topic, generally through the use of written questions, open and closed.

Figure 3.4 The questionnaire method is less formal and personal than an interview

Disadvantages of questionnaires

- A questionnaire with closed questions produces quantitative data; this type of questionnaire does not really go into detail and often tells us little about a person's beliefs and true personality.

- While open questions can produce richer qualitative data, these are very hard to analyse. Questionnaires that use open questions are very unreliable, and it is difficult to repeat them and obtain the same findings.

- Depending on when and where questionnaires are filled in, they can suffer similar problems to lab experiments and interviews. Such problems might include demand characteristics (social desirability bias), evaluation apprehension and researcher effects. If the participant fills in the questionnaire in the presence of the researcher, they may answer questions in a way that portrays them in a positive way, or they may work out what the focus of the questionnaire is and answer in the way they think the researcher wants them to. They may feel nervous in front of the researcher and not behave naturally. Finally, the appearance and personality of the researcher may have an influence on how they answer the questionnaire. All these issues then question the validity of the questionnaire method. If questionnaires are posted, to be filled in and returned, not everyone may return them which can then lead to a biased sample.

- The questions used on the questionnaire might be ambiguous and might be interpreted incorrectly.

- By the way they are phrased (leading questions), questions may lead to biased answers and interpretations – for example, 'Ninety per cent of people questioned claimed they eat healthily. Do you?' This hints at the fact that if you do not eat healthily you are not part of the majority, and most people want to be part of the majority. Also the question asked is somewhat ambiguous – what does it mean by 'eat healthily'? What type of food is the question referring to? Does it mean eating healthily all the time, at every meal?

Figure 3.5 John Merrick, the 'elephant man'

Case studies

A case study involves observing what happens to or piecing together the case history of a single person or a group of individuals – for example, the study of a severely disabled adult, his/her past history and any rehabilitation and development. A case study was conducted in the case of John Merrick, the 'elephant man', who was discovered working as a sideshow freak. After being rescued from this dreadful existence, his background and life were researched to discover the cause of his physical abnormality.

Such research often helps to shed light on general psychological issues, such as the nature/nurture debate on mental illness or intelligence. John Merrick was found to have a higher-than-average IQ, despite his dreadful life.

A case study can be carried out in different ways, by using a person's or a group's own memories (if they are alive), or by using the recollections of friends or past records or documents of various types. Most case studies use a descriptive method: the focus is narrow on one person's or one group's behaviour, and a high level of detail is provided. This method may involve taking the opportunity provided by a one-off event, offering an unusual example of a person's behaviour, as was the case with John Merrick.

The case study is an exploratory method and can be carried out using interviews and observations; both subjective and objective data are collected. The case study provides qualitative data and is often used within clinical psychology. The approach plays a major role in diagnosis and in the planning of therapy or treatment of a single person or a group of people. Case studies may also be carried out on the typical representatives of a group – for example, the effects of isolation on young children, so that generalisations can then be made.

> ### Key term
>
> **Case study –** generally this is an in-depth study of just one person or group, collecting detailed information.

Over to you

If you were doing a case study on Adolf Hitler to assess his psychological state during the Second World War, what would you need to know about him? Consider the following:

1   History of his childhood.

2   His relationship with his parents.

3   His interests and careers.

4   Specific experiences that may have had an effect on him.

5   His sexual preferences and social and intimate relationships.

All this information would give us a detailed account of Hitler's life – a case study – and from this evidence we could put together a psychological profile of him.

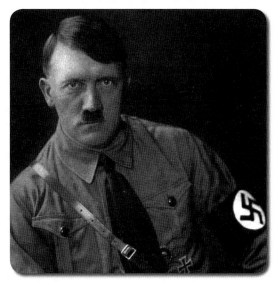

Figure 3.6 How would you assess Hitler's psychological state?

Advantages of case studies

- They allow for a detailed qualitative analysis of the person or persons being studied that can highlight strange behaviour and therefore stimulate new research.

- The case study can investigate behaviour which it would be unethical to create artificially.

- Research from case studies can confirm or challenge a theory and can provide a wealth of information (e.g. the findings may contradict or support a well-established theory).

- The case study can take on board the experiences and feelings of the subject, so it is very subjective in nature.

- Because this method acknowledges the importance of subjective information, it accepts individual differences – the fact that we are all different in our beliefs, feelings and behaviour.

Disadvantages of case studies

- They often rely heavily on the memory of the person being studied, or close family and friends, which means that objectivity is lacking and recollections may be inaccurate.

- No two case studies are ever the same and this has a negative effect on reliability and validity.

- This method relies on the interpretation of the evidence by the person undertaking the study which is often very subjective and therefore may be biased. The final report may only contain what the researcher has selected.

- Often case studies are done on atypical individuals (e.g. John Merrick), so the findings cannot necessarily be generalised.

Summary

Observations
There are different types of observation: naturalistic – observing behaviour in a natural environment with no interference; participant – where the researcher is part of the group he or she is observing; and non-participant – where the researcher observes a group without participating.

Interviews
Interviews can be structured or unstructured, and may contain open or closed questions. They allow the researcher to explore behaviours that are often private, but they are open to interviewer bias and interpretation.

Questionnaires
Questionnaires are often a cheap and easy way to collect data, but can lead to biased samples and rely on participants to interpret the questions correctly.

Non-experimental methods

Correlation studies
These are used to establish a relationship between two variables; however, they cannot tell us much about cause and effect.

Case studies
Case studies of groups or individuals allow researchers to study situations it would be unethical to recreate, but they often rely on recollections, thus lacking objectivity. They are usually based on atypical individuals, meaning that it is difficult to generalise findings

4 Ethical issues and ways of overcoming them

INTRODUCTION

This chapter deals with the ethical issues that arise within psychological research and how these can be dealt with. Ethical issues refer to the moral guidelines or principles that any society tries to adhere to. Within psychological research, this includes lack of informed consent, deception, confidentiality, right to withdraw and protection from harm. The chapter describes each ethical issue, discusses how each issue can be dealt with and how successful the method used to deal with the issue is.

OBJECTIVES

The specification requires you to have an awareness of the following:

● Ethical issues and ways of overcoming these issues.

Ethical issues

There are several main ethical issues within psychology, and other issues may stem from these. The main ethical issues are:

1 Informed consent – if it is not possible to obtain informed consent, then prior consent or presumptive consent can be sought and a debrief given at the end.

2 Deception – it is often very difficult to avoid this, although it can be dealt with by offering to debrief the participants.

3 Confidentiality – participants are made aware that any information they provide will be treated in the strictest confidence; they can be informed at the start of the study or, if this is not possible, at the end of the study in the form of a debrief.

4 Withdrawal – participants are made aware at the start that they can withdraw from the study at any time, or they are informed in a debrief at the end, when they are told that they can withdraw their data.

5 Protection from harm – every effort is made to stop any harm, either psychological or physical; when this is unavoidable, counselling can be offered at the end of the study.

Ethics are a set of moral principles used to guide human behaviour. In our society, the term 'ethics' is used generally when we are referring to the behaviour of doctors or lawyers. A doctor must not betray the confidence of a client; this is considered unethical. A lawyer must defend his or her client to the best of his or her ability, even if he or she knows the client to be guilty; to do otherwise would be considered unethical.

The term 'morals' refers to our everyday understanding of what is right and what is wrong. Some of these morals are written as laws – for example, we know it is against the law to commit murder or to steal from someone, but a lot of morals are unwritten laws and are dictated by the society we live in, which socialises people into behaving in certain ways. These unwritten moral codes can include a wide range of actions, such as not lying to your friends, not betraying someone's trust or helping someone in distress. If you do not perform these actions you are not breaking the law, but you are going against the behaviour that society says is morally right or wrong. Sometimes morals are a controversial issue, provoking debates about whether something should be done for the greater good. Examples might be sacrificing one life to save many, or carrying out experiments on animals in order to develop life-saving drugs for humans – does this imply that a human life is more important than the life of an animal, or does it depend on the type of animal used?

When applying and carrying out research on human beings, the relevance of ethics is paramount and control is needed. This need for ethical control led to the establishment of

Figure 4.1 Is the life of an animal less important than that of a human?

Remember

The relevant body for psychology in Britain is the British Psychological Society (BPS).

You can view the BPS ethical guidelines on the web at www.bps.org.uk/the-society/code-of-conduct/code-of-conduct-home.cfm

a set of rules or ethical guidelines which can be used to judge whether the research carried out is acceptable or not. These guidelines are derived from the Nazi trials at Nuremberg. It was found that the Nazis conducted many horrible experiments on concentration camp prisoners during the Second World War. After these Nazis were put on trial at Nuremburg, it was decided to draw up a code of practice, as a guide to what is acceptable in scientific research. This led to the Nuremburg ten-point code, which has since been adapted by professional bodies all over the world.

Most professional bodies also have their own ethical committees, which review all research proposals and attempt to make sure that any research conducted is ethically acceptable. The power of these committees is unclear, however, and in the case of the British Psychological Society (BPS), a lot of members of the committee may also be psychologists who may not wish to turn down important psychological research.

Generally, the guidelines for psychological research are just that – guidelines. Anyone who does not adhere to them is not breaking the law, although they may be struck off by their relevant committee or society. The guidelines might be too rigid in some areas and may prevent relevant and much-needed research; in other cases they are not clear enough and allow researchers to find ways round them to carry out their research regardless.

Remember

One way to deal with any ethical issues is to adhere to ethical guidelines set up by the BPS.

In life there are no universal, ethical truths and what might be considered to be unethical in one society or culture is ethically acceptable in another. These guidelines need to be reviewed constantly and adapted as societies and attitudes change.

Protection from physical/psychological harm

'The risks that an individual may be exposed to during a psychological investigation should not be greater than the risks they might have already been expected to face in their everyday life' (Eysenck 2005)

The first and most important ethical issue is protection from physical and psychological harm. The key question to be asked with any research is whether the harm that might be caused during the research is greater than that encountered in ordinary life.

Physical harm is fairly easy to measure because the effects can be seen easily, but psychological harm is harder to report. This might include stress, which we know is a psychological state but which also has physical symptoms.

So the questions arises, does the study cause psychological harm? This is harder to evaluate than physical harm and the effects of the study on the participants, unless demonstrated in their behaviour, are hard to record or monitor. Most researchers, though, agree that psychological harm can be caused by any research that increases levels of stress, affects a person's self-esteem or causes any kind of embarrassment or distress. Again, the main rule that researchers should follow is whether the risk to the person is greater than he or she would experience in everyday life.

Other issues, such as confidentiality and the right to privacy, can lead to the issue of protection from harm – for example, passing on sensitive information about a person may cause that person distress. Also, the right to privacy is linked to protection from harm – for example, filming or watching someone in a private place without their permission might lead to participants suffering harm.

Ways of dealing with harm

There are several ways of dealing with this issue.

Figure 4.2 Research participants should be protected from any harm arising from experiments

- If the harm is caused indirectly (e.g. through the use of deception, lack of informed consent, invasion of privacy or disclosure of private information), participants can be dealt with using the methods specific to those issues and hopefully this will solve the protection from harm issue as well.

- One way to deal with protection from harm specifically is to do a cost-benefit analysis – do the benefits of the research outweigh any potential costs to the participants? This is often carried out before the research is done, so it lacks validity – it is quite difficult to judge accurately the effects of a study on participants before you have actually carried out the study.

- Another way is to debrief participants at the end of the study. The main aim of any debriefing is to restore the participants to the same state they were in before they took part in the study. A problem with debriefing is that it is difficult to judge how successful a debriefing may be.

- A debriefing could also just inform the participants about the study in its entirety, in order to set their minds at rest about what they have just participated in, assure them that everything will be dealt with in the strictest confidence, and offer them the right to withdraw their data if this would make them feel better. Anyone truly traumatised after a study could be offered counselling to help restore them to the state they were in before the study took place.

- Another way to protect participants from harm is to inform them that they can leave the study at any time.

- A possible indirect way to protect participants from harm would be to inform them about the study beforehand to see if they would be happy to take part; often this is not possible, however, so presumptive consent or prior general consent can be used (see page 36 on dealing with informed consent).

Remember

Some establishments have their own ethical committees, which can be used to judge whether a study is ethically acceptable before it takes place.

Informed consent

[Consent is] 'an ethical requirement which demands that all participants or clients should agree to the procedures which are to take place. Within a research context this also implies that participants should be free to withdraw from the study at any time without undue pressure being put upon them to continue' (Cardwell 2003)

A lack of informed consent can be linked to protection from harm, since without this consent, the participant might also lose the right to privacy and the right to confidentiality.

Figure 4.3 All research participants should be fully informed about what will take place

Informed consent means informing the participant about the research, including what the research will require, the purpose of the research and the rights the participants has – for example, the right to confidentiality, the right to withdraw at any time and only to take part when informed consent has been sought and obtained.

If someone puts themselves forward for an experiment, we might think that they know precisely what is going to take place. Unfortunately, this is not always the case. Without total informed consent about all parts of a study prior to an individual taking part, it becomes impossible for the person to make a reliable judgement about their agreement to participate. Informed consent means that participants give their informed consent before they take part in any study. The word 'informed' is a major part of this ethical issue; this shows that the participants have been told about all the essential details of the study – what they will have to do and what might happen to them. They also know that they have obvious rights, such as the right to withdraw and rights of confidentiality. Experimenters should also be made aware that there are several specific groups that might not be able to give their consent – for example, the elderly, children under 16 and those with special needs.

Dealing with lack of informed consent

Each participant must give their consent to take part; if this is not possible, presumptive consent or prior general consent must be sought and then a debrief carried out.

Often revealing the true nature of any research through consent may negate the specific study; it is for this reason that other options can be used. One is the use of presumptive consent. Presumptive consent is when you take a selection of participants from your chosen target population (e.g. if the research is targeted at sixth-form students, you would take a sample of sixth-form students) and ask this sample if they would have consented to take part in a study that used deception and/or could possible cause some harm; if they agree and state that they would have given their voluntary informed consent, we can reasonably assume that they speak for the opinions of the target population.

A second method would be to use prior general consent. With this method, participants who might be used in a study are told that sometimes subjects are misinformed about the real nature of a study. Only those who agree that such a practice is acceptable would be chosen to take part. Therefore they have given general informed consent, but they do not know whether the actual research they are taking part in uses misinformation. A similar method to this would be obtain informed consent from participants several weeks before the study is to take place, in the hope that they might have forgotten what they were told (i.e. they forget they are being deceived).

A third way would be to just debrief participants after the study has taken place (see page 39) and give them the chance to withdraw their data if they wish to do so. Of course, the researcher should allow participants to leave at any time if they have given their consent to take part in a study initially, but later realise that they would like to recall that consent.

Deception

> [Deception is] *'the deliberate misleading of participants during a research study, either through telling them lies or by omitting to tell them some important details of the research such that they are unable to give their full informed consent'* (Cardwell 2003)

Participants who take part in any research must not be deceived if at all possible. When participants are deceived, we take away their chance to give their fully informed consent to take part in the study. (There are obviously some times when deception is inappropriate and some times when it may be more admissible.)

Unfortunately, it seems to be the case with most research that it cannot avoid deception, as this would have a negative effect on the results. If this is the case, participants must be debriefed after the study and informed of the real aims/hypothesis; they must then be allowed to withdraw their data if they so wish. (Wherever possible, all participants must be made aware that they can withdraw from the study at any time.)

Dealing with deception

There are several ways of dealing with the issue of deception. One way is to use role play. The participants are told all about the study beforehand and about any manipulations that might take place – for example, they might be told that someone is going to pretend to be upset in order to measure their reactions. The participants are told to act as if they did not know what was really happening. A problem with this is that the behaviour can never be guaranteed to be natural or real, since the participant is only playing a role.

Another option to deception is to inform the participants about the general nature of the study (not the detailed hypothesis being tested) and, again, ask them to act out the experimental procedures as though they were naive partici-pants. Would their behaviour be more natural if they were not told exactly what is being measured, or would the behaviour still be artificial?

Alternatively, the participants can be deceived and given a full debriefing at the end of the study (see page 39) and offered the option to have their results removed.

Confidentiality

'participants or clients have the right to expect that information gathered during the research or therapy session will not be made public without their consent' (Cardwell 2003)

All participants must be made aware that any information they provide will be treated in the strictest confidence.

Any knowledge obtained about a participant during a study should be kept confidential unless otherwise agreed beforehand. Participants taking part in any psychological research have a right to expect that information they provide in the form of data or results will also be treated confidentially and, if circulated, will not be identified as theirs.

Figure 4.4 It is vital that all research information gathered from participants is treated in the strictest confidence

Dealing with confidentiality

The main ways of dealing with the issue of confidentiality are to inform the participants that their names and all their results will be kept in total confidence, and offering them the opportunity to withdraw their data. During any study, participants should be referred to as numbers rather than names; this helps to keep information confidential.

Right to withdraw

'the option for the participant to withdraw from the research at any time should be made clear from the outset. Also, the participant has the right to withdraw their data or any consent previously given' (Twining 1998)

Before the outset of any study, the researchers should make it clear to the participants that they have the right to withdraw themselves at any time during or after the study, and that the knowledge and/or data can also be removed from the study and the final results.

Dealing with the right to withdraw

At the beginning of any research, participants are told that at any time during the study they have the right to withdraw themselves and their data. It should be made clear that there is no pressure for them to continue, whether they decide to withdraw at the start of the study, halfway through or right at the end. Even after participants have been debriefed, if they are still unhappy, they have the right to require that their data be withdrawn and destroyed in their presence.

Figure 4.5 Participants have the right to withdraw themselves and their data at any time

Debriefing

[Debriefing is] 'a post-experimental interview in which the experimenter tries to restore the participant to the same psychological state they were in when they entered the experiment' (Cardwell 2003)

Debriefing is an important part of any psychological research, especially where deception or some kind of physical or psychological harm has taken place. Debriefing participants has the following functions: it aims to restore them to the same state as when they entered the investigation, and it can help a good researcher to regard participants as colleagues and not as objects to be used solely for the ends of the experimenter.

However, debriefing does not provide a justification for any unethical aspect of the investigation. Often it is seen as adequate merely to inform participants of the true nature of the investigation, but in some circumstances this would be insufficient. If a participant is traumatised during a piece of research, merely debriefing them about what a study was about would not resolve this issue.

One way in which psychologists have attempted to deal with these ethical concerns has been to devise a set of ethical guidelines; a summary of these guidelines is shown in Table 4.1.

Remember

Debriefing is not an ethical issue; it is a way of dealing with ethical issues.

Key example

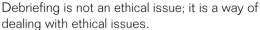

Milgram (1963): Behavioural study of obedience

Milgram's (1963) study on obedience was said to suffer from many ethical issues. Participants were deceived into thinking that they were giving real electric shocks to other participants, who were really confederates. Milgram was also critised for the severe distress that this study caused the participants. Milgram argued that all these ethical issues were dealt with, stating that the participants were fully debriefed after the study and that they were all given a psychiatric examination one year later, which revealed no psychological damage. Nearly 74 per cent of the participants stated that they were happy to have taken part in the study.

Table 4.1

CONSENT	CONFIDENTIALITY	PROTECTION FROM HARM	WITHDRAWAL	DECEPTION
Are the participants volunteers? (Exceptions include children, the elderly and those with special needs)	Respect participants' privacy and keep data confidential; do not break the law (e.g. on data protection) **(protection from harm)**	Being professional in the way you behave and being honest about your own competence	Making sure that participants can drop out at any time **(consent)**	Always debrief participants at the end of the study
Have participants been told what the research is about?	Ensuring participants cannot be identified	Treating participants with respect and having due regard for their rights and welfare	Being prepared for people to say no **(consent)**	Explain exactly what the study is about
Has informed consent been obtained?	Get participants' agreement if you are to discuss their data	Maintain the highest standards of safety for equipment, etc.		Be prepared to answer any questions
Are you sure that no deception has taken place?	All records should be kept safely and not left where others might have access to them	Do not allow participants to attempt tasks that are embarrassing, dangerous, painful or illegal		Make participants' results available to them
Are participants aware they can withdraw at any time? **(withdrawal)**	Controlling who else will see the data	Not causing stress, discomfort or embarrassment; allowing participants to withdraw **(withdrawal)**		Participants should have the right to withhold their results **(withdrawal)**

Summary

Protection from physical/ psychological harm
The most important of the ethical problems is how to protect participants from physical or psychological harm, which is linked to many of the other issues. The key question with any research is whether the harm that might be caused is greater than what a participant might encounter in ordinary life. Psychological harm is harder to report than physical harm.

Ethical issues
Ethics can be controversial – what should be sacrificed for the greater good? But when carrying out research with human participants, ethical issues are paramount.

Right to withdraw
Participants should have the right to leave a study at any point.

Debriefing
Debriefing at the end of the experiment is a way of dealing with some of these ethical issues. It aims to return participants to the state they were in before they took part in the research.

Ethical issues and ways of overcoming them

Informed consent
This involves making sure a participant knows exactly what is involved in an experiment. This may mean it is difficult to get people to take part; presumptive consent and prior general consent are ways round this issue.

Confidentiality
Results and personal information gained in an experiment should be kept confidential and anonymous.

Deception
Participants should not be deceived as to the nature of an experiment; however, this can affect the results. Alternatively, if deception is necessary, the participants should have a full debrief at the end of the study.

5 Operationalisation of variables

INTRODUCTION

This chapter covers all other major areas within the topic of research methods. The chapter describes how variables can be operationalised and the problems that arise when trying to define behaviour correctly. It also explains ways in which confounding variables can be controlled. Standardised instructions and procedures are explained, as well as the different sampling methods that can be used when choosing participants. These sampling methods include random sampling, self-selected sampling, systematic sampling, opportunity sampling and stratified sampling. These sampling methods are discussed in terms of their advantages and disadvantages.

OBJECTIVES

The specification requires you to have an awareness of the following:

● Operationalisation of independent variables, dependent variables and co-variables

● Ways of overcoming confounding variables

● Procedures, including sampling and choice of apparatus.

Operationalisation of variables

A correlational hypothesis does not have an IV or a DV because the variables are not being manipulated. A correlation is looking for a relationship between two variables. For example, there is a correlation between the two variables of self-esteem and how attractive someone is. These two variables are known as co-variables – they may vary together.

As we have already seen, any kind of hypothesis can be tested, but it must first be **operationalised** – that is, it must be made clear what is being manipulated, measured, controlled or correlated.

'Noise affects memory'. This hypothesis is not very clear. What do we mean by 'noise'? What do we mean by 'memory'? A better way to express this hypothesis would be: 'The level of noise (loud/quiet) has an effect on the memory recall of a list of ten words.'

Within psychology we measure many abstract terms, such as 'self-esteem' and 'aggression', and often there is no one clear definition of the behaviour to be measured. The term 'operationalised' generally refers to the dependent variable (what is being measured), but we need to be clear about the meanings of any variables within a study. For example, a person's aggression is affected by their self-esteem. In this case we need to be clear about what we mean by aggression and by self-esteem. If we cannot measure self-esteem (the IV), how can we manipulate it to see its effect on aggression (the DV)? If we take a correlational hypothesis – 'There is a relationship between self-esteem and aggression' – we are not measuring these variables, but seeing how much they co-vary, but we still need a clear definition of what we mean by self-esteem and aggression so we can measure them to test for a relationship.

Let us take the example of a study observing aggressive behaviour. The study must state what is being observed and how. Aggression is being measured, so we must define what we mean by aggression, what behaviour indicates aggression and at what level. This might lead to a list of behavioural categories that encompass the behaviour that is to be observed. The aggressive categories might include shouting, swearing, pushing and physical assault.

Key term

Operationalised – gaining a precise definition of variables that are being manipulated, measured, correlated or controlled, and defining each variable of interest in terms of the operations taken to measure it.

Figure 5.1 How would we define aggression if we were measuring it?

Over to you

Can you think of any other behaviour that might be encompassed by the term 'aggression'?

Over to you

How could we define and measure the term 'fear'?

Key example

A study is carried out to test the hypothesis that gender affects levels of aggression. To begin this research, the term 'aggression' has to be operationalised – that is, the variable aggression must be defined in terms of the operations taken to measure it. The researcher designs a schedule of aggressive behaviour, ranging from low aggression to high aggression. The researcher then states the hypothesis: 'Gender has an effect on a person's level of aggressive behaviour as measured by an aggressive schedule'.

So any behaviour or topic that is going to be studied first needs to be operationalised; it must be defined so that it can be measured. Most behaviour cannot be easily defined so that one term or phrase encapsulates every aspect of a particular behaviour; therefore it often has to be categorised into different types. Using the example of aggression, this might include lots of different behaviours, such as pushing, hitting and kicking. You will often need to produce categories that cover all the different levels/definitions of a specific behaviour.

Remember

Pilot studies allow researchers to check out the procedures and general design of their study using a small sample of participants. This method can highlight any problems with a specific design. With a lab experiment, for example, unforeseen extraneous variables can be identified. With a questionnaire or interview, a pilot study could highlight any issues with specific questions, such as leading or ambiguous questions. With an observation, some part of the chosen behaviour to be observed might not have been coded.

Overcoming confounding variables and other uncontrolled factors

Some people argue that you can never totally control all extraneous variables, so every study will have some confounding variables. Table 5.1 shows issues that may arise with each research method and how these might be controlled.

Table 5.1

RESEARCH METHOD	CONTROL OF EXTRANEOUS VARIABLES AND OTHER UNCONTROLLED FACTORS
Lab experiments:	
1 Demand characteristics/ experimenter bias	A single-blind method in research means the participants are not told the true aim of the study. A double-blind method means that the experimenter will not know either; therefore he or she cannot give cues about the aims of the study.
2 Experimenter effects	The instructions given to each subject must be identical, as should the procedure used for each subject and the scoring techniques. The experimenter tries to behave as normally as possible and just follows the standardised procedures (see page 46) for the experiment (a pilot study could be run).
3 Evaluation apprehension	The experimenter reassures participants that results will not reflect badly on them, that all results are kept in confidence and that the participant can leave the study at any time.

RESEARCH METHOD	CONTROL OF EXTRANEOUS VARIABLES AND OTHER UNCONTROLLED FACTORS
4 Social desirability bias	The experimenter reassures participants that results will not reflect badly on them and that all results are kept in confidence.
5 Lack of ecological validity	There is no way round this in a lab setting, except through having good mundane realism.
Experimental designs:	
1 Independent/individual differences	No matter what sampling method you use (e.g. random), individual differences may still exist between your two groups of participants.
2 Repeated measures/order effects	Counterbalancing.
3 Matched subjects/individual differences	No matter how well subjects are matched (e.g. using identical (MZ) twins), individual differences may still occur.
Field experiment:	
1 No control over extraneous variables	No way to resolve this issue with a field experiment.
2 Demand characteristics and experimenter effects	Experimenter remains concealed.
3 Lack of internal validity	No way to resolve this with a field experiment.
Natural experiment:	
1 No control over extraneous variables	No way to resolve this issue with a natural experiment.
2 Demand characteristics and experimenter effects	Experimenter remains concealed.
3 Lack of internal validity	No way to resolve this issue with a natural experiment.
Correlation:	
1 A third variable may be causing the correlation	No way to resolve this issue with a correlation.
Observation:	
1 Behaviour being observed not accurately measured	Run a pilot study to test observation categories.
2 Lack of reliability in behaviour being observed	Inter-rater reliability.
3 Effects of being observed	Make sure observation is covert.
4 Lack of internal validity	No way to resolve this issue with an observation.

RESEARCH METHOD	CONTROL OF EXTRANEOUS VARIABLES AND OTHER UNCONTROLLED FACTORS
Interview:	
1 Interviewer effects	The questions asked of each participant must be identical, as should the procedure used for each participant. The interviewer tries to behave as normally as possible and just follows the standardised procedures (see below).
2 Leading questions	Check for leading questions (pilot study could be run).
3 Biased analysis	Another researcher not involved with the study interprets the data.
4 Social desirability bias	Inform participants that all answers in the interview will be kept in confidence.
Questionnaire:	
1 Leading questions	When constructing the questionnaire, avoid leading questions and run a pilot test to test the questionnaire.
2 Social desirability bias	Inform participants that all answers on the questionnaire will be kept in confidence.
3 Experimenter effects	Allow participants to fill in the questionnaire in private.
Case study:	
1 Biased interpretation of data	Another researcher not involved with the study interprets the data.
2 Unreliability – no two case studies the same	Compare information gained from different cases based on a similar theory.

Remember

Some of the variables in Table 5.1 may not be truly considered to be confounding variables, but they are factors that could affect the accuracy of the results when using any different research method.

Standardised instructions and procedures

When carrying out any research there are instructions that must be followed to allow for good reliability and validity. These standardised instructions are mainly used with the experimental method, which sets out to give the experimenter and the participants specific instructions on how the experiment should be run. These instructions can be written down or spoken verbally. They often include what the participants are expected to do, any time constraints and awareness of any ethical issues. If followed carefully, these instructions will mean that everyone who takes part in the experiment will be treated the same, and this adds to the reliability and validity of the study.

Even with non-experimental methods, there must be some kind of instructions. In the case of questionnaires, there can be instructions at the top of the questionnaire, informing the participant how to fill it in.

There is slight difference in meaning when using the term 'standardised procedures'; this generally refers to how the administration of an experiment is conducted and also how it is measured and/or scored. This can also apply in the case of interviews and questionnaires: there can be some procedure in terms of the order in which questions are asked, what type of questions are asked and how they are asked.

In the case of observations, the procedure might state that the behaviour to be observed must have been clearly defined and categorised. It might also state how the behaviour to be observed should be carried out – for example, either time sampling or event sampling; again, this will add reliability and validity to the study.

So the procedures refer to how such measuring tools are designed, to support their reliability or validity.

Sampling

In order to begin to test any hypothesis or start any research, we need a sample of people or animals to study.

One of the main aims of research is to be able to generalise from our sample; in order to do this, we must identify our **target population**. The target population itself is too large for us to use every person; therefore we select a sample from it to work with. For example, a study on the attitude of teenagers in London to under-age drinking would have a target population of all the teenagers in London; obviously we cannot use all of these, so a sample would be chosen.

In choosing our sample we attempt to avoid using a biased sample, which would not be representative of our target population. The target population for each sample is often dictated by the hypothesis that is being tested. With any sample chosen we can never be fully sure that the sample is truly representative of the target population, so the aim of sampling is to remove as much bias as possible, to make sure that no members of the target population are more likely than any others to get into the sample.

There are several sampling methods.

Random sampling

Random sampling is where every member of the target population has the same chance of being chosen. The easiest way to do this would be to put all the names of the target population in a hat and pick out the number of participants that you need. Another way to select a random sample would be to give each participant a number and then take numbers from a random number table. A third way to select a random sample would be to use a computer that has been programmed to generate an endless string of random numbers.

The main advantage of using random sampling is that everyone in the target population has an equal chance of being chosen for the sample. A disadvantage with this sampling method is that, by chance, you might still end up with a biased sample – for example, if you wish to study attitudes to under-age drinking and your target population is the mixed sixth form of a school, the participants randomly selected might all turn out to be boys, meaning that your sample is not representative of the target population. Also with this method your target population/group might be too big to give everyone a chance to be randomly picked and it is impossible to carry out. A final disadvantage is that a person selected randomly may not want to cooperate with the study.

Figure 5.2 With random sampling, every member of the target population has an equal chance of being chosen

Over to you

A selection of 20 lines from movies are written on pieces of paper. How would you select one randomly?

Over to you

Choose every third name from the following list of participants:

- Jane Doe
- Ivor Train
- Daniel Craig
- Mary Roberts
- Jack Smith
- Keira Knightley
- Geoff Hilton
- Erin Lorien
- Pierce Brosnan
- Beverley Lewis

How could this lead to a biased sample?

Volunteer or self-selected sampling

To make sure the participants cooperate you could use volunteer or self-selected sampling. With this method the participants choose themselves by replying to an advertisement or a postal question-naire. An advantage of this method is that it is easy to use. A disadvantage is that it is not representative of the target population. In general, most people do not volunteer; therefore those who do tend to have different characteristics – for example, they are keen or want to impress.

Systematic sampling

Systematic sampling is when every third or fourth name is taken from a list made up of the target population. An advantage of this method is that it prevents bias in the way the researcher picks participants, but, again, you might end up with a biased sample whereby every third name selected may be male or have similar characteristics.

Opportunity sampling

Opportunity sampling is when the researcher takes advantage of having participants available at the time of the research. A study carried out at a university would use university students who are available. An advantage of this method is that it is the easiest to carry out, but a major disadvantage is that because participants are chosen indiscriminately, you may not be able to generalise your findings to the target population – you might have a biased sample. In the case of the university, all the participants are students and therefore do not represent the whole population, unless your study is focused specifically on university students.

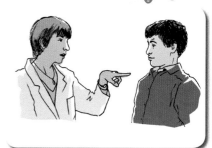

Figure 5.3 Opportunity sampling takes advantage of whatever participants are available at the time of the research

Stratified sampling

Stratified sampling is when the sample must contain all groups in the same proportion as in the target population. For example, if your target population is students at a school, the sample must include years 7, 8, 9, 10, 11 and sixth form. If all year groups contain 400 students, except sixth form which contains 200 students, your proportional sample would include four students in every year but only two in the sixth form. This sampling method is very time-consuming and difficult to do, and you are still not guaranteed a representative sample.

Key term

Apparatus – a collection of equipment used for a particular purpose.

Over to you

How would you systematically select four or five movie quotes from a list of 20?

Quota sampling

Quota sampling is obtaining the sample through selecting a quota of people roughly in proportion to their occurrence in the population.

Apparatus

Apparatus refers to any resources needed to run a study successfully. In the case of an experiment, it would involve the use of a laboratory, an artificial environment; this would contain any measuring tools needed to collect data, such as stopwatches, psychometric tests and questionnaires. It is important that all apparatus or materials are listed to allow for good validity and reliability if the study were to be repeated. Even in the case of interviews, questionnaires and observations, the apparatus can refer to the measuring tools being used – for example, the actual questionnaires or the behavioural categories designed for the observation.

Figure 5.4 The apparatus of an experiment refers to the resources needed to run the study successfully

Summary

Standardised instructions and procedures
There should be clear instructions to the experimenter and to participants as to how the experiment is run. Standardised procedures should also be in place to control how results are measured.

Operationalisation of variables
Operationalisation means gaining a precise definition of which variables are being controlled, which are being manipulated and what is being measured.

Operationalisation of variables

Overcoming confounding variables and other uncontrolled factors
The type of confounding variable depends on the sort of experiment being undertaken, as does the method that can be used to overcome them.

Apparatus
This refers to any tools needed to collect data, including stopwatches, psychometric tests and questionnaires.

Sampling
Participants for an experiment can be chosen in a number of ways: random sampling, volunteer sampling, systematic sampling, stratified sampling and opportunity sampling. Each method has its advantages and disadvantages.

6

Descriptive and inferential statistics for analysing data

INTRODUCTION

This chapter looks at the data gained from research and how it can be analysed. It begins by explaining how quantitative data can be analysed. Descriptive methods, such as the mean and the mode, are explained and also how this kind of data can be displayed on scattergraphs and bar charts. The chapter then discusses how qualitative data can be analysed, using content analysis. It then moves on to how quantitative data can be analysed for its significance and to show if a specific hypothesis has been proved or not. This includes explaining levels of significance and levels of measurement. When analysing psychological data, five specific statistical tests are used; these are explained, along with the reasons why and when each test is used. Statistical tests discussed

in this chapter include chi-squared, sign test, Mann-Whitney U, Wilcoxon matched pairs and Spearman's rank order. The chapter then discusses the terms 'reliability' and 'validity' and how these can be applied within psychological research. The chapter ends by explaining the differences between findings and conclusions.

OBJECTIVES

With any kind of quantitative data (numbers) we can carry out some descriptive analysis; **descriptive statistics** provide ways in which data can be summarised. Two ways of doing this are by using measures of central tendency and measures of dispersion.

The specification requires that you have an awareness of the following:

- Statistical tests, for example, chi-squared
- Levels of measurement
- Levels of significance
- Descriptive and inferential statistics for analysing data
- Issues relating to reliability and validity.

Key term

Descriptive statistics – ways of describing the data gained through the use of measures of central tendency and measures of dispersion.

Measures of central tendency

Measures of central tendency analyse the results and give average values. There are three measures of central tendency:

- The **mean** is the arithmetic average, which is worked out by adding up all the scores and dividing by the number of scores which gives us the average.

- The **mode** is the most recurring score in a set of data.

- The **median** is the middle score when all scores are lined up, lowest to highest.

Each measure of central tendency has its own advantages and disadvantages.

Table 6.1

DESCRIPTIVE METHOD	ADVANTAGES	DISADVANTAGES
Mean	The mean makes full use of all available data. It is the most powerful measure of central tendency available.	It is a very sensitive measure and can be affected by extreme outlying values.
Mode	The mode does actually occur in any sequence of data, unlike the mean or possibly the median.	It is a sensitive measure and small changes in results can affect the mode value. The mode tells us little about the other values in the data set.
Median	The median is unaffected by any outlying values.	The median does not work well with small data sets and is affected by changes in the central values. The median tells us little about the other values.

Over to you

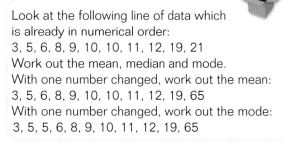

Look at the following line of data which is already in numerical order:
3, 5, 6, 8, 9, 10, 10, 11, 12, 19, 21
Work out the mean, median and mode.
With one number changed, work out the mean:
3, 5, 6, 8, 9, 10, 10, 11, 12, 19, 65
With one number changed, work out the mode:
3, 5, 5, 6, 8, 9, 10, 11, 12, 19, 65

With the mode, if there is more than one number that appears the most, then you may have two modes; this is called bi-modal. For example, look at the following line of numbers: 2, 4, 5, 5, 5, 6, 7, 7, 7, 8, 9; bi-modal = 5 and 7.

If there is an even number of scores, then to work out the median you take the two middle scores, add them up and divide them by their number. For example: 2, 4, 5, 6, 8, 9; median = 5 + 6 = 11 divided by 2 = 5.5.

The range

The measure of dispersion we will look at is the range. The range is very simple to work out: it is just the highest score minus the lowest score, with 1 added if whole numbers are used. For example: 5, 7, 8, 9, 21, 45, 55; range =55 − 5 + 1 = 51. This means that there is a possible range of 51 scores in this data set.

The advantage of the range is that it is very easy to calculate. The disadvantage is that the range ignores all values except the two extreme ones and is seriously affected by any outlying values.

Visual images

Any descriptive data can also be displayed using visual images.

Scattergraph

Correlations measure the relationship between two variables. For example, if shoe sizes are related to height, a scattergraph can be used to display this correlational data.

The two variables are plotted against each other; you can see if there is a correlation just by looking at the spread of the data plotted, and you can also see whether the correlation is positive or negative or whether no correlation exists.

The correlation results found after a statistical test has been carried out give a score between −1 (negative correlation) and +1 (positive correlation); this is called a correlation coefficient. For example, a score of +0.87 is a strong positive correlation.

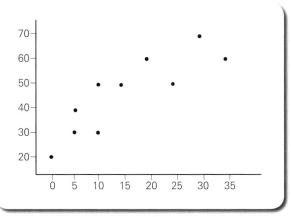

Figure 6.1 A scattergram is used to display correlational data

Bar chart

Bar charts are used to display data in separate categories – for example, non-continuous data.

The columns on the bar chart do not touch each other, indicating separate data. For example, gathering data on what 18-year-olds do on a Friday night can be graphically represented: four stayed in, two went to a party, three went to the cinema, three went to a club, four went to the pub and four went for a meal.

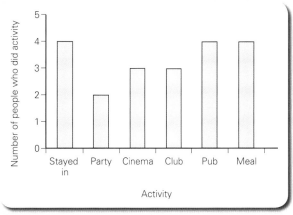

Figure 6.2 A bar chart is used to display data in separate categories

Histogram

Histograms show continuous data – for example, data measured on a continuous scale of measurement such as time. The histogram can show a type of frequency distribution, with a vertical column representing the number of scores in each category – for example, predicted downloads of a record from iTunes between 2011 and 2015.

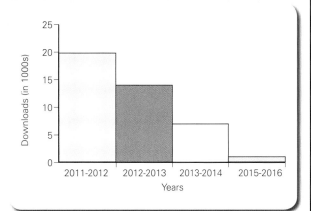

Figure 6.3 Histograms show data measured on a continuous scale

Qualitative data

Content analysis

Content analysis is a general term that refers to collecting data from people and society indirectly through work produced by that person or society. Through this method it is possible to understand a person or society's psychological state or make-up. It can be used to analyse messages in the media, including stories published in newspapers and speeches made by politicians.

Your sample of qualitative data could be taken from the media or from an interview – for example, looking at children's adverts and finding that in these adverts the boys' toys seem to be 80 per cent based around aggression. The content analysis would use a coding system such as a definition of an aggressive toy (a list of these toys would be compiled). This coding system provides an objective, systematic and descriptive record of events, allowing for a methodology that is replicable. The data collected are then analysed to see how often each coding unit occurs – that is, counting how often the particular item of interest occurs. The research methods that use content analysis include observations, interviews and questionnaires where the questions are open.

The advantages of content analysis are that it allows patterns in the data to be analysed and summarised; once you have numerical data some kind of statistical analysis can take place. Content analysis is also considered to be valid as it is based on material gained from the real world.

The disadvantages of this technique include the loss of detailed information when changing qualitative data into quantitative data. Also, when coding behaviour, the definition of behaviour needs to be clear, otherwise scoring of behaviour becomes subjective. Many behaviours are difficult to define clearly. How do we define self-esteem, for example? How many codes would there be?

Categorisation

Categorisation is another way of analysing qualitative data. This involves grouping similar items together. For example, if you were interviewing a soldier about his experiences in the Second World War, you would group together statements by the interviewee about particular subjects, such as the emotions he felt and his relationships with other soldiers. This method is very subjective and the data gathered are often biased by the researcher's own interpretation of the data. The method can be used to analyse data from interviews, observations and case studies.

Levels of significance

When carrying out research on human behaviour there are no certainties, even when carrying out controlled experiments that produced detailed quantitative data. Most of the behaviour that psychologists research is abstract in nature and therefore hard to quantify. Therefore, any quantitative data that is collected during psychological research is put though the rigours of a test of significance. This is generally applied only to experimental methods and correlations. A statistically significant result is one which is unlikely to have occurred by chance. We can never be totally certain that chance has not played a part in the results, but when these chances are proved to be very slim, we can accept the experimental hypothesis and reject the null hypothesis.

How do we decide when to accept the experimental hypothesis and reject the null hypothesis? To answer this question we need to look at the level of significance. Generally in psychology we accept the 5 per cent (0.05) level of significance, which means that the probability that the results were arrived at by chance is 5 per cent or less, making the results at least 95 per cent accurate. At times, more stringent levels of significance are used: 1 per cent (0.01). How do we know our results are significant at the 5 per cent level? We must put the results through statistical analysis, such as a statistical test; the test we choose will depend on the research method used and the level of measurement of the data. We will consider the level of measurement first.

Levels of measurement

Any quantitative data found in psychological research will be at one of four levels. It is important to identify this; if you want to know if your results are significant or not, you must select the correct statistical test to analyse your data and this will depend on the level of measurement and the research method used.

Nominal level

The first and easiest is the nominal level, when data simply fall into categories – for example, asking ten students what they did on a Friday night: three stayed in, two went to the pub, two went out on dates and three went the cinema. The data is in frequency form – in separate, exclusive categories.

Ordinal level

The next level of measurement is the ordinal level, when you can put results in some kind of order – for example, from highest to lowest. If you were to give students a spelling test and the score is out of 20, you would put the scores in order from highest to lowest. This tells us the order of the participants but does not tell us anything about the distance between these different positions. For example, consider a study that measures aggression on a scale from 1 to 100, where one participant gets a score of 10 and another a score of 20. This does not tell us that the second person is twice as aggressive as the first. This is because the study has

Figure 6.4 The level of measurement of data allows us to choose a statistical test

used a scale invented by the researcher and we cannot assume that intervals along its length are equal.

Interval level

The next level of measurement is interval level, when fixed units of measurement are used that have equal distances between all points on the scale concerned. Interval data lacks a real zero, though – for example, temperature can fall below zero into minus temperature.

Ratio level

The fourth kind of data is at the ratio level, which is similar to interval level; it has fixed units with equal measurement, but with **ratio data** you have an absolute zero – for example, height in centimetres or time in seconds. We can compare a person's height with that of the average of the population, and we can make such statements as 2 metres being twice as tall as 1 metre.

Of the four levels of measurement available to the psychologist, nominal data is the weakest. Information is allocated into categories by counting frequencies of occurrence within each category.

Ordinal data can be meaningfully compared with each other; one value might be higher than the other.

Interval and ratio data are both measured in fixed units with equal distances. Interval data has a zero which is not meaningful (e.g. temperature), but with ratio data, the zero is meaningful (e.g. time in seconds).

Statistical tests

Once we know the level of measurement of our data, we can consider which statistical test to apply to our results, to see if they are statistically significant or not.

In order to obtain the probability level of a set of results occurring through chance, an appropriate inferential statistical test needs to be selected and applied. There are five important statistical tests:

1   Chi-squared test

2   Sign test

3   Mann-Whitney U test

4   Wilcoxon matched pairs signed ranks test

5   Spearman's rank order correlation coefficient.

The test we choose depends on two factors:

- The level of measurement of the data obtained.

- The type of data obtained (e.g. the research method used).

Table 6.2

RESEARCH METHOD	NOMINAL	ORDINAL, INTERVAL OR RATIO
Independent data/independent groups design	Chi-squared test	Mann–Whitney U test
Related data/repeated measures design	Sign test	Wilcoxon matched pairs signed ranks test
Correlational		Spearman's rank order correlations coefficient

As we can see from Table 6.2, we simply look at the level of measurement of data required and then cross-reference this with the research method used to acquire that data, and therefore the type of data (related, independent or correlational) – this gives us the statistical test we need to apply.

Once it has been applied, every statistical test will give an observed value which is then compared to the critical value. Depending on the specific test, if the observed value is above or below the critical value this will either accept or reject the null hypothesis and either accept or reject the experimental hypothesis (see Table 6.3).

Table 6.3

STATISTICAL TEST	OBSERVED VALUE EQUAL TO OR BELOW CRITICAL VALUE	OBSERVED VALUE EQUAL TO OR ABOVE CRITICAL VALUE
Chi-squared	Accept null	Accept experimental
Sign test	Accept experimental	Accept null
Mann–Whitney U	Accept experimental	Accept null
Wilcoxon matched pairs	Accept experimental	Accept null
Spearman's rank order	Accept null	Accept experimental

Over to you

Why do we use statistical tests and how do we decide which one to use?

Key example

A researcher at a university carries out a study on memory, testing the hypothesis: 'Gender has an effect on memory recall'. Twenty participants are chosen (ten male and ten female), using opportunity sampling. The researcher simply stands by the door of his lab and asks the first ten men and ten women who go past to take part in the study. Memory is tested by getting participants to recall a list of ten randomly chosen words of equal length. The participants sit in a quiet room and are given the list of words to study for one minute. They are then given one minute to recall as many words as possible. As the data collected are at the ordinal level and the experiment is an independent groups design, the researcher analyses the results using a Mann-Whitney U test and finds that his results are significant at the 5 per cent level. He retains the experimental hypothesis, 'Gender has an effect on memory recall'.

Reliability and validity

Any findings need to be checked for their reliability and validity before any firm conclusions can be drawn. As we have seen throughout the first few chapters, each research method has different advantages and disadvantages when it comes to checking the reliability and validity of the results obtained. Also different methods have different levels of **reliability** and **validity**, with lab experiments having good internal validity and reliability, and naturalistic observations having good ecological validity. There are several ways that researchers can improve the validity and reliability of these results, irrespective of the research method chosen, you will recognise some of these from the material you studied for your AS PY 2 exam.

Ways of ensuring reliability

One of the main aims of most research is to be able to conduct studies in such a way that once a study has been carried out, other researchers who follow the same set of procedures and methods can obtain similar findings.

Split test

In a split test, items for any kind of test are divided and looked at separately. In the case of a questionnaire the questions are split – for example, all the even questions are put on one test and all the odd questions on another test. One person does both tests at the same time, and the scores from both tests are then compared to see if the results are consistent. Another example might be to consider a questionnaire based on ageing. Are all the questions asking about ageing? After the data are gathered, the results from the questionnaire are split in half and compared; if they are similar, this would indicate reliability. This tests the internal reliability – how consistently a method measures within itself.

Test-retest

This is simply the same test given to the same participant at different times to see if the results are similar. This tests external reliability – how consistently a method measures over time. This can also be applied when testing in different locations and across the population.

Inter-observer reliability

This is the extent to which observers agree on the behaviours they have observed. Any behaviour to be observed must first be clearly defined, and all types of that behaviour coded or put into categories so that any observer can use the coding system devised to obtain similar results. Two observers can then carry out the same observation and their ratings can be compared to provide a measure of inter–observer reliability. A lot of behaviour to be observed may be very complex. For example, if you were interested in observing attraction, what does this mean? What is attraction? Is it a look someone gives, some kind of body language?

Ways of ensuring validity

Most researchers are keen to show that their results are valid (i.e. accurate), but there are two kinds of validity and it is often very hard to achieve both.

Internal validity

This kind of validity is only really achievable within the lab setting. To achieve this, the experimenter must make sure that he or she has:

1 controlled all variables to prevent confounding variables

2 reliable and consistent measures in place

3 standardised instructions and procedures

4 obtained a random sample

5 controlled for experimenter effects/bias, demand characteristics and evaluation apprehension.

Three ways to test validity are content validity, concurrent validity and construct validity.

- **Content validity** – does the test represent the topic or subject being studied? This may involve a more rigorous look at the measuring instrument – for example, all parts of a questionnaire are examined, and each question is looked at carefully for its content.

- **Concurrent validity** – two sets of scores are taken at the same time, one from the new experiment and one from an already established experiment. The results are then checked to see whether they correlate. If one test on aggression gives a participant a high aggressive score and another test also gives the participant a high aggressive score, we have concurrent validity.

- **Construct validity** – does the test actually measure what it sets out to measure? For example, if a test measures aggression then that person should naturally behave as aggressively as the test results state.

Ecological validity

This refers to being able to generalise any findings from a study to any population group and any real-world setting. Lab experiments lack **ecological validity**; the only way round this is to carry out either a field experiment or a natural experiment, both of which have greater ecological validity, as they generally take place in a natural environment. Naturalistic observations can also be said to have greater ecological validity.

Findings and conclusions

A distinction has to be drawn here between findings and conclusions. Findings refer to the results of any particular study. The findings of any study can be quantitative or qualitative in nature.

The conclusion refers to the inferences you make about a set of results. The results are summarised and statements are made about their meaning which might be generalised to the rest of the relevant population.

Summary

Descriptive data

Descriptive data includes mean, mode, median and range, as well as how data can be displayed (e.g. bar charts, scattergraphs and histograms).

Analysing qualitative data

This includes content analysis, which allows qualitative data to be coded in an objective and measurable way, although coding is often difficult. Categorisation – grouping similar items together – can also be used to analyse qualitative data.

Inferential statistics

This involves drawing conclusions about a wider population from a sample of that population. We must consider both levels of significance and levels of measurement and their advantages and disadvantages.

Descriptive and inferential statistics for analysing data

Statistical tests

Once we know the level of measurement for our data we must use a statistical test to see if our results are significant. The five important tests are the chi-squared test, the sign test, the Mann-Whitney U test, the Wilcoxon matched pairs signed ranks test, and Spearman's rank order correlation coefficient.

Findings and conclusions

Findings refer to the results of a particular study and can be either quantitative or qualitative. The conclusion refers to the inferences made about a set of results.

Ways of ensuring reliability and validity

Before drawing a conclusion, we must look at the reliability and validity of our results. Reliability could be tested using split test, test-retest and inter-observer reliability methods. With validity we must look at internal validity (the control the researcher had over the experiment) and ecological validity (how readily results can be extrapolated to the wider population).

Exam focus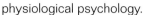

Exam structure: Chapters 1–6

PY 3 is split into three sections: A, B and C. Sections A and B are the research methods questions, where you will need the material covered in chapters 1 to 6. A research method will be described and then there will be a range of short, compulsory questions about research methods; some of these will be specific to the research method described, while others will be based round the general topic of research methods.

Each of the questions will be worth about 25 marks. There will generally be two questions worth 25 marks each, giving a total of 50 marks. The marks will based around three skills, as set out below:

AO1: Knowledge and understanding of science and how science works
- Knowledge and understanding of psychological theories, terminology, concepts, studies and methods in all of the following areas of psychology: cognitive, social, developmental, individual differences and biological.
- Further development of knowledge and understanding of psychological principles, perspectives and applications from at least two of the core areas: cognitive, social developmental, individual differences and biological.
- Being able to communicate this knowledge and understanding of psychology in a clear and effective manner.

AO2: Application of knowledge and understanding of science and how science works
- Analysis and evaluation of psychological theories, concepts, studies and methods in at least two of the areas of psychology: cognitive, social, developmental, individual differences and physiological psychology.
- The ability to analyse and evaluate psychology principles, perspectives and applications in relation to research issues, debates and controversies in psychology.

AO3: How science works – psychology
- Designing, conducting and reporting psychological investigation(s); choosing from a range of methods; and taking into account the issues of reliability, validity and ethics.
- Drawing conclusions from data with precision and accuracy.
- Analysing, interpreting, explaining and evaluating the methodology, results and impact of investigative activities in a variety of ways.
- Designing investigations and drawing valid conclusions from them; analysing data, including the use of inferential statistics; and understanding the scientific nature of psychology.

For sections A and B, the weighting of the skills will be 20 marks for AO1, 20 marks for AO2 and 10 marks for AO3.

Exam tips
1 Carefully read the piece of research described – some of the questions will refer to this directly.
2 Make sure you can identify the research method used.
3 Look at the marks for each specific question: make sure you write enough for the number of marks.
4 Carefully read each question: if it asks for two advantages or two ethical issues, make sure you write two – do not repeat yourself.

7 Issues in research

INTRODUCTION

This chapter covers the **issues** that can occur within psychology, especially when carrying out scientific research and when applying the findings of such research to the real world. The first two issues include the advantages and disadvantages of using scientific methods in psychology. This also refers to specific studies that can be deemed to be scientific, and the advantages and disadvantages of these. The next two issues include ethical issues that arise when using human participants in research, the ways of dealing with these ethical issues and how successful these methods are. This also refers to specific studies to illustrate the ethical issues that research has caused, alongside other studies that have attempted to deal with these ethical issues, and their successes or failures. The last two issues include ethical issues that arise when using non-human animals, again referring to specific studies and research, and the arguments for and against using animals, along with ethical issues arising from two applications

of psychology to the real world, again referring to relevant studies and/or examples of real-world applications.

OBJECTIVES

The specification requires you to have an awareness of the following:

- The advantages of the use of the scientific method in psychology.

- The disadvantages of the use of the scientific method in psychology.

- Ethical issues in the use of human participants in research in psychology.

- Ways of dealing with ethical issues when using human participants in research in psychology.

- Ethical issues in the use of non-human animals in research in psychology.

- Ethical issues arising from two applications of psychology in the real world.

The first four essays follow a similar kind of structure. Candidates will be asked to discuss/explain/consider the topic in question, often backing up their answer with reference to relevant theories and/or studies.

This chapter covers section C in the PY 3 exam paper. At the end of this chapter on page 78 you will find an explanation of section C and some hints about tackling it.

Key term

Issue – an important subject requiring a decision, an outcome or consequence.

Advantages of the scientific method

Within psychology many studies have used scientific methods to collect data and carry out research. The use of these methods has many advantages. The most scientific method in psychology is obviously the lab experiment, but in fact any kind of experiment is generally considered to be scientific. This is not to say that other methods are not also scientific – for example, an observation can also be considered to be scientific if some of the scientific methods such as control are applied.

There are many **advantages** of using the **scientific** method, including greater control over **extraneous variables** in order to produce fewer confounding variables. This greater control also allows the researcher to establish a cause-and-effect relationship.

With research methods, the lab experiment has the greatest control and allows the experimenter to control and manipulate the IV in order to see its effect on the DV. It can be argued that other methods used within psychological research also have good control and use scientific application. For example, Milgram's 1963 study on obedience had good control despite using an observational method. It might also be argued that Zimbardo's (1973) prison role-play study had a certain level of control. The lab experiment is still recognised as the most scientific, however.

Any control allows for greater accuracy in the results – in this case, greater internal validity. It also allows for better reliability – that is, the experiment can be repeated and the same results achieved, therefore making the results more consistent. The scientific method also allows for greater **objectivity**, often using **standardised instructions** and **procedures** more than other subjective research methods such as the case study.

The scientific method allows researchers to use scientific equipment to carry out their research. It also allows the researcher to gather more data that can be analysed. It is especially good for acquiring quantitative data, which can be subjected to statistical analysis to see if the hypothesis can be accepted or rejected. It is argued that the scientific method gives more credence to psychology as it can be backed up by scientific evidence. Both the behavioural and biological perspectives adhere to the scientific approach and its methods.

Key terms

Scientific – using scientific methods and equipment, not only in terms of a laboratory experiment, but any methods that are deemed scientific. Scientific method consequently refers to a method that is used to prove or disprove a theory or hypothesis. For a method to be deemed scientific, it must collect data in an objective, controlled fashion. It must have the potential to be disproved – that is, falsifiable – and it must be carried out with set procedures and instructions in a way that allows for reliability, so that it can be repeated and similar results gained.
Advantages – benefits; in this case how using the scientific approach benefits psychology.

Key terms

Extraneous variables – any variable other than the IV (being manipulated) that could in all truth affect the DV (being measured).
Objectivity – in research terms this means applying and analysing research without any emotion or personal bias.
Subjectivity – in research terms this means applying and analysing research in a way that is affected by a researcher's emotions and prejudices.
Standardised instructions – a set of instructions generally used in experiments that are consistent in wording and content for all participants across all different experimental conditions.
Standardised procedures – a set of rules and procedures set down to indicate how a study should be administrated and/or scored.

Referring back to the definition of 'scientific', any research method can be considered scientific as long as it collects data in an objective, controlled manner. The following research methods have been put in order of how scientific they can be considered to be, with lab experiments considered the most scientific and observations generally the least scientific (although this is not set in stone):

Figure 7.1 Interviews and questionnaires allow us to gain information in written or verbal form

1 **Lab experiment**

2 **Field experiment**

3 **Natural experiment**

4 **Interviews/questionnaires**

5 **Observations**

Summary of the advantages of the scientific method

- Internal validity – the effects on the DV are a product of the manipulation of the IV.
- Reliability – the use of the scientific method allows for good reliability. Similar results can be obtained using the same participants because scientific methods tend to have standardised instructions and procedures, allowing for good replication, especially with lab experiments. However, even observations can have standardised procedures in terms of how behaviour is observed, making sure it is coded correctly and allowing for inter-rater reliability.
- Good control – scientific methods have good control over most extraneous variables, especially in the lab experiment.
- Fewer confounding variables – with the lab experiment especially, because of the level of control there is less chance of confounding variables than with other less scientific methods; this means that we can state that it is the IV causing changes in the DV.
- Cause and effect – the scientific method lets us state that it is the IV causing changes in the DV.
- Quantitative data can be collected – this quantitative data can then be analysed using descriptive and inferential statistical tests, which can then be used to prove or disprove a hypothesis.
- A lot of apparatus can be used – a lot of research equipment can be used to collect data (e.g. measuring instruments).
- Participants can be chosen – with scientific methods, especially lab experiments, you can choose the participants that best represent your target population.
- Animals can be studied – you can study and control animal behaviour in a scientific setting.

- All behaviour can be observed – in a controlled setting you are less likely to miss any behaviour displayed; all behaviour can be recorded.
- Experimental realism – with some experiments the participants can be fooled into believing that the artificial set-up is real.
- Mundane realism – the artificial situation or activity can be made to resemble a real-life situation.
- More objective and more controlled – in comparison to other less scientific methods, such as observations and case studies, the scientific method is more objective and allows for more control.

Over to you

What advantages did each of the following studies have?

- Milgram's (1963) study on obedience
- Asch's (1951) study on conformity
- Sherif's (1935) study on conformity
- Selye's (1936) study on stress
- Peterson and Peterson's (1959) study on duration in short-term memory
- Ainsworth and Bell's (1970) study on attachments
- Loftus and Palmer's (1974) study on eyewitness testimony.

Key term

Disadvantage – an unfavourable circumstance, situation, thing or person – in this case, how using the scientific approach can disadvantage or handicap psychological research.

Remember

Stick to the essay title. If you are asked to discuss the advantages of a certain study or method you will not receive any credit for discussing disadvantages. Do not start discussing whether or not psychology is a science – that is a different essay on a different paper.

Disadvantages of the scientific method

The main disadvantage of the **scientific** approach is that it is artificial. Psychology is all about human behaviour. Is it possible, therefore, to use scientific methods to study it? Again, the scientific method does not just apply to experimental methods; it can also be applied to any research method that uses scientific applications, such as controlled observations; these are also disadvantaged because their control makes them less natural, and therefore they are also artificial.

The use of the scientific method leads to low ecological validity – for example, any behaviour observed in a lab is not the same as behaviour observed in the natural environment. The use of the lab as a research method has the least ecological validity. Many factors make the lab experiment artificial, including the actual study itself – for example, Asch's (1951) study on conformity; we do not all generally conform by looking at lines on a board and judging their length (lack of mundane realism).

The actual environment of lab experiments can also affect the behaviour of the participants. This can happen in several ways:

- experimenter bias
- experimenter effects
- demand characteristics
- evaluation apprehension.

The experimenter themselves may behave in such as way as to affect the results. They might be rude or their appearance or gender might influence the participants' results. The experimenter might also be biased and interpret the results in such a way as to fit in with what they expected.

Demand characteristics may occur within a lab or artificial setting if the participants know they are in a study. They may try to work out what the experimenter is trying to prove and give answers to support or discredit the study. The participants might also pick up subtle cues from the experimenter. This would make any results invalid.

Due to the artificial nature of the study, participants may suffer evaluation apprehension. They might become nervous because they feel they are being evaluated. Again, in these circumstances the results would not be valid.

The participants may also try to portray themselves in a good light and therefore not demonstrate natural behaviour (social desirability bias). Also the scientific approach does not apply to all the perspectives within psychology, such as the psychodynamic and humanistic approaches.

Key terms

Mundane realism – when an artificial situation closely resembles a real-life situation (e.g. the participant is carrying out an activity that is similar to what they do in real life).

Experimental realism – when participants are fooled into believing that an artificial set-up is real.

Demand characteristics – participants attempt to work out the hypothesis being tested and either give the results expected or the opposite. The participant looks for cues from the researcher (e.g. their tone of voice or body language) or simply from the questions asked.

Experimenter effects – the experimenter's behaviour, appearance, and so on may have an effect on the participants' behaviour and, consequently, the results.

Experimenter bias – when the experimenter treats the participants and the results in a way that supports his or her own view.

Evaluation apprehension – participants are apprehensive about being judged and this may affect the results.

Social desirability bias – participants change their normal behaviour in order to be viewed in a more favourable light.

Summary of the disadvantages of the use of the scientific method
- Lack of ecological validity – not a real-life setting.
- Lack of generalisability – your sample of participants cannot be generalised to the rest of the population.
- **Demand characteristic** – participants' reactions to being part of a study.
- **Experimenter effects** – the experimenter's behaviour, and so on, and its effect on the participants.
- **Evaluation apprehension** – participants' apprehension at being part of a study.
- **Experimenter bias** – the effect of the experimenter treating participants and/or results in a biased way.
- **Social desirability bias** – participants behaving in a way that portrays them in a positive light.
- Lack of **mundane realism** – activity or exercise that in no way reflects normal everyday life.
- Lack of experimental realism – participants do not believe that the set-up of the study is real (they are not fooled).

Over to you

What disadvantages did each of the following studies have?

- Milgram's (1963) study on obedience

- Asch's (1951) study on conformity

- Sherif's (1935) study on conformity

- Selye's (1936) study on stress

- Peterson and Peterson's (1959) study on duration of short-term memory

- Ainsworth and Bell's (1970) study on attachment

- Loftus and Palmer's (1974) study on eyewitness testimony.

Remember

Stick to the essay title. If you are asked to discuss the disadvantages of a certain study or method, you will not receive any credit for discussing advantages.

Over to you

What advantages would there be if you were asked to use a scientific method to find out:

- how many pints of beer would impair a person's ability to drive a car

- the most boring book in the country

- the maximum amount people can remember watching a ten-minute film.

What disadvantages would there be to using a scientific method?

Ethical issues in the use of human participants in research

If you have already studied chapter 4 in this book the issues arising from the use of human participants in psychological research will already be familiar to you. This is because these issues are relevant for both the Research methods sections and the Issues in Research sections of the PY 3 exam.

Within psychological research ethical issues have arisen when using human participants. These issues include:

- deception

- lack of protection from harm (physical and psychological)

- lack of informed consent

- lack of the right to withdraw

- lack of confidentiality.

The debate rages about the ethical issues within psychological research, with researchers arguing that it is essential that certain studies are carried out to allow theories to be tested. Some studies are criticised for causing ethical issues, while researchers argue that the issue did not exist or was dealt with before, during or after the study. Many studies in psychology cause the issue of deception, as often it is not possible to inform participants about the true nature of a study without negating the effects of the study. For example, Asch's (1951) study on conformity had to use deception or it would not have worked; because of the issue of deception, you also then have the issue of a lack of informed consent.

A major ethical issue arises with many studies if it is deemed that the study has caused harm to the participants – for example, research by Milgram (1963) and Zimbardo (1973). Again, studies criticised for causing harm have refuted these accusations by stating that the participants were in no way harmed, or, if they were, they were debriefed and counselled afterwards in order to counter any negative effects.

Lack of protection from harm (physical and psychological)

The first and most important ethical issue is protection from physical and psychological harm. The key question to be asked with any research is whether the harm caused during the research was greater than that experienced in ordinary life.

With this issue, physical harm is fairly easy to measure because the effects can be seen easily, but psychological harm is harder to report. This may include stress, which we know is a psychological state, but which also has physical symptoms.

Deception

Participants who take part in any research must not be deceived if at all possible. When participants are deceived we take away their chance to give their fully informed consent to take part in the study. There are obviously some times when deception is inappropriate and some where it may be more admissible.

Lack of informed consent

Informed consent means informing the participants about the research. This would include what the research will require, the purpose of the research and the rights the participants have (e.g. right to confidentiality, right to withdraw at any time and only to take part when informed consent has been given).

Lack of right to withdraw

Before the outset of any study the researchers should make it obvious to the participants that they have the right to withdraw themselves at any time during

or after the study, and that the knowledge and/or data acquired can also be removed from the study and the final results.

Lack of confidentiality

Any knowledge obtained about a participant during a study should be kept confidential unless otherwise agreed beforehand. Participants taking part in any psychological research have a right to expect that information they provide in the form of data or results will also be treated confidentially, and, if circulated, that it will not be identified as theirs.

Some studies countered these claims of ethical issues. How did the following studies deal with the claim that they had caused ethical issues?

- Milgram's (1963) study on obedience

- Zimbardo's (1973) study on conformity.

Over to you

What ethical issues did the following studies have?

- Milgram's (1963) study on obedience

- Zimbardo's (1973) study on conformity

- Asch's (1951) study on conformity

- Watson and Rayner's (1920) study on classical conditioning

- Bandura's (1961) study on social learning

- Landis's (1924) study on emotions and facial expressions.

Remember

Stick to the essay title. If you are asked to discuss the ethical issues that arise, you can mention how some researchers dispute these issues in terms of their studies. Do not start discussing how these issues can be dealt with – that is another essay title.

Figure 7.2 A cost-benefit analysis is a way of dealing with the issue of protection from harm

Dealing with ethical issues when using human participants in research

Ethical issues have arisen when using human participants in psychological research. These issues include deception, lack of protection from harm (physical and psychological), lack of informed consent, lack of the right to withdraw and lack of confidentiality. If the material in this section seems familiar to you, it may be that you have already covered it in chapter 4. This is because dealing with ethical issues is important for parts A and B, as well as section C, of the PY 3 exam. There are several ways of dealing with these ethical issues.

Let us first take the issue of a lack of informed consent. Many studies cannot fully inform the participants about the true aims of the study beforehand, as this would affect the validity of the results through demand characteristics and social desirability bias. Therefore we can use presumptive consent and prior general consent. Any study that does not get informed consent will have to address the issue of deception. One way around this is to debrief the participants at the end of the study. Another way is to use a role-play method; hopefully each participant will adopt the role that he or she is given and will act according to that role. There are several ways of dealing with the issue of protection from harm, including doing a cost-benefit analysis or carrying out a debrief of the participants. All ethical issues can also be dealt with through the use of ethical guidelines and ethical committees.

All these ways of dealing with ethical issues have been supported or criticised for their effectiveness. For example, some researchers argue that

protection from harm can be resolved by a debrief, but does this really return a participant to the same mental and physical state he or she was in before a study began? Another example is the use of presumptive consent – can we state that getting the consent of people similar to the sample to be used is really getting informed consent?

Dealing with protection from harm

There are several ways of dealing with this issue. If the harm is caused indirectly – through the use of deception, a lack of informed consent, invasion of privacy or disclosure of private information – it can be dealt with using the methods specific to those issues, and hopefully this will solve the issue of protection from harm.

One way to deal with protection from harm specifically is to do a cost-benefit analysis – do the benefits of the research outweigh any potential costs to the participants? This is often carried out before the research is done, so it lacks validity – it is quite difficult to judge accurately the effects of a study on participants before you have actually carried out the study.

Another way is to debrief participants at the end of the study. The main aim of any debriefing is to restore the participants to the same state they were before they took part in the study. Again, a problem with debriefing is that it is difficult to judge how successful it is.

A debriefing could also simply inform the participants about the study in its entirety, to set their minds at rest about what they have just participated in and offer them the right to withdraw their data and assure them that everything will be kept in confidence. Anyone truly traumatised after a study could be offered counselling to help restore them to the state they were in before the study took place.

Remember

Some establishments have their own ethical committees, which can be used to judge whether a study is ethically acceptable before it takes place.

Another way to protect participants from harm is to inform them that they can leave the study at any time.

A possible indirect way to protect participants from harm would be to inform them about the study beforehand to see if they would be happy to take part. Often this is not possible, however, so presumptive consent or prior general consent can be used (see below for dealing with a lack of informed consent).

Dealing with a lack of informed consent

Each participant must give their consent to take part. If this is not possible, presumptive consent or prior general consent must be sought and then a debrief must be given.

Often, revealing the true nature of any research through consent may negate the specific study; for this reason there are other options that can be used. One is presumptive consent; this is when you take a selection of participants from your chosen target population and ask this sample if they would have consented to a take part in a study that used deception and/or could possibly cause some harm. For example, if the research were targeted at sixth-form students, you would take a sample of sixth-form students. If they agree and state that they would have given their voluntary informed consent, then we can assume that they speak for the opinions of the target population.

A second method would be to use prior general consent. With this method participants who might be used in a study are told that sometimes subjects are misinformed about the real nature of a study. Only those who agree that such a practice is acceptable would be chosen to take part in the study. Therefore they have given general informed consent, but they do not know whether or not the actual research they take part in uses misinformation. A similar method would be get informed consent from participants several weeks before the study is to take place, in the hope that they might have forgotten what they were told (i.e. they forget that they are being deceived).

A third way would be simply to debrief participants after the study has taken place (see below) and give them the chance to withdraw their data if they wish to do so. Of course, the researcher should allow participants to leave at any time, even if they have given their consent to take part in a study, if they later realise that they would like to recall that consent.

Dealing with deception

There are several ways of dealing with the issue of deception – one way is to use role play. The participants are told all about the study beforehand and about any manipulations that might take place – for example, they might be told that someone is going to pretend to be upset in order to measure their reactions. The participants are told to act as if they did not know what was really happening. A problem with this is that the behaviour can never be guaranteed to be natural or real as the participant is only playing a role.

Another option is to inform the participants about the general nature of the study (not the detailed hypothesis being tested) and, again, ask them to act out the experimental procedures as though they were naive participants. Would their behaviour be more natural if they were not told exactly what was being measured, or would the behaviour still be artificial? Alternatively, the participants can be deceived and then given a full debriefing at the end of the study (see below), and offered the option to have their results removed.

Dealing with confidentiality

The main ways of dealing with the issue of confidentiality are to inform the participants that their names and all their results will be kept in total confidence, and to offer them the chance to withdraw their data at any time. During any study, referring to each participant as a number rather than a name will assist in keeping information confidential.

Dealing with the right to withdraw

At the beginning of any research participants are told that at any time during the study they have the right to withdraw themselves and their data. It should be made clear that there is no pressure for them to continue at any point, whether

at the start of the study, halfway through or right at the end. If participants are still unhappy after they have been debriefed, they still have the right to require that their data be withdrawn and destroyed in their presence.

Debriefing

[Debriefing is] 'a post-experimental interview in which the experimenter tries to restore the participant to the same psychological state they were in when they entered the experiment' (Cardwell 2003)

Debriefing is an important part of any psychological research, especially when deception or some kind of physical or psychological harm has occurred. Debriefing participants has two functions: it aims to restore participants to the same state they were in when they entered the investigation, and it can help a good researcher to regard participants as colleagues, not as objects to be used solely for the ends of the experimenter.

However, debriefing does not provide a justification for any unethical aspect of the investigation. Often it is seen as adequate merely to inform participants of the true nature of the investigation, but at other times this would be insufficient. If a participant is traumatised during some research, merely debriefing them about what a study was all about would not resolve this issue.

Remember

Debriefing is not an ethical issue; it is a way of dealing with ethical issues.

Remember

If an essay question asks you how ethical issues were dealt with, do not just describe the studies and state what the ethical issues were.

Over to you

How were ethical issues dealt with in the following studies, and were the methods used effective?

- Milgram's (1963) study on obedience
- Zimbardo's (1973) study on conformity
- Hofling's (1966) study on obedience.

Ethical issues in the use of non-human animals in research

This area requires a different approach to the other topics we have considered in this chapter. We need to look at the ethical issues that arise when using animals in research, including the arguments for and against the use of animals in research.

Within psychological research, ethical issues have arisen when using non-human animals, mainly in relation to protection from harm. Many studies have led to animals being harmed. The issue here is to discuss the harm that such research causes, and to consider the arguments for and against research that causes such harm.

Figure 7.3 What ethical issues arise from the use of animals in research studies?

A lot of psychologists argue that it is the responsibility of researchers to use animals whenever possible in their studies if such research could alleviate any kind of human suffering. Other psychologists have argued that it is ethically and morally wrong to abuse any animal simply because another species has greater power – that is, they claim that it is wrong for one species to consider itself more important than any other species on the planet (speciesism). Other researchers and psychologists take a third viewpoint and state that animal research should be undertaken, but that set guidelines should be followed so that only beneficial research is carried out, with strict controls over the amount of stress and suffering that is caused.

Over to you

What ethical issues arose from the following studies on animals?

- Seyle's (1936) study on stress using rats
- Seligman's (1974) study on learned helplessness using dogs
- Brady's (1958) study on stress and ulcers using monkeys
- Harlow's (1959) study on maternal deprivation using monkeys
- Pavlov's (1927) study on classical conditioning using dogs
- Skinner's (1938) study on operant conditioning using rats and pigeons.

Remember

The main issue with most animal research is protection from harm.

Arguments in favour of the use of non-human animals in research

- Greater control – when studying non-human animals the researcher has greater control over the animals.

- Objectivity – there is more chance of achieving this when studying animals; humans tend to have fewer expectations and biases about other species.

- Less of an ethical issue – we can do things to animals we cannot do to humans.

- Similarity – humans and non-humans are sufficiently similar in their physiology for us to be able to draw conclusions about behaviour; if certain behaviour is found in one species, it will repeated in another.

- Legislation and guidelines – the Animals Act 1986 protects the rights of animals, allowing for safer and more controlled research.

- Use of Bateson decision cube – if used correctly, this system will control any research carried out. The system assesses any animal research to be conducted by looking at three criteria:

1 The quality of research to be carried out has to be at the highest level.

2 Any animal suffering must be kept to a minimum.

3 The research must offer certainty of benefit to humankind.

Arguments against the use of non-human animals in research

- Cannot apply to humans – animals are so different to humans that the experiments conducted on animals are of little value to us.

- Speciesism – any harm caused to animals is similar to being racist, discriminating against one species for the benefit of another.

- Ethics – no research is worth the unnecessary suffering of animals.

> ### Remember
>
> This topic asks you to consider ethical issues that have arisen in research on non-human animals – it invites a discussion of these issues, both for and against.

Ethical issues arising from two applications of psychology in the real world

This topic also requires a different approach when attempting to answer questions on it in the exam.

When psychology has been applied to the real world, it has led to certain ethical issues – areas that spring to mind include warfare (interrogation, propaganda, dehumanisation) and advertising (the use of persuasive commercials).

Your essay must describe two real-world applications, as well as explaining the ethical issues they have caused. Your main focus will probably be the harm that was caused by the real-world application.

To take the example of advertisements, these attempt to persuade people to buy certain products. Much of the time they use physical attractiveness and expertise to try to make us believe in the product. Psychology has been used by advertisers to make potential customers develop a need for the product, to make the product stand out from others, to persuade us to buy the product and then convince us that we need to keep buying it. It can be argued that these techniques create ethical issues as they make us believe something that is essentially not true – that is, they deceive us.

Advertising uses similar methods to propaganda, which persuades recipients to adhere to or accept opinions as if they were their own. We can see the ethical issues that have arisen, especially when propaganda is used alongside politics and warfare – for example, Hitler and Nazi Germany in their persecution of the

Figure 7.4 Psychology can be applied to real-world situations, including warfare

Figure 7.5 Can psychological research be used to support racism and discrimination?

Jews. This moves us on to other areas that have used applications of psychology, such as the military. The military has used methods of psychology in interrogation techniques, involving methods of sensory deprivation and brainwashing, which obviously lead to the ethical issue of causing harm.

The use of research within psychology can also lead to more general ethical issues when it is applied to the real world. A lot of research has indirectly led to race and gender bias. Some research has stated that differences in IQ and behaviour exist between different races, and this evidence has often been used in support of racism and discrimination. A lot of research within psychology has also been male-based, so women have also suffered discrimination in the form of sexism.

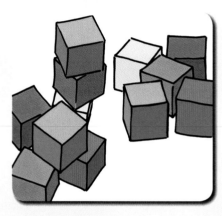

Figure 7.6 What ethical issues might arise in a study about child development?

Over to you

How did the following areas apply psychology to the real world, and what ethical issues have these caused?

- Advertising
- Military
- Psychological treatment
- Media (pop psychologists)
- Gender bias
- Cultural bias
- Child development.

Remember

Two applications of psychology in the real world need to be discussed in this essay, with a clear indication of the ethical issues they have caused. You could answer this question using applications from two different areas, such as the military and advertising, or you might use two different applications from the same area, such as the use of propaganda and of interrogation techniques within the military.

Summary

Issues in research

Advantages of the scientific method

The scientific method can refer to a range of experiment methods in psychology, not just lab experiments. It has many benefits, including good internal validity, good reliability and a high level of control by the researcher.

Ethical issues in the use of human participants in research

There are a number of ethical issues to deal with when using human participants, although some argue that behaving in a completely ethical way, getting informed consent and avoiding deception would affect results.

Disadvantages of the scientific method

Because scientific environments are artificial, the scientific method might suffer from low ecological validity and evaluation apprehension among participants, as well as experimenter bias.

Ethical issues when applying psychology to the real world

The main ethical issue is protection from harm: how research, theories, techniques, and so on, within psychology can lead to ethical issues when applied to the real world – for example, the use of psychology within the military (psychological torture) and within the media and advertising.

Ethical issues in the use of non-human animals in research

Using animals rather than humans in experiments has various advantages. Some researchers argue that animals should be used whenever possible in order to spare human suffering, while others believe that since animals cannot give consent, using them is unethical. Others believe in strict guidelines to limit the pain or suffering of animals used in research.

Dealing with ethical issues when using human participants in research

Role play or debriefing can be used to overcome deception. Prior or presumptive consent or debriefing can be used to overcome lack of informed consent. Ethical guidelines or committees can be used to overcome many of the ethical issues, especially protection from harm.

Exam focus ▶

Exam structure: Chapter 7

Section C of the PY 3 exam, which Chapter 7 relates to, is assessing AO3 skill.

AO3: How science works – psychology
- Designing, conducting and reporting psychological investigation(s); choosing from a range of methods; and taking into account the issues of reliability, validity and ethics.
- Drawing conclusions from data with precision and accuracy.
- Analysing, interpreting, explaining and evaluating the methodology, results and impact of investigative activities in a variety of ways.
- Designing investigations and drawing valid conclusions from them; analysing data, including the use of inferential statistics; and understanding the scientific nature of psychology.

There are two essays, both worth 15 marks, making a total of 30 marks for section C. Marks for the paper (PY 3) are 50 marks for sections A and B, and 30 marks for section C, making a total of 80 marks.

Exam tips
1 Be aware of the time you have – about 15 minutes to spend on each essay.
2 Stick to what the question is asking.
3 If you have to begin by setting the scene, do it in just a few sentences.
4 Try to back up each essay with relevant studies and/or research.
5 Top answers may try to evaluate the studies or researchers referred to in the question.

8 Controversies

INTRODUCTION

This chapter covers six controversies that exist within psychology and looks at studies and research that can be used to discuss and explain each one. The chapter covers the status of psychology as a science and the arguments for and against psychology being considered a science. It also looks at the controversy around the use of scientific benefits measured against ethical costs. The chapter covers the controversies over the existence of cultural bias and gender bias within psychology research and/or studies. The controversy between free will and determinism is discussed. The chapter also covers the balance of genetic and environmental influences on human behaviour.

At the end of this chapter, on page 93, the Exam focus section explains the structure of the controversies question in PY 4 and gives you some exam tips.

OBJECTIVES

The specification requires you to have an awareness of the following:

- The status of psychology as a science.

- The balance of scientific benefits measured against ethical costs in psychology.

- The balance of genetic and environmental influences on human behaviour.

- Issues of cultural bias in psychology.

- Issues of gender bias in psychology.

- The question of free will and determinism in respect of human behaviour.

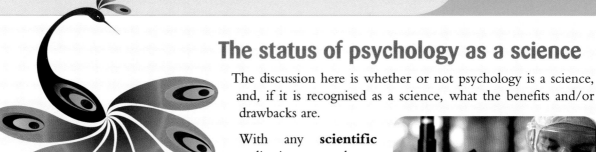

The status of psychology as a science

The discussion here is whether or not psychology is a science, and, if it is recognised as a science, what the benefits and/or drawbacks are.

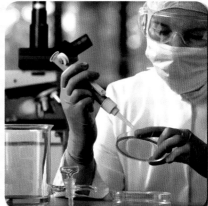

Figure 8.1 Is psychology a science?

With any **scientific** application, any theory that has been proven must also have the potential to be falsified, and any research carried out must have findings that it is possible to replicate. A major part of the scientific definition is the idea of falsifiability, the reasoning that any hypothesis, once proven, can then also be disproven.

For any area to be judged a science, it must have only one current explanation or theory. Any scientific study or research that is carried out must be done under objective conditions, unaffected by the biases or cultural expectations of the researcher. The scientific approach also makes the best use of control, particularly using the lab experiment, where all extraneous variables are under the direct control of the experimenter. The scientific method therefore allows hypotheses to be made and then tested, to be either proved or falsified; the use of the scientific method allows the hypothesis to be checked for its validity and reliability.

The evidence gained from the chosen sample of participants is often representative of the target population it has been drawn from; if the data are quantitative they can be subjected to statistical analysis and conclusions can be drawn. The data can also be referred to as being empirical (derived from experiments and observations). The analysis of such data can include inferential statistics to test if the results show any significance or if they are due purely to chance.

The scientific approach can therefore be used to reject certain theories. When upheld, scientific research can support statements about relationships between different events, allowing statements of cause and effect and predictions to be made.

Can psychology be considered a science? For anything to be deemed scientific, it must have

Over to you

Can psychology be deemed to be scientific? Does it have all the qualities that make a subject scientific? If psychology is said to be a science, should it have all these qualities?

Key term

Scientific – using scientific methods and equipment, not only in a laboratory experiment, but in terms of any methods that are deemed to be scientific. Scientific method consequently refers to a method that is used to prove or disprove a theory or hypothesis. For a method to be deemed scientific, it must collect data in an objective, controlled fashion. It must have the potential to be disproved (i.e. falsifiable), and it must be carried out with set procedures and instructions in a way that allows for reliability, so it can be repeated and similar results obtained.

objectivity, control and a clear explanation. Can this apply when studying human behaviour? All scientific knowledge comes from one specific explanation, but can we say this about psychology, which has five perspectives? A major component of something being deemed scientific is the establishment of a paradigm, one theoretical orientation that is accepted within the specific topic or subject in question. Unfortunately, within psychology we do not have this; what we do have are five existing theories that all explain behaviour in different ways. This goes against accepting psychology as a science.

Psychology does use a lot of scientific methods in its research, and the lab experiment is the desired method of many researchers because of the opportunities it offers for control and prediction. This supports the argument that psychology does qualify as a science. However, is the scientific approach the best way to study human behaviour, which in itself is not scientific? Should we use lab experiments to study human behaviour when these will always lack ecological validity?

Some parts of human behaviour can be studied in a scientific way – for example, assessing short-term memory – but the majority of human behaviour is very complex and difficult to study accurately in an artificial environment. The scientific method might be important for psychology in terms of validating results and showing that they are consistent, thereby giving the subject more credence. In studying human behaviour, however, other less quantitative methods should be used. We should avoid quantifying and measuring behaviour and allow more qualitative research methods, which provide knowledge of a person's behaviour, including their thoughts, perspectives and experiences. Unlike science, then, we should allow subjectivity to play a role.

Although psychology uses lab experiments to collect data, it also uses methods such as case studies, which are very subjective. It has been argued that using totally objective methods is impossible since any research will always be open to the interpretation of someone else and studying human behaviour is very subjective. Therefore, any research found must be backed up by separate findings from different studies to counter this individual interpretation bias that might occur.

When studying human behaviour, we are studying abstract terms which need to be clearly defined and categorised (operationalised). We need to clearly define all human behaviour so we can then observe it accurately. The scientific approach establishes causality within psychology; the only research method within psychology that does this is the lab experiment. To prove cause and effect in the lab, every variable that might affect the variable being measured must be controlled, but even in this artificial setting we can never be 100 per cent certain that all variables are controlled – we have no way of knowing all the possible ways in which one individual might be influenced to behave at any given time. This, again, supports the view that psychology is not a science.

Another part of the explanation for something to be considered to be scientific is the idea of falsifiability – that is, even when a theory has been supported, it is still possible to disprove it. Within psychology there exist theories and explanations that cannot be disproved – for example, the psychodynamic approach.

All the evidence seems to support using several approaches, making psychology part science (objective) and part non-science (subjective).

Evaluation

The status of psychology as a science

There seems to be support for and against psychology being a science. To some extent, psychology can establish causality when using highly controlled research methods. There are certain advantages when using scientific methods in psychology, the main one being that we can uphold or reject hypotheses. Another argument for psychology being a science is that psychology as a whole is generally scientific as many of the perspectives take a scientific standpoint (biological, behavioural and cognitive). Also with psychology being accepted as a science, it gives it more creditability and status.

The main argument against psychology being considered a science is that the focus of psychology is to study human behaviour – and it is problematic to study and research human behaviour scientifically. This is why it is impossible to prove a hypothesis in psychology because human reaction to any given situation is unpredictable and the best psychologists can hope for is a majority, especially in artificial situations.

The best way to study human behaviour naturally is to use naturalistic observations which are one of the least scientific research methods used within psychology. The question this controversy brings up is not 'is psychology a science' but 'should it be a science'. Science is concerned with the collection of data using methods that are valid and reliable to support and help establish theories of human behaviour and development. Psychology attempts to use scientific techniques to the best of its ability, but scientific methods do not give us a true insight or explanation into natural human behaviour. Often what is important in explaining any observed behaviour is the subject's own experiences, views and opinions, a subjective approach as opposed to the scientific objective approach.

Key terms

Scientific benefits – the usefulness of using lab experiments to show cause and effect, and to prove hypotheses and gain useful research data from which conclusions can be drawn.

Ethical costs – the ethical issues that may arise from carrying out scientific experiments, such as deception and lack of informed consent.

Genetics – the study of hereditary, genetic features and the constitution of a single organism.

Environmental – the external conditions and or surroundings.

The balance of scientific benefits measured against ethical costs

This is quite a broad area to cover and a lot of relevant studies may already have been covered at AS and A2 level. This controversy looks at research that has been carried out and tries to see if the effect of such research was beneficial – in other words, did the benefits outweigh the costs?

For any piece of research, the **ethical costs** must be measured against the actual scientific benefits in terms of results and any conclusions that are drawn. You could use knowledge acquired from other parts of the syllabus here, especially PY 3, but here the idea is to see if the benefits outweigh the costs. You could discuss research that used human participants or animals, or you could refer to research which by its nature is socially sensitive, considering the costs and benefits and whether these balance out.

Table 8.1

RESEARCH	COSTS	BENEFITS
Milgram (1963)		
Zimbardo (1973)		
Selye (1938)		
Watson and Rayner (1920)		
Brady (1958)		
Pavlov (1927)		
Bandura (1961)		

Over to you

What ethical issues would need to be overcome in a research study looking into the stress felt by school children taking exams?

Over to you

Think about the pieces of research in Table 8.1, copy out the table and fill in the costs and benefits for each one.

Evaluation

The balance of scientific benefits measured against ethical costs

A lot of research has been criticised for being ethically dubious, the main example being Milgram. But many argue that such research is needed and it was not the specific research that caused the ethical issues, but the actual subject of the research – in this case, obedience.

A lot of social research causes ethical issues because they raise important questions about human behaviour in certain social situations. The more important the issue, and therefore the more benefit society might gain from it, the more likely it is that the research will cause ethical issues. It can be argued that it is a moral responsibility for researchers to carry out such research and therefore ask difficult questions. Just because a certain topic may lead to ethical issues arising does not mean the research should not be carried out. What we have is a conflict between gaining valuable research for society and the ethical responsibilities of the researcher.

In the case of animal research there may be different questions to ask. Certain studies do seem to cause a certain level of harm to the animals used, with some studies even causing the death of the animal (Brady, and the use of monkeys to study how too much control can cause stress). The argument here is whether animals should be used at all. Can we compare their behaviour to non-animals? Does the research benefit us, and even if it does, should we still carry it out? Are we the most important species on the planet? Bateson's cube tries to address these questions with any research having to address three issues: the quality of said research, the degree of animal suffering caused within the research, and the certainty of benefit to animals and non-animals from the results of the research. Each piece of research therefore needs to be considered independently and if the decision cube was applied to research already carried out, would that research have been done? There are also issues with using Bateson's decision cube as it is difficult to judge whether research will have any benefits before it is carried out. Also how much animals might suffer may be hard to gauge, depending on what is being measured. It is clear if physical harm is being done, but it is hard to measure any psychological harm being caused to the animal, such as stress. Humans may react differently to stress than other species.

The balance of genetic and environmental influences on human behaviour

This actually refers to the nature/nurture debate – how much of our behaviour is determined by nature (hereditary) and how much is determined by nurture (learning and the environment)? This is an important debate: if we are born with all our behaviour (i.e. it is innate), then no form of intervention will affect our development; therefore, the environment we are brought up in or how we are taught will have little effect on our development. The opposing view is that everything is learnt; therefore, everything affects our development, with our environment and the way we are brought up both playing a major role in the development of our behaviour. Some researchers argue that any development is a combination of nature and nurture working together to influence a person's development and behaviour. A person may be born with a natural ability (nature), but that ability must be developed (nurtured).

One argument that elaborates this is the issue of phenylketonuria (PKU), a genetic disorder. If PKU is detected early enough, it can be dealt with by changing a child's diet, therefore showing an interaction between inherited nature (PKU) and environmental nurture (changing someone's diet).

Figure 8.2 Can race have an impact on people's personalities?

Throughout psychology, lots of topics bring up the issue of the nature/nurture debate, including language development, the development of aggression and gender roles. These are important issues which can highlight the nature/nurture debate and its significance. If aggression is learnt then we must control a person's upbringing and or environment to control this, but if aggression is down to heredity then none of these changes will affect the person and some sort of biological treatment may be needed. This debate has caused a great deal of controversy, especially when the issue of race is debated – for example, research considering whether certain races are more intelligent than others has led to increased discrimination against a particular race.

Supporters of the nature argument discuss the genotype – a person's genetic make-up – and the phenotype – the observable features of a person that are caused by an interaction between their genes and the environment. An example of phenotype is skin colour – you are born with a certain colour of skin, but this might be affected by the amount of sunshine in the environment you live in which makes your skin tan.

Figure 8.3 Identical or monozygotic (MZ) twins

Within this controversy it is very hard to study either nature or nurture in isolation. We cannot bring up a newborn baby in total isolation to see how he or she develops. For example, if language is innate, it might be argued that a person brought up in isolation will still develop language skills without any influence from the environment. Obviously such studies would be unethical and can only be used when they happen naturally. For example, in the case of Genie, a young girl who was kept in isolation from birth for many years. When she was first discovered, Genie could not speak or understand language. Even if this were to happen, we still cannot be totally certain that environmental influences have not affected that person. As soon as a baby is conceived, its development in the womb can be affected by its mother's behaviour – diet, stress, and so on.

A lot of research in this area has looked at identical, or monozygotic (MZ), twins, who share almost 100 per cent of the same genes. The research has also tried to focus on MZ twins who have been reared separately, in an attempt to isolate the nurture element. Problems arise with such research, however: the sample size is very small as there are not many MZ twins within a population, and an even smaller number that have been separated at birth; also there are still slight differences in MZ twins, so we can never totally state whether some behaviour is learnt or innate.

Within psychology, different perspectives take different standpoints when it comes to this debate, with the biological approach supporting nature and the behavioural approach supporting nurture. The other three approaches (psychodynamic, cognitive and humanistic) support both nature and nurture, giving them different values according to their own theories and research.

One way to resolve this issue is with the diathesis stress model, which offers an explanation for this controversy by stating that any behaviour is a combination of both nature and nurture. For example, it has been argued that there is a genetic link to schizophrenia. This argument would suggest that if one MZ twin has the disorder then so must the other twin, but research has not found this to be the case in all MZ twins. This is because some kind of stressor is needed to trigger the disorder, and this trigger would naturally come from the environment. Therefore, any disorder can be caused by both nature (a genetic predisposition) and nurture (stressors in the environment).

Evaluation

The balance of genetic and environmental influences on human behaviour

It seems apparent that both genetics and the environment play a role in defining a person. Human behaviour seems to be a complex mix of cultural, environmental and genetic influences and it is impossible to say which is stronger. This controversy has important practical consequences, for if only genetics affect human behaviour, then changing a person's environment (upbringing, schooling) will have no effect on their development. But on the other hand, if the environment does play a role in a person's development then their upbringing and schooling will have an effect on their development.

In light of this issue, when research is considered we must view it in terms of its social and political context. Research supporting the genetic argument may be influenced by the views of the specific government in power. Also any research in this area has to take on board any cultural or sub-cultural differences that may affect the findings. Jenson's (1969) study on IQ differences between white and black people in America found that black people on average were less intelligent than white people and these findings were consequently used to support the importance of the role of genetics. Many of these black people, though, had had poor education and therefore scored low in the IQ tests, indicating the importance of environmental influences not genetic influences.

Cultural bias

The controversy here is the existence of cultural **bias** within psychology. The trouble with studying different cultures to see behavioural differences is that variations between cultures can also exist within one culture, between so-called subcultures. The behaviour of a specific **culture** might also be affected by the political associations of society, which might constrain the natural behaviour of that culture – for example, use of control in a country ruled by dictatorship. Consider the differences between individualist cultures based on democratic politics and collectivist cultures based on the politics of communism.

It is argued that within psychology that there exists a culture bias – that is, a foreign immigrant in a western culture may receive a diagnosis of having a mental illness simply because their behaviour fits a specific mental disorder; when viewed within their own culture their behaviour might be considered normal. Some disorders may also exist within one culture that are simply not recognised in another.

Within psychology, the emic/etic distinction refers to how human behaviour is analysed differently. The etic approach looks at general human behaviour that is supposed to exist in every country, irrespective of culture, such as the development of morals. Moral development is seen as a universal process – no matter where you are in the world, you will develop morals through the same

Key terms

Culture – the artistic and social pursuits, expression and behaviour valued by a society or class at a particular period.

Bias – irrational preference or prejudice.

developmental processes. An emic approach, on the other hand, would look at how behaviour varies in different cultural settings.

It is argued that most psychological research uses the etic approach and explains all human behaviour throughout the world using research and theories mainly developed from the western world; this assumes that everyone should behave in the same way as they do in a western country. This means that whatever has been used to measure behaviour in one culture can be used to measure the same behaviour within another culture. Problems can occur even when studies rely on evidence actually gained from different cultures. There might be a problem with the accurate replication of the study, for example, which is done to check for reliability and validity. This might be caused by translation, as some psychological terminology may not translate well from one language to another, especially in terms of instructions. Also, the operationalisation of certain variables, such as the IV and the DV, might be difficult across different cultures.

A lot of research in psychology has been based around genetics, with some results reinforcing differences in intelligence levels between countries. Past research has found that the intelligence levels of certain cultures were inferior to others; despite the fact that this testing was found to be flawed, it was still used in support of discriminating against specific races.

Remember

Research findings that supported racial discrimination have led psychologists to try to prevent research from being racist or biased.

As we have seen, culture bias may even play a role when it comes to diagnosing mental illness. Some illnesses have be found to be specific to certain cultures – for example, Amok, which when found in Asia describes wild and aggressive behaviour. Perhaps these disorders do exist across different cultures but we define them in different terms; or maybe certain disorders exist only in specific cultures and this needs to be recognised, as a lot of countries have many non-indigenous people inhabiting them. In the UK it has been found that if you are African-Caribbean, you are seven times more likely to be diagnosed with schizophrenia. This suggests that cultural bias is taking place. During diagnosis, the behaviour of non-indigenous people that is considered a symptom of schizo-phrenia may be viewed as something else, or possibly even normal, in their own country. A way to reduce this problem would be for the medical professionals to become familiar with typical behaviour of certain social groups and to adjust any language differences, so that more reliable and valid diagnoses may be given.

Evaluation

Cultural bias

When psychological research uses the etic approach, ideas about human behaviour in one culture are used to explain human behaviour in a different culture, it is clear that cultural bias will exist within that research. Even studies that use an emic approach, which looks at how behaviour differs across cultures, could still suffer from culture bias because, no matter how hard the researcher tries, they still can never really detach themselves from the culture in which they were brought up. Even though researchers understand that behaviour may be different across different cultures, the design of a particular study or measuring tool is based on western society and may not apply or even be understood by participants from a different culture.

Most theories and ideas on psychological processes have been developed by western countries, especially the USA, and so consequently have many measuring tools that psychologists from these

countries are used to using. Also, research may have been manipulated in several ways to serve the political and social beliefs of a particular society.

Research may exaggerate cultural differences between societies or results may lend support to racist views, such as Jenson's (1969) study that measured IQ between white and black Americans. The black Americans were found to have lower IQ but two factors may have caused this – one being the poor education they had received in the USA, and the second that the measurement of IQ was developed to measure the IQ of white Americans and not black Americans.

Gender bias

The controversy here is the argument that within psychology, **gender** bias exists. Two issues seem to arise when it comes to gender and psychology. The first is that there are theories and research that just ignore the differences that exist between men and women – this is called the **beta bias**. Then there are theories and research that exaggerate these differences – this is called the **alpha bias**. With beta bias, all research ignores any differences between men and women, with most research being carried out on men and the results applied evenly to men and women, with no thought of any differences that might exist. Some psychological research has been carried out on males, giving an androcentric view of human behaviour, when the research only represents half of the population, and, in some female-dominated countries (loss of men through war), less than half. While alpha bias does the opposite, stating that real differences do exist between men and women, the research carried out often exaggerates these differences. The results from such research can be used either in a negative way, to devalue women, or in a positive way, to increase their value.

There are several other types of gender bias that researchers argue are present in psychological theories. Androcentric theories define all behaviour in terms of results purely from research with men. While gender-centric theories explain male and female development as two isolated variables, this view tends not to reduce

Figure 8.4 Are gender roles biologically determined?

the importance of women, rather emphasising how men and women develop differently. Ethnocentric theories also assume that all research, wherever it was carried out, can be applied across any gender, population, race or country. Even though most research has been carried out in the western world, this view assumes that all findings can be applied anywhere. Also, most research is based on heterosexual participants. This is viewed as the norm; therefore, a homosexual lifestyle is viewed as abnormal, with it even being diagnosed as a mental illness in the past.

Intrapsychic theories base the development of any individual on internal factors, blaming these for whatever problems the individual might have. It puts little emphasis on external factors. Finally, the deterministic view argues that all behaviour is determined for us; this means that gender roles are determined and therefore inevitable.

One way round this gender bias within psychological research is to generate bias-free theories, and there are several ways of doing this. One way is to use gender-free theories that prevent stereotypes that might benefit one sex more than another. Another way would be to use a flexible theory that can be related to any person, irrespective of their age, race, gender or sexual orientation, without devaluing any individual because of any differences in their age, gender, race or sexual orientation. It is also possible to ensure that a theory is interactionist in the way that it acknowledges that behaviour can be understood by looking at the interaction between person-centred aspects, such as a person's thoughts, experiences and personality, and external causes, such as the environment and other relationships. A final way would be to use the lifespan approach, which states that modifications to behaviour can happen at any time in a person's life, not just at critical periods such as childhood or adolescence. We can also accept that in person's lifetime the social political climate may change and this might influence a person's behaviour – for example, the changing role of women in many societies (less homemaker, more independent, career-driven).

Over to you

Think about all the psychological studies you know. How many of these have gender bias? How could the researcher have got round this issue?

One of the biggest issues with psychological research is the use of the lab experiment, which has been used to give credence to conclusions from research into human behaviour and gender differences. The problem with this method is that it is artificial – it studies a person's behaviour with no reference to any cultural or personal context, and the gender differences that are detected are therefore probably more a reflection of the participants being studied than of gender differences across societies.

Over to you

There is also the issue of gender bias in psychology itself because most psychology students are female, but most research that has been published has been conducted by males. Is this an issue that is being addressed?

When any research has been carried out on females, it has been done by males, who have their own gender biases which affect their treatment of the participants and, consequently, the results found. Women have therefore been classified as emotional and lacking the intelligence of men. Certain ailments that are feminine-based have also led to these negative labels and stereotypes – for example, premenstrual syndrome. When studying certain behaviours, there are stereotypes that exist, as well as pre-existing theories; consequently, research findings have tended to be based around these pre-existing stereotypes and theories, again, with a lot of research just using male participants.

As we have seen, a way round this would be to use a more flexible theory when doing research, looking at a spread of women – for example, social class, age and culture – and also studying women at a more subjective level, taking on board their experiences and opinions while ignoring conventional stereotypes, and also studying women in the context in which they live (again, using an interactionist approach).

Gender bias also seems to exist within certain diagnostic systems. For example, a woman is more likely to receive a diagnosis of anorexia than a male. There are two possible reasons for this: first, it is a genuine finding that the disorder is more prevalent among females; and second, it may be due to gender biases that exist within psychology. These exist because often during diagnosis, the environmental circumstances in which the disorder is found is ignored – for example, females may have more to cope with than males (multiple roles as career woman and homemaker). The female's symptoms are interpreted in line with gender stereotypes – for example, a woman's behaviour is interpreted as over-emotional because women are seen to be more emotional than men.

Evaluation

Gender bias

Within psychology, issues of gender bias do exist, but it is not just the research that is biased, it is the society itself. Historically, most societies have been dominated by men and even with more of a move towards equality, mainly in western society, most women would still argue that they are discriminated against. The research within psychology may be gender-biased because of the society in which the research is designed. Most research designs and measuring tools have been developed by men and therefore cannot be applied to women. The research may be designed to study human behaviour but actually it is studying male behaviour. Many of the findings of cognitive and emotional functioning for women may be inaccurate because of the flaws in the methodologies used. Some research may also be driven by the social and political climate of any society at one specific time, such as Bowlby's research on maternal deprivation. Research clearly does contain gender bias and it is more obvious when the research has what we call beta bias – the study is only carried out on men yet the results applied to everyone, ignoring how gender may have affected such results. Asch studied conformity using males, Zimbardo studied conformity to social roles using males and Milgram studied obedience using only males, and from this research, ideas about how humans conform and obey were developed.

Free will and determinism

According to the deterministic point of view, everyone's behaviour has been determined by external forces – a person's upbringing, environment, and so on – and internal forces – genetics, chemical imbalance, and so on.

According to the free will point of view, all behaviour is down to the individual's own conscious thought and decisions.

The deterministic approach argues that if you study behaviour by applying scientific methods, you must adopt a deterministic view – if psychology does not have a deterministic approach then it is not scientific (this is another issue). Several of the perspectives within psychology support the deterministic approach. The biological approach argues that all behaviour is determined by internal factors (e.g. genetics, chemical levels) – this is referred to as physiological determinism. The behavioural approach also supports a deterministic approach, stating that all behaviour is determined by learning and the environment; this is known as environmental determinism. The psychodynamic approach also supports the deterministic approach, affirming that all behaviour is determined by our personality, which is a consequence of our early childhood (again, all determined); this is called psychic determinism. The cognitive approach is mechanistic in its function and is therefore deterministic, as the mechanical approach maintains that all actions have certain results.

Over to you

Is our behaviour a consequence of our free will or is it determined?

Key terms

Free will – the apparent human ability to make choices that are not externally determined.
Determinism – the idea that all acts, choices and events are the inevitable consequence of internal/external causes.

Figure 8.5 Do we have free will or is our behaviour predetermined?

There does seem to be a less rigid approach in the case of soft determinism, which states that some behaviour is controlled by the situation (external factors), while other behaviour is only slightly controlled. Soft determinism takes the view that how much of our behaviour is determined is connected to the situation in which behaviour has occurred. For example, a driver is speeding down a road when he spots a police car; he slows down either because he might be pulled over and get a speeding ticket (highly constrained) or because he realised that he has been driving too fast and feels bad (modestly constrained). Supporters of the free will argument maintain that a major issue with determinism is that it is not possible to carry out any kind of test to measure determinism; therefore it cannot be measured.

Most people would like to think that they have some kind of free will, otherwise they would feel like robots, behaving in an automatic way. The humanistic perspective reinforces the idea of free will. This perspective states that we all exercise individual choice in our behaviour and that any arguments to the contrary – for example, affirming that behaviour is determined by internal and external causes – would dehumanise behaviour.

Free will has disputed that the deterministic approach is scientific, as precise predictions about human conduct have been extremely difficult to make. Even well-established sciences such as physics have not always been able to show 100 per cent cause and effect.

Even though the biological perspective supports determinism, any physiological factors seem to be more applicable to non-human animals, which apparently lack the self-awareness that is related to will; humans have this self-awareness and consciousness, and therefore have a will. So a lot of research and findings from the biological approach supporting determinism is not applicable to humans. The behavioural approach takes more of a middle ground, seeing some learning as having free will and not being totally governed by determinism. Bandura put forward the idea of reciprocal determinism, whereby our environment affects our behaviour and our behaviour affects our environment – the environment affects our reactions (determined), but we also choose to react within our environment (free will). Even the Freudians believe that we have the possibility for free will, as a lot of behaviour has several causes, some of which are conscious causes, therefore supporting the notion of free will.

Supporters of the deterministic viewpoint argue that several problems exist within the free will approach, the main one being exactly what is meant by the term 'free will'. If it cannot be accurately defined, how can it exist? Free will is an abstract word, but, like determinism, it is difficult to measure or study in any scientific way in order to prove its existence. Determinism argues that all behaviour has one or more causes, but free will argues that there are no causes. Therefore, within free will, all behaviour is aimless. Many people would claim that their behaviour is not random and has a reason, a cause, but it has not been stated how free will causes any behaviour.

Some argue that free will and determinism are actually linked and are not separate points of view. Our behaviour is determined by external factors – our past experiences and genetics (deterministic

Remember

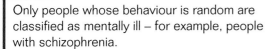

Only people whose behaviour is random are classified as mentally ill – for example, people with schizophrenia.

view) — but it is also affected by internal factors — our personality and thoughts at the time (free will view). Another way of looking at this is to say that our thoughts and personality (free will) are all shaped by past experiences and memories (determined), and therefore free will can exist, but it is also determined! According to this viewpoint, free will is part of the deterministic argument.

Over to you

If behaviour is determined, how can criminals be imprisoned for doing something that was determined by their genes or behaviour they have learned?

Evaluation

Free will and determinism

This debate is one that does not give us a clear answer although many would argue that determinism is the stronger position. Both free will and determinism are abstract terms and are therefore hard to quantify and measure. No scientific experiment will ever be able to accurately measure either of these terms so this is a controversy that will never have an answer. A lot of research does seem to support determinism, with free will actually being part of the deterministic viewpoint. Behaviour can be determined in part by how much free will we have and this free will is determined by our upbringing and the society we live in. Therefore people who live in so-called collectivistic societies (determined politically – communistic countries) will have less free will than people from individualistic societies (determined politically – democratic countries). Also as far as individual development goes, a person brought up to follow strict family rules will feel they have less free will than someone brought up in a more relaxed family unit who will feel that they have more free will (free will has been determined by the environment, in this case upbringing by the family). So far from being two different viewpoints, all behaviour is determined – even if it is deemed free will!

Summary

Controversies

The status of psychology as a science

Psychology uses many scientific methods, but in studying complex human behaviour, it often lacks the empiricism of 'true' science; it does not have one 'paradigm', as a science should have, but rather five different theories on how to look at human behaviour.

Genetic vs environmental influences on human behaviour

Is it nature or nurture that makes us who we are? Many researchers believe that it is a combination of the two, and it is impossible to study either in isolation. Experiments involving MZ twins are very important in this debate.

Cultural bias

Behaviour differs between cultures and between subcultures. Psychology is accused of having a culture bias: by applying a set of norms, behaviour that would be completely normal and acceptable in an individual's own culture can be perceived as abnormal and dangerous.

Scientific benefits vs ethical costs

How far should we sacrifice our ethics to achieve results that will prove or disprove our hypotheses?

Gender bias

There are several types of gender bias that researchers argue are present within psychology, ranging from ignoring the differences between men and women (beta bias), to exaggerating them (alpha bias).

Free will and determinism

The deterministic argument states that all human behaviour is determined by external forces, while the free will argument states that behaviour is down to an individual's choices. Various schools of thought support each theory.

Exam focus

Exam structure for PY 4

Only two of the controversies outlined in this chapter will be set in the exam and you must answer just one, allowing yourself about 40 minutes to do so.

The question is marked out of 25:

- 3 marks are awarded for AO1: simple description of the actual controversy in question.
- 7 marks are awarded for AO2: evaluating the controversy.
- 15 marks are awarded for AO3: clearly interpreting and analysing the evidence for and against the specific controversy.

Exam tips

1 Read the question carefully.
2 Clearly outline and evaluate the controversy.
3 Refer to evidence that illustrates the controversy; analyse and criticise this evidence.
4 Watch the time – spend about 40 minutes on each question.

9 Memory

INTRODUCTION

There has been a great deal of research into memory and how we retain information. Research into memory has investigated how we encode, store and retrieve information. Most research has tended to be conducted in laboratories, using tight controls; therefore, questions can be raised as to the ecological validity of such research. Look out for research that has been conducted in natural conditions, where ecological validity will be high.

There are some psychologists who think that our memory is divided into separate sections, or stores, where information is sent from one store to another. The multi-store model of memory aims to show how memory works using a very simple model.

The working memory model shows how short-term memory is much more complicated than the multi-store model suggests.

The levels of processing idea questions the view of fixed memory stores, and suggests that it is the way we process information that leads to lasting memories or failure to recall.

Chapters 9 to 13 relate to part B of the PY 4 exam, at the end of Chapter 13, on page 166, you will find information on exam structure and exam tips.

OBJECTIVES

The specification requires you to have an awareness of the following:

- Multi-store model of memory (e.g. Atkinson and Shiffrin)

- Alternatives to the multi-store model of memory (e.g. levels of processing – Craik and Lockhart; working memory model – Baddeley)

- The role of emotion in memory (e.g. flashbulb memories, repression, depressive state)

- Explanations of forgetting (e.g. decay, displacement, context dependency, interference)

- Explanations of memory disorders (e.g. amnesia, Alzheimer's disease).

Multi-store model

This model of memory is a representation of memory, based on the idea of having more than one store for information. As can be seen in Figure 9.1, Atkinson and Shiffrin suggested there were three kinds of memory store: sensory memory, short-term memory and long-term memory.

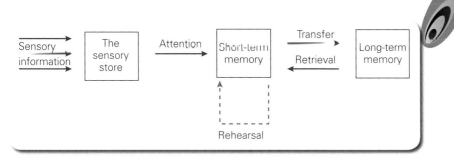

Figure 9.1 Atkinson and Shiffrin's multi-store model

Sensory memory

The first stage of the model is sensory memory, and this is the first port of call for any information that is received by the senses. Research into sensory memory has mainly been based on the visual and auditory senses. Information is only held in sensory memory for a very brief period of time before it is lost, 1–2 seconds at the most. If attention is paid to the information, a small fraction of it is transferred to short-term memory (STM).

Research into sensory memory

Key example

Sperling (1960): The information available in brief visual presentations

Aim: To find out how much people can remember when presented with visual information for a brief period of time.

Method: A lab experiment using a tachistoscope to present participants with three rows of four mixed letters (12 letters in all) for 50 milliseconds. This is so brief that it is impossible to focus on individual letters to read them. The participants then heard a tone (high, medium or low) to indicate to the participants which line they were to recall.

Findings: Participants were able to recall 80 per cent of the letters on the row selected by the cue if they were asked to recall the letters immediately. Participants reported seeing more letters than they could recall, indicating that the capacity of sensory memory is large but decays rapidly. Information in the sensory system lasts about one-quarter of a second.

Conclusions: Given that participants did not know beforehand which row was going to be selected for recall, they managed to recall the information well. This suggests that all the information was available in the sensory system at one point, but is very easily lost, as information in the sensory system fades away rapidly.

Evaluation of this research:

- Sperling's work is the basis of the view that sensory memory stores are very large but decay very rapidly.
- Later research has shown that it is possible for information in sensory memory to last up to four seconds.
- This is evidence for a sensory memory system.

Short-term store

Atkinson and Shiffrin suggested that short-term memory is also limited in capacity and duration, and is very easily disrupted. Short-term memory can hold a little more than sensory memory, but experiments have shown that it is still limited in what it can hold. According to this model, the information to be remembered is passed on to long-term memory (LTM) if it is rehearsed.

Research into short-term memory

Research into short-term memory has mostly been conducted in laboratory conditions. The way that short-term memory has been investigated is through encoding, capacity and duration. Experiments in this area show that short-term memory is mostly encoded acoustically through sound; the capacity is about five to nine items and the duration is approximately 18 seconds.

Long-term store

Long-term memory has the potential to last indefinitely and has an unlimited capacity. Most long-term memory research has tended to look at relatively short time spans. Even studies of long-term memory tend to be limited to time spans of just a few weeks, and only a handful have reported on memories for events more than a year after the event. However, Bahrick *et al.* (1975) investigated memories of people who had left school many years before and found that, with prompting, even very long-term memory can be activated by cues.

Distinguishing between short-term and long-term memory

The evidence for separate stores in memory comes from research studies that demonstrate the way memory is encoded, the duration of memory and the capacity of memory. These studies support the multi-store model of memory because they show that STM and LTM are separate stores in memory.

Key term

Encoding – the way that information is changed into a form in which it can be used and stored in memory. This may be based on sound (acoustic code), sight (visual code) or could even be the meaning attached to information (semantic code). Studies have shown that short-term memory tends to be encoded acoustically, while long-term memory is more semantic.

Research into encoding of short-term memory

Key example

Baddeley (1966): The influence of acoustic and semantic encoding

Aim: Research conducted into short-term memory by Conrad (1964) found that participants made mistakes when immediately recalling words that sounded similar (acoustic similarity). Baddeley aimed to investigate this further by testing the effect of acoustic similarity on long-term recall. He also aimed to see what the effect of semantic encoding (by word meaning) had on STM and LTM.

Procedure: Two lab experiments were conducted, with one experiment testing STM (recall tested immediately) and the other testing LTM (recall after 20 minutes).

Participants were split into four groups and each group was shown different sorts of words: group 1 was shown ten acoustically similar words (e.g. man, can, ban), group 2 was shown ten acoustically dissimilar words (e.g. hit, cow, jog), while group 3 was shown ten semantically similar words (e.g. large, huge, broad, wide), and group 4 was shown ten semantically dissimilar words (e.g. work, hot, tidy).

Findings: In the experiment testing STM, group 1 (acoustic similarity) participants recalled approximately 55 per cent of the words. In the experiment testing LTM, group 3 (semantic similarity) also recalled 55 per cent of the words. The recall of all the other groups in both experiments was 75 per cent.

Conclusions: The findings suggest that in STM information is encoded acoustically, which is why the words that sounded similar were confused. In LTM the information is encoded semantically, which explains why words with similar meanings were difficult to remember.

Researchers have investigated the separate areas of memory; through this research we have gained insight into the way that memory works.

All the research evidence showing memory as having different stores supports the multi-store model.

Key terms

Duration – how long a memory is stored. Short-term memory only lasts a short time, about 18 seconds, whereas long-term memory potentially lasts for ever.

Capacity – how much can be held in memory. STM has a limited capacity, which Miller estimated to be 7 +/–2. The capacity of LTM is probably unlimited.

Research into long-term memory

Key example

Bahrick, Bahrick and Wittinger (1975): Fifty years of memory for names and faces

Aim: They aimed to investigate recall of information over a very long period of time in order to test very long-term memory (VLTM). They particularly wanted to investigate the sort of memories that happen in everyday life rather than in laboratory conditions. Therefore, they wanted to see if memories can last several decades and to test VLTM in a way that showed external validity.

Procedure: 392 (162 male and 230 female) participants were selected from high school graduates, with an age range from 17 to 74. The participants were asked to name (first and last names) all the students in their graduating class, and then to pick out the portraits of classmates selected from yearbooks, where some of the photographs had been replaced or supplemented with photographs from other yearbooks that were unfamiliar to the participants.

Findings: Those participants who had graduated from school less than 15 years before were about 90 per cent accurate in identifying names and faces. This declined to about 80 per cent for names and 70 per cent for faces after 48 years. Participants could recognise and match names and faces for a few hundred classmates, but could only remember a small number of names.

Conclusions: This study showed that participants were able to remember information over a very long period of time. Recall was not related to class size or recognition performance. Although memory for classmates was not perfect, this study supports the existence of very long-term memory in a real-life setting.

Evaluation of this research: This study had high ecological validity because it investigated memory in a real-life setting and gives us information about how memory functions in the real world, where participants are motivated to recall information.

Memory research

Research into memory has mainly been conducted using laboratory studies. This has the obvious advantage of being able to determine cause and effect. On the other hand, there is the loss of ecological validity, as memory in everyday life may not work in quite the same way as the experimenters had thought.

Any of the studies researching memory that show sensory memory, STM or LTM as separate stores provide support for the multi-store model; this includes research into forgetting.

Over to you

How would you investigate memory?
How would you ensure that what you were measuring was a true reflection of memory?
Would it be easier to investigate long-term memory (LTM) or short-term memory (STM)?

Evaluation

The multi-store model

This model was the first widely accepted model of how memory works and has been very influential. The most important factor, that information must pass through all stages in order to for it to enter long-term memory (LTM), is questionable. For example, the levels of processing model would argue that it is the depth of processing that is important for retention. The model also suggests that rehearsal is needed for information to be stored in LTM. However, it is impossible for some information to be rehearsed, such as smells, as shown in the research of Pointer and Bond.

The multi-store model (MSM) has enabled psychologists to construct research into the different stores. This gives credence to the model as the research clearly shows that there are different types of memory store: sensory, short-term and long-term. There are case studies (see the section on amnesia) that give further support to the distinction between the different memory stores. These case studies show that there are some people who have an intact short-term memory (STM) but defective LTM and others where this is reversed.

The model is too simplistic and suggests there is a single short-term store which does not show the true complexity of human memory. The working memory model shows that STM is a complex system that allows people to use different sensory modalities. A good deal of the evidence for the multi-store model comes from laboratory studies which are artificial and may not reflect the true nature of memory in everyday life.

Alternative models of memory

Working memory model

The working memory model was first proposed by Baddeley and Hitch (1974); it is a model of a short-term memory store that is actively selecting and processing information. Baddeley and Hitch suggested that the short-term store is actively engaged in any cognitive task and is not just a temporary repository store, as the multi-store model would suggest. In addition to this, they argued that short-term memory is a complex, multi-component system. The working memory model has been revised through a series of experiments over the years, but the basic components have remained; these are: the central executive, the phonological loop (which incorporates the inner voice and the inner ear) and the visuo–spatial sketchpad.

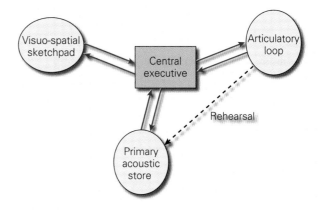

Figure 9.2 Baddeley and Hitch's working memory model

The central executive

This is the main component of the model and can be thought of as the slave master of the other components, as it directs attention and controls and coordinates the other systems. It is the most important part of the model as it is involved in any demanding cognitive task. The central executive has a limited capacity and Baddeley suggested that it is more like an attention system that can process information and can even store it for a short period of time.

The phonological loop

This is divided into two separate components. The first is the articulatory process, which can be thought of as the inner voice. When we repeat a telephone number or shopping list in our heads, we are using the articulatory process. The articulatory process is also used to store the words we are preparing to say when we are about to speak out loud.

The second part of the phonological loop is the phonological store. This functions as the inner ear and holds speech-based information in an auditory form. Items held in the phonological store decay in about 1.5–2 seconds unless held in the phonological loop by rehearsing them sub-vocally and using the articulatory process to keep them in the loop.

The two parts of the phonological loop work together in tasks such as reading, where the articulatory control system is used to convert the written word into a sub-vocal form used by the phonological store.

The visuo-spatial sketchpad

As the name would suggest, this deals with visual and spatial information. It can receive visual information directly from the visual perception or from long-term memory. In everyday life, the visuo-spatial sketchpad might be used to think about all the possible routes from home to college, and determine the best way to reach college in time for the first lesson. In this way, the visuo-spatial sketchpad can be thought of as the inner eye.

Over to you

Which of the components of the working memory system would you use if:

- you were listening to directions of how to get to the local library?

- you were in the shopping centre, picking out an outfit for a wedding and trying to imagine what you will look like wearing it?

- you have to remember a telephone number until you can find a pen to write it down?

- you are listening to a story?

Research into the working memory model

Key example

Baddeley and Hitch (1974): Working memory

Aim: To provide evidence for the different components of the phonological loop.

Procedure: Participants were asked to perform two tasks at the same time; these are known as concurrent or interference tasks. This is because it is assumed that each component in working memory has a limited capacity to process information. So if two tasks make use of the same component, then performance on one or both tasks would be worse when they are performed together than when they are performed separately.

The tasks were a digit span task, which required participants to remember a list of numbers, and a reasoning task, in which they had to answer 'true' or 'false' to a statement such as 'BA: A follows B' or 'AB: B is not proceeded by A'.

Findings: As the number increased in the digit span task, participants took longer, but only fractions of a second longer.

The number of mistakes in the reasoning tasks remained fairly constant. This shows that one component of the working memory system can be working on the digit span task while another component can be working on the reasoning task.

Conclusions: These results cannot be explained by the unitary short-term system proposed by the multi-store model, as only a multi-component system can make sense of these results. When the component working on the digit span task reaches its limit, another component can still be working on the reasoning task.

The working memory model

This is a more credible model than the multi-store model as it shows that STM is capable of both temporary storage and active processing. The model attempts to explain how memory functions. Evidence from PET scans shows that different areas of the brain are used in visual and verbal tasks and these areas may be the components of the working memory.

The most important component of the model is the central executive (CE), but how it functions is unclear. Baddeley suggested the CE has a limited capacity, but measuring the capacity is problematic as it is impossiblc to measure it independently of the other components. This means that least is known about the most important part of the model.

There is evidence to suggest that the phonological loop helps comprehension of complex text and the ability to learn spoken vocabulary. It plays a key role in the development of reading and some children with dyslexia have problems with the phonological loop.

The model for working memory did not adequately address the interaction with LTM which is a problem that stemmed from the idea that the central executive was a purely attentional system. To allow for this and other issues, in 2000 Baddeley added a fourth component: the episodic buffer. This is a third slave system which has a limited capacity store that binds together information from integrated episodes. The episodic buffer is a crucial feature of the capacity of working memory and acts as a workspace and could be regarded as the storage component of the central executive.

Levels of processing

Craik and Lockhart (1972) questioned the view of fixed memory stores and put forward the idea that it is the level at which the information is processed that makes a difference to the likelihood of retaining the information. What they meant by that is that it is what a person does with the information when it is received – that is, how much attention is paid to it and how deeply it is thought about – that determines how much is remembered.

They identified various levels at which information could be processed, from very deep to extremely shallow. For information to be transferred to LTM, information needs to be thought about, understood and related to a past memory to be given meaning. They suggested that the more deeply something is processed, the more likely it is to be remembered. This deeper level of processing made the memory stronger, more durable and longer-lasting.

- Structural level – very shallow processing (e.g. glancing at what the words look like)

- Phonetic level – processing what the words sound like

- Semantic level – deep processing (e.g. thinking of the meaning of the words)

Evidence for levels of processing comes from research conducted by Craik and Tulving (1975) where they tested the effect of the depth of processing on memory by giving participants questions to answer. The way the question was worded would make a difference to the way the participant processed the information. Participants were presented with words (e.g. road) and then asked either structural-, phonetic- or semantic-level questions about each word.

- Structural level: Is the word in capital letters?

- Phonetic level: Does it rhyme with 'toad'?

- Semantic level: Does it fit in the sentence 'The man walked down the _____'?

Participants thought they were being tested on reaction times to answer yes or no to each question. Later they were given an unexpected test of recognition and it was found that those words processed at the semantic level were recognised more often than the structurally processed words.

In considering the levels of processing model, keep the following points in mind:

- Many studies have been conducted that have confirmed the idea of 'deep' semantic processing for remembering information.

- Later research has found that processing is more complex than levels of processing suggests.

- There are problems with defining deep processing because it is vague and therefore difficult to measure.

Evaluation

Levels of processing

Research evidence for levels of processing comes from research conducted by Craik and Tulving, which is low in ecological validity as they only tested memory of words. The time taken to process words may affect the recall, which makes it difficult to tell whether it is the level of processing or the time taken to process that is the cause of recall.

The levels of processing theory was the first to investigate the processes that occur when memories are laid down. It offers a useful alternative to the very simplistic multi-store model as it successfully explains why some things are remembered better than others. The fact that things are more easily remembered if they have meaning to the person doing the remembering can be used in educational settings, especially when it comes to revision.

However, the levels of processing explanation is problematic as there is no objective description of semantic processing, as different types of semantic processing lead to different levels of recall. Research has shown that the type of memory test given affects the ability to recall information. Another problem with levels of processing is a lack of evidence to support the distinction between short and long-term memory. For example, Clive Wearing could semantically process new information but this had no effect on his ability to recall it later, which suggests that there is more to memory than merely processing information.

A very important criticism of the levels of processing explanation is that it states that information that is elaborated will be better remembered, but then it fails to explain why this happens – it describes rather than explains memory.

The role of emotion in memory

Flashbulb memories

Sometimes people have a distinctly vivid, precise and long-lasting memory of personal circumstances surrounding a shocking event. It is as though the mind has taken a picture of circumstances in which the information surrounding the event was revealed. This is why these memories are known as flashbulb memories. People remember very clearly the context in which they first heard the news – things like what they were doing, where they were and the people they were with at the time.

Flashbulb memories are associated with important events that are historical or autobiographical; these might include the London bombings in 2007, the Twin Towers attack in 2001 or the death of Princess Diana in 1997. It is the emotional arousal at the moment the news of the event is registered in the memory that makes flashbulb memories special. It is the emotions brought out by a flashbulb memory event that increase the ability to recall the details of precisely what was happening at the time of the event.

Figure 9.3 Flashbulb memory is likened to a snapshot photograph

Brown and Kulik (1977) asked people questions about ten major events and found that the memories for the events were exceptionally vivid, detailed and long-lasting. The things people remembered about these events were: where they were at the time they heard the news; how they heard the news; what they were doing at the time; and the emotion they felt at the time they heard about the event.

Brown and Kulik suggest that these memories are special and differ from other memories because there is a specific mechanism in the brain that is activated at times of great emotional arousal that are viewed as important.

Bear in mind the following in relation to flashbulb memories:

- One reason why flashbulb memories may be remembered is because they tend to be talked about over and over again. The news is so important that people like to talk about it repeatedly, and in doing so, they retain the information long after other memories would have faded into the background.

- Sometimes these memories are not necessarily accurate. Studies have shown that accuracy reduces during the first three months and levels at about twelve months.

- Although not as accurate or permanent as people think they are, the forgetting curve for flashbulb memories is far less affected by time than for other types of memory.

Repression

The idea that we push memories out of consciousness into the unconscious was proposed by Freud. He suggested that forgetting is motivated by the desire to avoid unpleasant or anxiety-producing experiences. Repressed memories have not disappeared, but have been pushed into the unconscious.

Levinger and Clark (1961) conducted research into repression in order to test Freud's theory that uncomfortable memories are repressed. They gave participants lists of neutral words and negative, emotionally charged words. They found that participants took longer to react to negative, emotionally charged words. Levinger and Clark concluded that Freud was correct in thinking that uncomfortable memories are repressed.

This research was a laboratory experiment and is not true to life. The negative, emotionally charged words are not as stressful or upsetting as real-life events would be, and therefore they have a much lower emotional threat than real-life, anxiety-provoking events.

Repression is sometimes called 'motivated forgetting' and is an ego-defence mechanism. Repressed memories have not disappeared, but have an accumulative effect and show themselves as dysfunctional behaviour. Repressed memories may appear in altered forms, such as dreams or slips of the tongue, known as Freudian slips.

The following are important points to remember about repression:

- Experimental evidence is difficult to obtain because the repressed memories are not easy to retrieve.

- It would be unethical to create the kind of traumatic memories needed for repression.

- The results of studies that have been carried out show mixed results, and where repression has been found, there has been a debate over the cause.

Depressive state

Many people suffering from depression lose their appetite; their sleep patterns are disturbed and they have difficulty initiating tasks, making decisions and, organising thoughts; in addition, their memory is affected. When a memory is encoded, along with the visual and auditory material, the mood the individual is in is also stored. This means that an individual's present mood will affect the memories that are most easily available. When in a good mood, good memories are likely to be recalled; in the same way, an unhappy mood would bring up unhappy memories. Eich (1995) created either good or bad moods in participants, then gave them neutral words and asked them what memories came to mind. The findings were that participants associated the words with similar moods to those that had been induced.

Depression affects memory by bringing up sad memories. A person with depression tends to recall negative and unhappy experiences. This reinforces the individual's negative view of life and therefore increases the unhappy mood.

Depression impairs the ability to create long-term memories; this may be because the individual's attention is elsewhere and the memories that other people create are not being registered by the depressed person.

Positron emission tomography (PET) scans show that brain cell activity in the frontal lobes is often reduced in people with depression. Serotonin helps to regulate arousal – the ability to be interested in normally pleasurable experiences. People with depression generally have decreased levels of serotonin which may account for the reduced brain activity.

Explanations of forgetting

Decay

Trace decay theory suggests that memories cause a physical change in the neural network of the memory system which creates a memory trace. Hebb (1949) called this trace an engram, and suggested that an engram occurs when a group of nerve cells excite and stimulate one another. According to Hebb, trace decay only occurs in STM, as the changes in LTM would be more structural.

Displacement

Displacement is based on the idea that STM has a limited capacity for information and that, because of this, new information displaces or overwrites existing information. The old information that has been displaced is forgotten.

Waugh and Norman (1965) tested this theory by presenting participants with a list of 16 digits. They were then given one of the digits and told to repeat the digit that came after it. They found that recall was better when participants were asked to recall from the end of the list. Waugh and Norman suggested that this showed that earlier digits were being displaced by later ones.

Context dependency

Context dependency is the idea that memory is improved if recall occurs in the same place as the information was learnt. Godden and Baddeley (1975) tested this using scuba divers, who were presented with lists of words either underwater

Figure 9.4 Major events may cause flashbulb memories

Figure 9.5 Smell is a good aid to memory

Figure 9.6 Scuba divers remembered more in the place where they learnt the material, whether underwater or on dry land

or on dry land. They found that what was learnt under water was best recalled underwater, and vice versa. They concluded that recall is better if the environment is the same as the place the information was first learnt.

Pointer and Bond (1998) investigated the sense of smell and colour on memory recall. The participants were asked to read a piece of prose; depending on the condition the participant had been randomly allocated to, the passage would have been printed on either a yellow page or a white page impregnated with a smell. The participants were allowed two minutes to learn the prose passage.

Participants in the smell-context condition were given either a blank sheet of white paper impregnated with peppermint essence (odour-odour) or an unscented white sheet (odour-no odour). Participants in the colour-context condition were given either a blank sheet of canary-yellow paper (colour-colour) or a white sheet of paper (colour-no colour). The participants were instructed to write down as much as they could remember of the prose passage, word for word as they remembered it.

The findings were that in the smell condition, participants remembered far more than the participants in the colour condition. Pointer and Bond concluded that the effectiveness of the smell condition provides support for the suggestion that context-dependent memory processes may underlie odour-evoked autobiographical memory.

Both these experiments give credence to context dependency.

The fact that Godden and Baddeley's experiment was carried out in a natural setting (for scuba divers) gives it ecological validity.

Over to you

Try carrying out a replica of Godden and Baddeley's context-dependent memory study. Obviously you cannot use scuba divers, but you could try it in different rooms or floors to see if that makes a difference.

Remember

The study of context-dependent memory shows us that things are easier to remember if we are in the place where we first learned them. As this is usually impossible in an examination, try to imagine yourself in the room where you learned the material – either in school or at home doing revision.

Interference

This happens when similar memories in LTM get in the way of each other. They can either be retroactive, where more recent information gets in the way of older information, or proactive, where previously learnt information gets in the way of newer information.

McGeoch and McDonald (1931) gave participants lists of adjectives to learn; when they could recall them perfectly, some participants spent ten minutes resting, some learnt new material that was very similar, and others learnt new material that was very different. Those participants who had been resting had the best recall, and those who had learnt the similar material had the lowest recall. This supports the idea of retroactive interference.

Hugo Munsterberg first observed interference theory in the nineteenth century. For many years he had kept his pocket watch in one pocket. He then changed it to a different pocket and, when asked for the time, he first went to the pocket he had kept his watch in for years. This could be explained by saying that he had learnt an association between the stimulus of being asked the time and the response of removing his pocket watch. After changing the pocket, the stimulus remained the same, but a different response was now needed.

Research into this area was conducted by Underwood and Postman (1960), who found that proactive and retroactive interference are more likely when two different responses have been associated with the same stimulus.

Evaluation

Explanations of forgetting

Trace decay suggests that a physical memory trace is formed in the brain and for something to be remembered it must be recalled many times to strengthen the trace. This does not explain how elderly people can recall events from their youth in great detail, even incidents that they have not thought about for years. Trace decay has difficulty explaining why some people recall things in great detail while others have poor recall. Another problem for trace decay is that it is nearly impossible to test.

Displacement theory provides a good account of how forgetting may take place in the multi-store model. However, this model has been shown to be too simplistic and so this explanation may not be sufficient. There is difficulty in deciding whether forgetting in STM is due to displacement or trace decay.

Context dependency shows that if the information is recalled in a different place to that in which it was learned, it is likely to be forgotten. The research evidence for this by Godden and Baddeley has ecological validity and therefore is likely to be how information is recalled in real life. This shows that if information is forgotten it may be wise for the person to imagine themselves back in the place that the memory was formed. Pointer and Bond's research shows how important smells are for recall and how information may be forgotten until the smell associated with the memory is present.

Research into interference has been conducted in laboratory experiments and therefore has low ecological validity. However, interference may happen when learning languages. For example, if someone has previously learned French and starts to learn German, it is possible that the French words interfere with the German ones needed, or vice versa.

Forgetting may also be evaluated using evidence from patients with amnesia as this is a form of forgetting.

Explanations of memory disorders

Amnesia

> ### Key term
>
> **Amnesia** – People suffering from amnesia have extensive memory problems; sometimes these are so bad that they have no recollection of eating a meal or reading the newspaper not long after they have done these things. There are many reasons for amnesia, the most common form being head injury.

Anterograde amnesia

Anterograde amnesia is the result of brain injury and is a selective memory deficit in which the individual has problems creating new memories. They remember things that happened before the injury, but events that occurred after the injury may be forgotten. Short-term memory might function quite well and the individual may be able to carry on a conversation; soon after the conversation, however, they may forget having had the conversation.

There are three distinct brain areas that may be damaged in cases of anterograde amnesia.

- The hippocampus appears to act as the instrument through which new information passes before being stored in memory. If the hippocampus is damaged, no new information can be formed, but memories that are already formed are not damaged.

- The hippocampus and the medial temporal lobes of the brain are associated areas; damage to these areas may result from stroke or aneurysm to one of the arteries that supply blood to these areas.

- Another area of the brain that may be damaged due to aneurysm is the basal forebrain, as the anterior communicating artery supplies blood to the basal forebrain.

Retrograde amnesia

Retrograde amnesia is a form of memory loss where the individual finds it difficult to retrieve memories from before the incident in which they suffered a head injury. In some instances the individual never recalls the events just before the incident. People with retrograde amnesia do not lose all their memories.

Retrograde amnesia may also be caused by disease, but the details of the physical changes in the brain that cause retrograde amnesia are not known. Individuals with retrograde amnesia can often remember things that happened in their childhood, but events near to the time of the event that caused the memory loss are lost. Usually, memory loss is worst for events leading up to the injury.

Clive Wearing, after a viral infection which caused encephalitis, completely lost his memory. This virus causes damage to areas in the

Figure 9.7 Clive Wearing lost his memory after a viral infection which caused encephalitis

brain including the temporal lobes, occipital, parietal and frontal lobes, thalamus, hypothalamus and amygdala, and completely wipes out the hippocampus. These structures are what are used for recall and remembering, and laying down new thoughts. Before the infection, Clive Wearing had been a conductor and BBC music producer. After the infection he could not remember anything. The only person he recognised was his wife, and if she left the room to go to the bathroom, when she came back he greeted her like she had been away for a long time. He had no memory for anything before the infection and could only remember anything for about 20 seconds.

Korsakoff's syndrome

Korsakoff's syndrome is caused by chronic alcohol abuse. In the case of Korsakoff's syndrome, the amnesia usually has a gradual onset, although this is not always true. It is caused by an increasing deficiency in the vitamin thiamine (B1). The brain damage of individuals with Korsakoff's is widespread, with damage caused to structures within the diencephalon, such as the hippocampus and the amygdala, which are vital to memory. In addition to this, the frontal lobes are often damaged.

Childhood amnesia

Childhood amnesia is the inability to remember events from early childhood. Studies into this area have shown that the average age of the earliest childhood memory reported is about 3½ years old. In general, women have better memories for early childhood than men. There are far fewer memories for men and women before the age of 8 years than for other periods.

Freud suggested that childhood amnesia is due to sexual repression, but modern research has disputed this. Another theory suggests that childhood amnesia is due to a lack of language skills before the age of 3. This theory argues that memories need to be stored conceptually and associated with words and meanings, but as a child younger than 3 years has not developed language, it is difficult to store the memories until this age.

Another theory suggests that the brain has not developed sufficiently to store memories properly. A baby is born with about a billion brain cells, but there are few connections between them. Between 8 and 24 months, the brain increases neurological function in the frontal cortex, growing more connections. This demonstrates that neurological immaturity may be one of the factors that limits early memories.

Transient global amnesia

Transient global amnesia is usually linked to psychological trauma, but sometimes occurs after a medical procedure or vigorous exercise. The individual may question repetitively and show confusion. They do know who they are, however, and the amnesia usually only lasts for 4–12 hours. If the individual forgets who they are, this is known as a fugue amnesia, which is due to severe psychological trauma. The memory usually returns slowly, although memory of the trauma may never return completely.

The fugue state has no known physical cause, but usually the memory loss is triggered by a traumatic life event. Psychological factors interrupt the neurobiological memory retrieval. Once the individual emerges from the fugue state, the memory system returns.

The fugue state may last anything from several hours up to a few months. The individual forgets who they are and leaves their usual surroundings, sometimes assuming a new identity. Fugue state often remains undiagnosed until after the individual has emerged from it and knows their real identity. They are often surprised to find themselves in strange surroundings when they emerge from the fugue state. Traumatic events in the individual's life are the usual cause of fugue state. The condition is common in war veterans or those who have experienced natural disasters.

Alzheimer's disease

Alzheimer's disease is a form of dementia affecting around 456,000 people in the UK. There is steady deterioration of the brain, with memory impairment in the early stages, followed by more general cognitive impairment as the disease progresses. As the disease develops, numerous senile plaques and tangles grow in the structure of the brain, which leads to the death of the brain cells. Plaques are deposits of the protein beta-amyloid that accumulates in the spaces between nerve cells. Tangles accumulate inside the nerve cells and are deposits of the protein tau. One theory suggests that the plaques and tangles block the ability of the nerve cells to communicate with each other, making it difficult for the nerve to survive. However, research is continuing as to how plaques and tangles are related to Alzheimer's disease.

Problems with memory are among the first symptoms of Alzheimer's disease. Individuals with Alzheimer's show symptoms of severely damaged recall and recognition memory. While there are some common symptoms of Alzheimer's disease, not everyone with the disease experiences the same problems.

Causes of Alzheimer's disease

Age is the greatest risk factor for Alzheimer's, with those over 65 more likely to be diagnosed; however, there are around 16,000 people under the age of 65 who also have the disease. The cause of the disease is not known, but it is likely that combinations of factors are responsible.

There is some evidence to suggest that Alzheimer's disease is inherited through genes. Using genetically engineered mice, Andrews-Zwilling *et al.* (2010) studied the apoE4 protein, which is carried by 65 per cent of people with the disease. They found that a loss of a particular type of neuron in the brain can impair apoE4-dependent memory functions. There are some families, usually where the disease appears early in life, where the inheritance of Alzheimer's disease is very clear from one generation to the next.

LeBlanc, a neuroscientist, discovered that an enzyme in the brain called Caspase-6, which normally plays a role in inflammation, will bring about Alzheimer's in some individuals (LeBlanc *et al.* 1999). The enzyme causes the senile plaques that clog up the brains of people with Alzheimer's.

Evaluation

Explanations of memory disorders

The causes and effects of amnesia are often difficult to identify. Clive Wearing, for example, lost a whole lifetime whereas another person may lose a few minutes worth of memory.

Anterograde amnesia is often due to a brain injury, but it may also be the result of drug or alcohol abuse. For example, drinking too much alcohol stops new memories forming by blocking the neural pathways while intoxicated. The individual may talk and interact quite normally, but the next morning they will be unable to remember any of the happenings of the night before past a certain point. Drugs, including recreational drugs such as cocaine, LSD, PCP and mescaline, may also lead to amnesia, as may some prescription medication, such as barbiturates, bromide, digoxin, diuretics and trycyclic antidepressants. Drug-impaired memory, like alcohol-induced amnesia, is usually resolved once the drug is discontinued. Another cause of this type of amnesia is shock or an emotional disorder.

Less common is retrograde amnesia. This is usually caused by damage to the areas of the brain near the hippocampus, as long-term memories are stored in the synapses of different brain regions. For example, damage to Broca's area of the brain, which is where language is produced, would lead to language-related memory loss.

However, it is important to remember that with both anterograde and retrograde amnesia it is the explicit, or episodic memory, which is normally lost. Amnesia patients usually retain their personality and identity and their implicit, or procedural memory, because these memories are stored in a separate area of the brain. This explains why Clive Wearing can still play the piano but has no memory of being a prominent musician with a long and distinguished career.

Scientists are still investigating Alzheimer's disease and the genetic factor is one area they are looking at. There are some families where it is clear that the disease has been passed on from one generation to the next. In these cases the disease usually appears fairly early in life.

The likelihood of inheriting the disease for the vast majority of people appears to be small. Even if a parent or other relative has Alzheimer's disease, the chances of developing the disease is only a little higher than if there were no cases of the disease in the immediate family.

A few years ago it was thought that exposure to aluminium may cause Alzheimer's disease but this has now been mostly discounted. This means that no environmental factors that may contribute to the disease have yet been identified.

Other factors that increase the risk of developing Alzheimer's disease are smoking, high blood pressure, high cholesterol levels and diabetes. People with Down's syndrome who live into their fifties and sixties have an increased risk of developing Alzheimer's disease as do people who have had a severe head injury.

There is no cure for Alzheimer's disease at present, but drug treatments are available that may alleviate some of the symptoms and even slow down the progression of the disease in some people. Drugs such as donepezil hydrochloride, rivastigmine and galantamine have been shown to work by maintaining acetylcholine in people with the disease. This is because people with Alzheimer's have been shown to have a shortage of acetylcholine.

Summary

Multi-store model of memory (e.g. Atkinson & Shiffrin)

Atkinson and Shiffrin suggested there were three kinds of memory store: sensory memory, short-term memory and long-term memory. Any research that shows one of these stores supports this model.

Alternatives to the multi-store model of memory (e.g. working memory model – Baddeley)

Working memory has a central executive, a visuo-spatial sketchpad and a phonological loop – these are all part of a complex short-term memory. Although it is an alternative to the multi-store model, this model adds to it as it is a model of STM; however, it allows for far more detail than the multi-store model.

Explanations of forgetting (e.g. decay, displacement, context dependency, interference)

There is evidence for each of these explanations of forgetting, and it may be that different mechanisms activate different ways of forgetting. It is possible that they all have a part to play.

Memory

Explanations of memory disorders (e.g. amnesia, Alzheimer's disease)

Amnesia has many causes: head trauma, stress, alcohol abuse (Korsakoff's syndrome) and Alzheimer's disease, which is a form of dementia.

The role of emotion in memory (e.g. flashbulb memories, repression, depressive state)

There is conflicting evidence for the role of emotion. Flashbulb memory would suggest a deep, long-lasting memory; repression would suggest the memory has been forgotten, or buried deep within the subconscious in order for it not to harm the ego; depressive state brings to mind bad memories.

Alternatives to the multi-stores model of memory (e.g. levels of processing – Craik & Lockhart)

Levels of processing: deep processing; shallow processing; structured level.

The idea is that the deeper the processing, the more likely that it will enter long-term memory. There is no real distinction between short-term and long-term memory; the way that the information is processed determines whether or not it is remembered.

10 Relationships

INTRODUCTION

Relationships are very important for psychological health. If you are in any doubt about this, think of the worst punishment meted out to prisoners who have misbehaved in prison – solitary confinement. This is a really hard punishment psychologically, because it is difficult for anyone to live without other people.

There are many different kinds of relationship. If you think of your own interactions with people, you can see that you have a variety of relationships, some very close and some mere acquaintances. Relationships vary from casual acquaintances to intense romantic partnerships. Psychologists have investigated what it is that makes us form relationships with some individuals and not others.

There is research evidence to show that the attachment a person has to their main caregiver as a baby affects the romantic attachments they form as adults.

OBJECTIVES

The specification requires you to have an awareness of the following:

- Explanations relating to the formation of relationships (e.g. sociobiological explanations, attraction, social exchange)

- Explanations relating to the dissolution of relationships (e.g. Lee's model, Duck's phase model, predisposing factors)

- Benefits of relationships on psychological well-being (e.g. self-esteem, buffering effects from stress)

- Research relating to under-studied relationships (e.g. homosexual relationships, mediated relationships)

- Cultural variations in relationships (e.g. intra- and intercultural variations).

The formation of relationships

Early stages in the formation of relationships – attraction

Physical attraction is the most highly rated feature in the likelihood of developing a relationship. Physical attraction was studied by Berscheid *et al.* (1971), who found that physical attractiveness is very important to 18-year-old American college students in deciding who they want to date. In order to find this out, Berscheid *et al.* ran a 'computer dating' dance, where people were matched up with others based on attractiveness criteria. They found that those who were of similar attractiveness were more likely to continue dating afterwards.

Over to you

Is physical appearance the only thing that matters when you meet someone?

Evaluation

The formation of relationships

A strength of the research by Berscheid and Walster is that it is not gender-specific as it used both males and females. Research into homosexual relationships has shown that physical attraction is still important when forming a relationship. This suggests that the idea of physical attraction is universal and can be applied to both genders.

A criticism of the research by Berscheid and Walster is that there are issues of cultural bias as the research was carried out in America and may not apply to other cultures. Studies conducted in western societies (individualistic cultures) may not be applicable in other non-western cultures. This is especially the case when looking at the formation of relationships as many non-western cultures depend on arranged marriages. This means that the research by Berscheid and Walster is culturally specific.

Another criticism of research into physical attractiveness is that the role of significant other people, such as friends and family, are not taken into account when studies are carried out in this area.

Hazen and Shaver put forward the theory that romantic partners form similar relationships to those they had with their caregiver when they were babies. They noticed that the way romantic partners interacted shared similarities to interactions between children and caregivers. For example, they have a desire to be close to each other and feel anxious when apart. The closeness gives them a secure base to help them cope with the challenges and opportunities life presents to them.

Figure 10.1 Men prefer to choose a younger female for a mate

Sociobiological explanations

Generally, men prefer to choose a younger female for a mate, while women favour older men. Buss (1990) suggested that males (unlike females) are able to reproduce throughout their adult lives, and this is why they are attracted to younger women who are able to bear their children. Women are attracted to men who are good providers for them and for their children. This is an evolutionary explanation, as it suggests that the selection of mates is purely for reproductive purposes, in order to pass on genes to the next generation.

Over to you

Collect a number of newspapers in which people advertise for partners.
Do they fall into the stereotypes that you would expect (women looking for well-off men who work hard, men looking for good-looking, young women)?

Key example

Schmitt *et al.* (2004): Sociobiological explanations of cheating ('Patterns and universals of mate poaching across 53 nations: The effects of sex, culture, and personality on romantically attracting another person's partner', *Journal of Personality and Social Psychology*, 86, 560–84)

Aim: To find out about those who cheat in relationships from a sociobiological approach.

Method: 16,954 participants from 53 countries were given an anonymous survey about experiences with romantic attraction.

Findings: Romantically attracting someone who is already in a relationship (mate poaching) was most common in Southern Europe, South America, Western Europe, and Eastern Europe but did not happen as often in Africa, South/Southeast Asia, and East Asia.

Support was found for the sociobiological explanation of relationships. Men were more likely than women to report having engaged in short-term mate poaching.

Conclusions: Human mate poaching is mainly done by males and this supports the sociobiological explanation because males, according to this approach, are more likely to want as many mates as possible in order to pass on their genes.

Evaluation

Sociobiological explanations

The study by Buss was conducted on 10,000 people in 33 countries. This included different cultures, religions, races and economic groups indicating that Buss' study was diverse. In any one country, where more than one culture was represented, Buss used more than one sample to reflect cultural differences.

The samples used in some countries were very small and in others very large. It is difficult to say if the results would have remained consistent if larger, more representative samples had been used. Some of the questionnaires were translated into the local language and then translated back into English. This means that some information gathered may have lost something in the translation process. In addition to this, it is possible that the meaning given to a particular question may be different when translated to a different language.

Social exchange theory

Social exchange theory suggests that people are most attracted to relationships that offer them the best rewards. Thibaut and Kelly (1959) suggested that for a relationship to remain satisfactory, the rewards for each of the partners must

Over to you

Are all relationships based on what we can get out of them? Does research in this area reflect the true dynamic, interactive nature of relationships?

outweigh the costs. They also said that an important consideration is the availability of alternatives to the current relationship. Thibaut and Kelly suggest that people compare the relationship they are in with relationships they have had in the past and any alternatives that may be possible. If the current relationship is better than both of these comparatives, it will continue. On the other hand, if it does not compare favourably, it may come to an end.

Rusbult (1983) added to Thibaut and Kelly's (1959) theory by suggesting that possible alternatives do not represent the only consideration in regard to commitment to a relationship. She claims that the investments that those involved have put into the relationship also count. This means that the more heavily a person has invested in the relationship, the more highly they will be committed to the relationship. Rusbult defines investment as emotional energy, such as disclosures about the self or simply how much is shared between them – for example, possessions or friends. Investments are unlike ordinary rewards and costs, as they are unlikely to be easily taken out of a relationship and will be lost, or at the very least greatly diminished.

Key example

Social exchange theory: Rusbult (1983): A longitudinal test of the investment model

Rusbult (1983) found that during the early 'honeymoon' period of a romantic relationship, the balance of exchange was largely ignored. Only later were costs related to satisfaction with the relationship.

Aim: To find out if the investment model predictions are correct regarding the process by which satisfaction and commitment develop (or deteriorate) over time.

Method: A longitudinal study of heterosexual dating relationships with an equal number of male and female participants. A volunteer sample was used and participants were paid each time they completed a 25-minute questionnaire.

The questionnaires assessed the rewards and costs, alternatives, investments, satisfaction and commitment for the participants. Questions were based on how satisfactory the relationship was, how it compared with possible alternatives and how much the participant had invested in the relationship.

Findings: Support for the investment model was found with increases in rewards leading to greater satisfaction, but variations in costs did not significantly affect the level of satisfaction. This was true for those who were in the early stages in the relationship (one to two months) for men and women. However, in the later stages of a relationship (three to seven months), increases in costs led to a significant decrease in level of reported satisfaction.

Commitment increased with greater satisfaction (greater rewards), greater investment and lack of alternatives.

Conclusions: The study showed that long-term relationships can persist despite low satisfaction, if sufficient investment has been made and alternatives are perceived as being of poor quality.

The dissolution of relationships

Some researchers look at the lifespan of a relationship in terms of how it is formed, how it is maintained and how it ends. The idea of ending a relationship may sound sad, but it is possible that some endings may be joyful occasions.

The breakdown of relationships

Duck (1982) developed a four-phase model to explain the breakdown of relationships.

The intrapsychic phase

One of the partners becomes increasingly unhappy and dissatisfied with the relationship. At this stage, they are unhappy enough to complain to other people, but not to their partner, about their dissatisfaction. It could be anything in the relationship that set off the dissatisfaction – personal habits, a feeling of injustice at effort distribution or something else that upsets one of the partners. This stage is usual in most relationships and it only progresses to the next phase if the dissatisfaction grows.

Dyadic phase

This is where the person being complained about becomes aware that something is not quite right. They discuss the problems, and if the discussions are constructive, the relationship may continue and move on. However, if the dissatisfaction is not resolved in an acceptable manner, there is progression to the next phase.

Social phase

Other people become aware of the break-up and friends and family get involved; the couple are either helped to resolve their differences, in which case they stay together, or they find a way to break up. It is at this stage that the social implications of the break-up are faced – for example, arrangements for care of the children are negotiated.

Figure 10.2 The dyadic phase

Grave-dressing phase

People need to justify their part in the relationship breakdown and need to tell their side of the story. In this phase, the partners both publicise their own accounts of the breakdown. This is necessary both psychologically and socially, because they need to show other people that the breakdown was inevitable, either because of injustice done or through mutual agreement. This shows other people that the partner who was not to blame for the break-up would still be a suitable consideration for future relationships.

The model proposed by Duck has been useful in providing counselling for people who are going through a relationship breakdown. For example, Duck suggested that in the intrapsychic phase, the couple should concentrate on re-establishing liking for each other rather than trying to correct behavioural faults.

Hill *et al.* (1976) investigated factors that predicted break-ups before marriage in college students. They found evidence for exchange theory in that unequal involvement in the relationship was blamed. The timing of the break-ups was related to the school calendar, which pointed to external factors in the break-up.

Sequences of separation

1 **Dissatisfaction** – during this stage, the couple start to realise that there are problems in the relationship.

2 **Exposure** – the problems in the relationship are brought out into the open.

3 **Negotiation** – the problems are discussed and solutions sought.

4 **Resolution** – both partners try to work out a resolution to the problems.

5 **Termination** – if the problems remain and no solution can be found, the relationship ends.

Lee (1984) found that the stages of dissatisfaction, exposure and negotiation were the most intense and exhausting stages. Not all breakdowns use all the stages. It is possible that some relationships will end after the first stage with one of the partners walking out. Lee suggests that the intensity of the relationship determines the level of commitment. Those who went through all the stages, trying to resolve the issues in the relationship, reported more attraction for their former partner and the greatest amount of loneliness following the breakdown of the relationship.

> **Remember**
>
> Lee (1984) carried out a survey of 112 couples who were breaking up and discovered evidence for five distinct stages.

> **Remember**
>
> Both Duck's and Lee's research has had an impact on the way that counsellors help couples to identify areas in their relationship that have started to go wrong and help them to tackle these issues.

Evaluation

The dissolution of relationships

Duck focused on the breakdown of relationships. This has proved useful for marriage guidance as it enables counsellors to use the stages to determine where the couples are. Some of the factors that Duck described are present in relationships that are not at risk of breaking down. Duck's model concentrates on what happens after the breakdown, whereas Lee's model is concerned with what occurs leading up to the breakdown and neither explains why the breakdown occurred.

Exposure and negotiation were the most exhausting and negative stages but not everyone went through all these stages. This might happen when the relationship went directly from dissatisfaction to termination because one or other of the partners walked out. Individuals who walked out on the relationship reported feeling less intimate with their partner, even when the relationship was working at a satisfactory level. Individuals who had a prolonged and drawn out experience in the stages from dissatisfaction to termination reported the greatest attraction and more loneliness after the break-up.

Research shows that poor mental health increases the risk of dissolving a cohabiting relationship. Those with poor mental health before the breakdown are more likely to suffer depression afterwards than those who did not have poor mental health. There are gender differences too, as men are more likely to commit suicide after a relationship breakdown and are more likely to suffer depression than women in the same situation.

The role played by individuals in the decision to end the relationship was found by researchers to be a powerful indicator of how the break-up would affect them. Those who did not want the relationship to end were the most miserable while those who initiated the break-up tended to feel a little guilty but in the main were relieved it was over.

Research has shown that many people remain friends after the end of their romance and the most difficult task is working out how to tell their friends about their current friendship in a way that is believable. They feel a need to explain their friendship in a way that shows that it is not a disguised sexual relationship. Recent evidence suggests that the process of relationship dissolution is not simply an emotional decision but a long-term process with a need to account to other people.

Research in this area is very sensitive and usually conducted after the event. This means that researchers usually have to rely on the individual's memory of what happened and memory is not always reliable.

Benefits of relationships

Research has shown a link between the experience of stress and physical and psychological illness, and has also identified factors that may act as buffers against the harmful effects of stress. Social support has been shown to provide a protective function against stress and other illnesses. Support offered in relationships may take the form of practical help (e.g. help with shopping, DIY) or may be more psychological (e.g. listening to a friend in need).

Key example

Deci, E., *et al*., (2006): On the benefits of giving as well as receiving autonomy support: Mutuality in close friendships (*Journal of Personality and Social Psychology*, 32, 313–27)

Aim: To find out the benefits of receiving support from a friend and at the same time to find out the benefits of giving support to a friend.

Method: Participants were assessed on their emotional reliance, security of attachment, dyadic adjustment and inclusion of friend in self. It was also noted how much autonomy support each participant received and gave.

Findings: There was significant evidence to show that receiving autonomy support (that is unasked for support) provided need satisfaction and improved relationship quality and psychological health. Also, giving autonomy support to a friend improved the relationship quality even more than receiving support from the friend. When participants were giving and receiving support, giving rather than receiving was noted as the main improver of psychological health.

Conclusions: Receiving support from a friend improves the relationship and psychological health. Giving support to a friend improves the psychological health of the giver more than the receiver.

Brown and Harris (1978) conducted a longitudinal study in Islington on women with depression after a stressful life event (e.g. death of a spouse or parent), and found that the rate of depression among those with an intimate friend whom they could confide in was 10 per cent, whereas it was 37 per cent for women without such support.

House, Landis and Umberson (1988) found that support groups are a useful resource for people suffering from long-term stressors. They suggested that support groups can help people to cope because they not only provide other people to lean on, but also ways of learning to cope through sharing ideas with each other.

The benefits of family are often overlooked. Adolescents who have close family ties are less likely to engage in anti-social behaviour. They are also less likely to be emotionally upset or suicidal. High parental expectations, parents at home at key times and shared activities between parents and teenagers provide a certain amount of protection from high-risk activities such as fighting, cigarette smoking and alcohol and drug abuse.

The individual in a family learns communication skills and the norms of society from interactions within the family from an early age. This gives them an understanding of how to act while in the presence of others. Families offer a place to go in times of crisis and provide a certain type of social support unavailable from other people. Families carry the history of the individuals and generally share the future too. Reminiscence about childhood and connection to memories provides support and happiness as well as relief from stress.

In the same way, close friendships provide advantages for the individual as they provide a basis for close contact with a like-minded person. Friends also give individuals the knowledge that they are not alone

Remember

As we have read, social relationships are important for physical and mental health and well-being. This is why it is such a difficult punishment to go into solitary confinement in prison. It affects the way you think and feel, as well as your physical health.

and offer a shoulder to lean on in times of need and can give good advice. They also share good times and laughter together. They boost self-esteem and provide companionship and even help protect overall health and mental well-being.

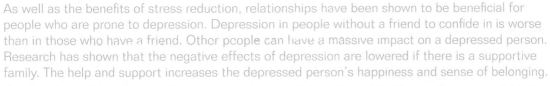

Evaluation

Benefits of relationships

As well as the benefits of stress reduction, relationships have been shown to be beneficial for people who are prone to depression. Depression in people without a friend to confide in is worse than in those who have a friend. Other people can have a massive impact on a depressed person. Research has shown that the negative effects of depression are lowered if there is a supportive family. The help and support increases the depressed person's happiness and sense of belonging.

Family relationships increase happiness, and research has shown that those who are married are happier and live longer than those who are not. This is evidence that there are health benefits from relationships. Family relationships are an excellent introduction to society. A child benefits from the socialisation process that happens in families. This is especially true if there are other children in the household, as brothers and sisters show each other ways of interacting in acceptable (and sometimes unacceptable) ways.

Friendships bring with them feelings of self-worth and acceptance. Good friends can help an individual celebrate during good times and offer support and guidance during bad times. In addition to this, friends prevent loneliness and provide companionship, increasing the individual's sense of belonging and purpose. They boost happiness, reduce stress and improve feelings of self-worth and help cope with distress in times of serious illness, job loss or other serious life events.

Research has shown that relationships have health benefits that can help people live longer. Relationships give individuals a sense of meaning and purpose and lead them to take better care of themselves. There is evidence to suggest that people with robust relationships are 50 per cent more likely to live longer than those who do not have links with family, friends, neighbours or colleagues. The increased risk of early death for those with no relationships is the same as smoking 15 cigarettes a day, not exercising, being severely obese or being an alcoholic.

Research shows that poor mental health is increased by the breakdown of a relationship which can reduce the chances of finding a new partner. Married people are more likely to have better psychological health than those who are not married. Studies have shown that cohabiting couples are usually between married couples and single individuals in terms of mental health.

Under-studied relationships

The term 'under-studied' means that there are some relationships that have not been as widely studied as others. Most research into relationships, until recently, has been conducted on friendships, mother–child relationships and romantic relationships. Research has tended to be thin on the ground in grandparent–child and boss–employee relationships, as well as arranged marriages, and, until quite recently, homosexual relationships and those based on texting and the internet. This is partly due to the fact that until a short time ago there was no such thing as an internet relationship. In addition to this, homosexual relationships were considered a taboo subject, because until 1973 homosexuality was considered a psychological disorder, and even after that was not accepted as 'normal'.

Mediated relationships

Figure 10.3 A Hindu wedding

Arranged marriage is the most common form of marriage partner selection worldwide. Ingoldsby (1995) found that in arranged marriages, the parents of the marriage partners usually have the most say, with friends and family also being influential. Ghuman (1994) found that for Sikhs, Hindus and Muslims living in Britain, the practice of arranged marriage was common, with families choosing the partners based on the grounds of social class, caste and religion. There was found to be some conflict for Asian parents, who were protective of their daughters, as the young people in westernised cultures wanted to choose their own marriage partner. It was found that Muslims were less likely to accept arranged marriages than Hindus and Sikhs.

Gupta and Singh (1982) conducted research into arranged marriages and voluntary marriages in India, and found that love in arranged marriages starts out very low, and in voluntary, romantic marriages it starts out very high. However, the love in arranged marriages grows steadily until, after a period of five years, it surpasses that of the voluntary, romantic marriages, with an even more significant difference after ten years. Divorce rates for arranged marriages are also lower than for voluntary, romantic marriages.

Electronic relationships are also on the increase and texting has transformed the lives of young people. A study from the Nestlé Social Research Programme found that many young people prefer to chat, flirt, make dates and even end relationships by text rather than mobile phone, email or landline.

Professor Haste (2005) suggested that texting is replacing speech for communication among young people. It is immediate, private and gives young people control over the way they communicate with their friends and family.

Access to a mobile phone is a key part in the life of young people, with 95 per cent owning a mobile phone. Texting is used at least once a day by nine out of ten 11- to 21-year–olds, and is a preferred way of chatting someone up for 55 per cent, of making a first date for 40 per cent, and even for ending a relationship for 34 per cent of boys and 23 per cent of girls.

Another form of mediated relationship is that of online or electronic mediated relationships. Online relationships can form and end faster than face-to-face relationships. People vary greatly in their ability to express themselves online and, although it can be learnt, some people are very good at it. The way that the meaning and mood of the written word is interpreted is also a personal thing, with some people being very good at 'reading between the lines'.

People online can express themselves and tell things about themselves that they would not disclose in face-to-face conversations. This allows for a deeper relationship, as people experience the other's message as a 'voice' inside their head and they may develop a mental image of the other person.

Some people find online relationships less stressful, especially those who are shy or have difficulty with verbal skills. The use of emoticons, trailers, caps and other keyboard techniques adds a variety of expression to the communication and allows the conversation to flow.

> **Remember**
>
> The problem with online relationships is that there is no guarantee that the people who are communicating are who they say they are.

Homosexual relationships

Before 1973 homosexuality was viewed as a psychological problem in the UK, and 'cures' were developed for people who were said to be suffering from this disorder. However, in 1973 it was removed from the DSM-II, which is a classification system of all mental disorders. Therefore, until the late 1970s, most psychological research showed homosexuals as pathological.

Gottman *et al.* (2003) published one of the first studies researching how gays and lesbians interact during conversations by monitoring facial expressions, heart rate changes, vocal tones and emotional displays. This study evaluated 40 same-sex couples and 40 heterosexual married couples on a cost-benefit analysis. They concluded that gays and lesbians are nicer to each other during arguments with partners, being significantly less domineering, less belligerent and using more humour. Lesbians use even more humour than gays. Gottman *et al.* concluded that there is a difference between relationship satisfaction for gay males and lesbians.

Figure 10.4 A homosexual couple

Lesbians put more importance on affection, while for gay men validation was more important than it was for lesbians; both show support for their partners, but in different ways.

Cultural variations in relationships

Intercultural variations: individualism/collectivism

Hui and Triandis (1986) conducted research into whether there was a consensus about what was meant by individualism and collectivism. They asked a sample of psychologists from all over the world to respond to a questionnaire in the way they believed an individualist and a collectivist would respond. They found that the responses converged, suggesting that there is a consensus about the meaning of these terms.

Hui and Triandis concluded that collectivism can be defined as concern by a person about the effects of their actions or decisions on other people. They are more likely to share material benefits and share non-material resources. There is a willingness of the person to accept the opinions and views of other people and a concern about self-presentation and loss of face. They believe in the correspondence of one person's outcomes with the outcomes of the group, and a feeling of involvement in and contribution to the lives of others. Individualists show less concern, sharing, and so on than collectivists.

In individualist societies, like the USA and Britain, each person is expected to be self-directing and self-sufficient. The 'I' comes before the 'we'. In collectivist societies, such as Japan, China or Korea, people are closely integrated in a unified social network. The 'we' comes before the 'I'. Relationships in individualist cultures are discontinuous, with the emphasis on individual happiness. If it does not work out, the relationship can be left and another one found.

In individualistic cultures, who an individual marries (if indeed they want to get married) is a matter of personal choice and desire. In collectivist cultures, marriage joins not just individuals but families, and is usually arranged by the parents of the two to be married. Relationships in a collectivist culture are continuous, and rules in relationships are important because of the need to maintain stable, long-term relationships. Respect for the wishes of elders, customs and traditions means that the marriage is arranged by the parents and other members of the family.

> ## Remember
>
> It is difficult, if not impossible, for a researcher from one culture to fully understand what is going on in another culture. This means that, even if a great effort is made, there may still be errors in the way a behaviour is viewed or reported in research from another culture.

> ## Remember
>
> Differences between western and non-western cultures can profoundly affect relationships.

Intracultural variations

Intracultural variations are the differences that occur within a culture. Such things as ideas, religious practices, attitudes and traditions are passed from one generation to the next and are resistant to change over time.

In contemporary Britain there is a great deal of cultural diversity, with many differences between various groups of people that can be viewed as intracultural variations. In London alone over 300 languages are spoken and, according to estimates in 2007, 31 per cent of London's population is from an ethnic minority (defined as non-white) and over 42 per cent is from groups other than white British.

British family life has been increasing in diversity since the early 1980s and relationships between couples have moved away from 'old-fashioned values', with more people preferring to live together rather than marry. Berthoud (2000) compared the family structures of ethnic minority groups in Britain with those of the white population. Caribbean people had low rates of marriage and high rates of single parenthood, and South Asians had high rates of marriage, but Berthoud considers that all groups are moving in the same direction, with Caribbean people ahead of the white trend and South Asians behind it.

The Caribbean community has a low rate of marriage and are less likely to live with a partner than white people. Those who have a partner are less likely to be married to them, and those who have married are more likely to separate or divorce.

In contrast to the Caribbean way, the key feature of South Asian relationships is the high rate of

> ## Remember
>
> Another consideration for intracultural relationships is social class. Hill *et al.* (1976) found that partnerships in which there was a discrepancy in age, educational aspirations and intelligence were more likely to end before marriage. With this in mind, it is likely that many relationships where class differences are apparent end before a long-term commitment is made.

marriage. Nearly all South Asians with a partner are married. South Asians are less likely than Caribbeans to have a white partner, but there are mixed marriages among Hindus and Indian Christians.

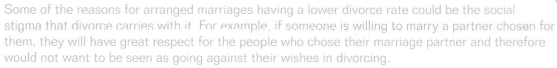

Evaluation

Under-studied relationships

Some of the reasons for arranged marriages having a lower divorce rate could be the social stigma that divorce carries with it. For example, if someone is willing to marry a partner chosen for them, they will have great respect for the people who chose their marriage partner and therefore would not want to be seen as going against their wishes in divorcing.

Gay and lesbian relationships are seen as different to heterosexual ones by some researchers and as the same by others. The shame of being homosexual is still felt by some people and this must put a strain on the relationship and make staying together more stressful.

Research in this area is fraught with difficulties because of the way that gays and lesbians are marginalised. There is also a need to protect the participants' identity from stigmatisation and further marginalisation. This may make people less likely to want to answer questions on their relationships and therefore data collected may not be as accurate as the researcher would like.

There are cultural differences between relationships. Research in non-western and western societies has found that there is evidence to suggest that western relationships are mainly concerned with the needs of the self. Relationships in the West are seen as voluntary and temporary in that the majority of relationships are viewed as easily terminated. On the other hand, most non-western relationships are concerned with the needs of other people with an obligation to serve them before self. They are also seen as lasting and permanent.

Research in the West has been ethnocentric and therefore has had restricted implications for non-western societies. It has also neglected some kinds of relationship in its own societies. Cross-cultural research has shown that the reason for failure in western relationships is due to individuals wanting independence, satisfaction of their own personal needs and personal control which contradicts the caring, sharing and compromise needed for a relationship to work.

There are some similarities between cultures as Buss found in his research. There was a universal tendency for men to prefer younger women and in most societies, with a few exceptions, women preferred men who were able to look after them. However, women and men in nearly all cultures valued kindness and intelligence more than age.

Summary

Explanations relating to the formation of relationships

Sociobiological explanations stem from the idea that humans have evolved to select a mate that will best pass on their genes to the next generation. This account, however, does not allow for couples who do not want children, or for homosexuality.

Attraction

Physical attractiveness is very important in deciding who to date. Walster *et al.* conducted a number of research studies in this area and found that people of similar attractiveness were more likely to be attracted to each other.

Research relating to under-studied relationships

Homosexual relationships were, until recently, under-studied, and this was probably because until recently they were considered unnatural and shameful. The change in the law in 1973 helped people begin to change their attitudes towards homosexual relationships.

Explanations relating to the dissolution of relationships

Lee's model and Duck's phase model have provided clear guidance on the stages that relationships go through when they break down, and, because of this, counsellors can establish a way to help those in the relationship stay together.

Social exchange

The relationships that give the best rewards and are better than anything else on offer are more likely to continue.

Relationships

Intra- and intercultural variations in relationships

There is a wide variety of relationships throughout the world and even within countries. Britain, for example, is a place where there is a great deal of cultural variation, not only in terms of ethnic differences, but also across different social classes.

Mediated relationships

Although arranged marriages are the most common form of mate selection in the world, there is not much research in this area. Research that has been conducted has found that in arranged marriages love grows.

Benefits of relationships on psychological well-being

Research has shown that relationships are a good way of keeping stress levels down and they also help people with depression. Research into marriage has shown that people who are married are more likely to live longer and be less depressed than single people.

Predisposing factors

Hill reported evidence for exchange theory in the breakdown of relationships where unequal involvement in the relationship was blamed for the breakdown.

11 Intelligence

INTRODUCTION

Intelligence is very difficult to define because there is no single definition. Some psychologists think that intelligence is a general ability to perform cognitive tasks, but others suggest that intelligence is the ability to learn from experience and adapt to the environment. Sternberg combined the two views and said that intelligence is the cognitive ability to learn from experience, remember important information and be able to reason well when coping with the demands of daily living. It is therefore necessary to look at cognitive development in order to understand how intelligence develops.

OBJECTIVES

The specification requires you to have an awareness of the following:

- Theories of cognitive development (e.g. Piaget and Vygotsky's theories)

- Theories of the nature of intelligence (e.g. Spearman's two-factor theory, Thurstone's multifactor theory, Gardner's multiple intelligences, Sternberg's triarchic theory)

- Issues relating to the measurement of intelligence (e.g. uses and limitations of IQ testing)

- The role of genetic factors in the development of intelligence (e.g. twin studies, family studies, adoption studies, genome research)

- The role of environmental factors in the development of intelligence (e.g. pre- and post-natal factors, cultural and subcultural factors).

Theories of cognitive development

The most comprehensive theory of development of intelligence was proposed by Piaget. Piaget was a biologist who acknowledged that the social and physical environment also had a role to play in cognitive development. Piaget said that a human baby is immersed in a social environment right from birth, and that this has an effect on the child and society, even more than the physical environment, changing the individual. Most of Piaget's work, however, focuses on the interaction between the individual and the physical environment.

Key terms

Schemas – little packets of knowledge that help us to understand and interpret the world. Piaget suggested that a schema is built up through experience and that new information is used to add to or modify previously existing schemas. For example, a child may have only ever have seen small dogs, and this would lead to the child having a schema of dogs as having four legs, a head and a tail, and being small. If the child then saw a large dog, the schema would be modified in order to include the new information.

Assimilation – the process of adding new information to previously existing schemas.

Accommodation – the change or alteration of existing schemas in the light of new information.

Piaget's theory

Piaget believed that knowledge is constructed and that from birth children actively select and interpret the information that is coming from the environment. Children do not passively absorb information, according to Piaget, as babies are born with the ability to adapt and to learn from the environment. This interaction between the environment and the individual is continued throughout childhood, through biological innate capacity and environmental information.

Over to you

If you went to the park and saw people sitting around, with a tablecloth on the grass, eating and drinking, what would you think they were doing? If someone were to ask you what they were eating, even if you had not seen it for yourself, you would know a good guess would be sandwiches. This shows that you have a schema for picnics and know what is usually eaten at a picnic.

Key term

Equilibrium – when a child encounters something new that does not fit into any of his or her existing schemas and an imbalance is created. This is rectified by the process of assimilation, by accommodating the new factor or creating a new schema to deal with the new information.

Sensorimotor stage – birth to 2 years

In this stage, babies learn about the world around them through action schemes such as sucking, grasping and hitting; they learn that they are agents of action and begin to act with intention. Babies also learn to differentiate self from objects in the environment. In this stage they learn that objects continue to exist even when they are no longer visible.

Pre-operational – 2 to 7 years

Children learn to think and use symbols and internal images, but their thinking is unsystematic and illogical and very different to that of adults. They have difficulty taking the viewpoint of others.

Concrete operational – 7 to 11 years

Children develop the ability to think logically, but only when they can refer to real objects and events. They can classify objects and order them into categories such as size or shape.

Formal operational – 11 years and up

Young people learn to develop the capacity to think systematically about abstract propositions, and they become concerned with the hypothetical, the future and abstract problems.

Vygotsky's theory

Vygotsky's theory is similar to Piaget's in that it emphasises the active nature of the child; however, they differ in the way they view the child. Vygotsky suggested that the social environment has a far bigger role to play than Piaget's theory allowed for. He claimed that language, attention and memory are mental processes that begin with interactions between the child and another person. He argued that while children may develop some concepts on their own through their day-to-day experiences, they would not develop abstract thought without instructions. According to Vygotsky, the child has a zone of proximal development, which is only achievable with the help and support of an adult.

A number of psychologists have developed Vygotsky's ideas; they stress the importance of collective learning, imitation and the role of culture on the developing child.

The importance of the role of parents or teachers in Vygotsky's theory has given rise to interest in the way that children learn in both formal and informal situations. Children learn by watching their parents or other adults and this type of learning is very effective; psychologists stress the importance of the interdependence of the shared problem-solving and guided activities with adults.

Comparing Piaget and Vygotsky

Piaget suggests that children interact with the environment, make their own discoveries and are independent. He does not say that children develop in isolation; although the social world is important, it is not as important as the development of a child's internal structures.

Vygotsky, however, argued that children are not simply the products of their own discoveries. He suggested that children need to have the conceptual tools

Figure 11.1 Play is very important to children's development

Remember

Piaget was a biologist and a psychologist, and believed that children process new information in order to make sense of the world around them. He suggested that all children pass through the stages of development in the same order, and that the way in which children think is different to the way adults think.

Figure 11.2 Help and support from adults is very important to children's development

Key terms

Zone of proximal development (ZPD) – the term that Vygotsky used to describe the things a child was capable of doing with help. 'Proximal' in this case means 'next'. The ZPD is the state of being able to do something with the help of an adult, as the next step towards learning to do it alone.

IQ – intelligence quotient is a score obtained from a standardised test designed to assess intelligence.

and knowledge that are given to them by other people. This helps children to develop ideas that they would not be able to have on their own.

Over to you

Piaget was an only child and Vygotsky was one of many children. Do you think this may have had an impact on the way they viewed childhood?

The theories of Piaget and Vygotsky are similar in their emphasis on the active nature of the child, on how knowledge is constructed through interaction and on qualitative changes in development. However, there is a major difference in that Vygotsky emphasised the role of culture and saw biology as less important than the maturation theory that Piaget proposed.

Evaluation

Theories of cognitive development

Piaget's theory has been very influential but in general there is little emphasis on social or emotional factors that may affect development. Later research has revealed greater sensori-motor abilities in babies than Piaget suggested. The idea of stages of development is unlikely to be as clear cut as Piaget describes and the performance of young children on Piaget's tasks can be improved by setting tasks that are familiar to the child's social and physical contexts. The exchange of verbal information between child and a more skilful person, as Vygotsky suggests, is limited to Western developed societies as in some cultures non-verbal communications are the norm for some tasks.

Research has shown that intensive tuition, where parents push their children to learn more quickly and earlier than is appropriate for their age (hot-housing), does not accelerate cognitive development all that much. However, cognitive development can be delayed by a deprived social and physical environment which shows that while genes are important, the environment is just as important, if not more so, in cognitive development.

There is evidence to suggest that cognitive development appears to be stimulated by the development of language. The language that a child hears at home plays an important part in the development of cognitive skills. There is a difference in the language heard by children from low socio-economic homes and those in high socio-economic homes. The quality of language available to the child and opportunities for enlarging vocabulary through practice is an important factor in the development of intelligence.

Theories of the nature of intelligence

Intelligence is a difficult concept to describe, but it is usually seen as the capacity for learning and reasoning, and other forms of mental activity such as the ability to understand facts.

Spearman's two-factor theory

Spearman analysed various tests taken by children and noticed that children who scored highly on one test generally scored highly on other tests. Spearman suggested that all aspects of intelligence are correlated with each other, although not perfectly. He believed that there are only two factors measured by intelligence tests: a general intelligence factor and a specific factor. He believed that both factors determine the measured value of intelligence on any particular test. The general intelligence factor (g) is common to all tests and will determine how well each individual performs cognitively; and the specific factor (s) is distinctive to each particular test and also influences the overall assessment levels. The implication of this is that people are intelligent, average or unintelligent, depending on their levels of general intelligence.

Thurstone's multifactor theory

Thurstone put forward a rival interpretation by focusing on the fact that the correlations between **IQ** subtests are not perfect. He noticed that some groups of test items correlated more highly with each other than other items in other groups of tests. He labelled these groups Number, Word Fluency, Verbal Meaning, Memory, Reasoning, Spatial Perception and Perceptual Speed. He believed that these clusters of correlated items indicated the existence of seven independent primary mental abilities. Someone who scored highly on Word Fluency, for example, would be expected to score highly on all the items that test Word Fluency, but the same person may or may not perform as well on items which test Number or Perceptual Speed.

> ### Remember
>
> There are ways of measuring people's cognitive ability, and this measurement is seen as intelligence. Certain levels of measured intelligence or IQ have labels attached to them. For example, those with an IQ of more than 130 have been seen as 'gifted'.

Gardner's multiple intelligences

Gardner's theory developed from research into cognitive ability. He suggested that children learn in different ways that are identifiably distinctive. He proposed seven learning styles that should be taken into account when teaching children anything. The most frequently used intelligences in schools are verbal–linguistic and logical–mathematical.

Visual-spatial

Architects and sailors are among the types of people who think in visual-spatial terms. These people are very aware of their environments and they like to draw and read maps. They find learning easier through drawing, verbal and physical imagery, models, graphics, charts and photographs.

Bodily-kinaesthetic

These people use their bodies effectively and have a keen sense of body awareness. They like touching things and can be taught using hands–on learning, role play and using real objects. The types of people in this category are dancers and surgeons.

Musical

People in this category are sensitive to rhythm and sounds. They love music and can be taught best by turning material to be learnt into lyrics, speaking rhythmi-cally using musical instruments or by listening to the radio.

Interpersonal

This type of person learns best through interaction with others. They have many friends and a great empathy for other people. They learn best through group activities, individual attention from the tutor and anything that uses other people, including computer conferencing and email.

Intrapersonal

These people shy away from others and are happy in their own company. They are in tune with their inner feelings and can be taught through independent study, reading books; they are the most independent learners.

Verbal-linguistic

Linguistic people have highly developed auditory skills and think in words. They like reading, playing word games and can be taught by encouraging them to repeat words, use computer games, books and lectures.

Logical-mathematical

People in this category like reasoning and calculating. They like to solve puzzles and enjoy logic games and mysteries.

Evaluation

Theories of the nature of intelligence

It is worth noting that there are two different ideas on the nature of intelligence. The first idea, that all intelligence comes from one general factor, known as g, has been researched by Spearman and Eysenck among others. This theory supposes that intelligence is mostly biological in nature and the speed of neural processing is at the heart of intelligence. However, the theory depends on psychometric tests and because of this it fails to take into account the many different talents that people have.

The second idea is that there is more than one type of intelligence and that there are different intelligences. The main problem with the psychologists who believe this is that they disagree on exactly how many intelligences there are. Some of the theories of multiple intelligences have too many concepts to measure, while Gardner's theory is difficult to confirm experimentally because of the complexity of the human brain.

Issues relating to the measurement of intelligence

Intelligence quotient (IQ) tests are measures of intelligence; different types of tests and subtests correlate with one another, even if they are different in

content. Most psychologists take the fact that IQ tests correlate with each other as evidence that they are all measuring a single common factor. Some people do not believe that IQ tests measure intelligence, but find it difficult to explain why it is that people who score highly on one test generally score highly on others, and people who score badly do so on all tests.

The accuracy of an IQ test consists of two main factors: reliability and validity. The reliability of a test should show consistency and stability with what it measures. If a set of weighing scales is a reliable measure of weight, then it should show consistency in results with different weighted objects. It should also provide stability by giving the same results if the same object is weighed on the scales on two separate occasions. If the scales are not consistent and stable, then it is not a reliable measure. The same notion applies to IQ tests: if an IQ test reliably measures general intellectual ability, then some test item scores should correlate highly with scores on other items. The scores on the test on two separate occasions should also correlate highly.

There are ways of establishing the reliability, and to measure the test's consistency researchers establish split-half reliability. The researchers give the test to a large group of people and record the score for even-numbered items and odd-numbered items, each representing half the test. For the test to be reliable, the participants should score the same on both the odd-numbered and the even-numbered items. If the scores are low on odd-numbered items and high on even-numbered items, or vice versa, then the test is not reliable.

Another way of checking the reliability is test-retest, as this is a measure of the test's stability. Researchers give the test to large groups of people on two separate occasions and work out their scores. If the scores on the second test are consistent with the scores they had on the first test, then the test is said to be reliable. If the scores are not consistent, the test is not reliable.

Children who do well at school should do better on IQ tests than those who do badly at school. To check the validity of an IQ test, researchers give the test to children of different ages or different levels of educational attainment. If the IQ test is a valid measure of intelligence it should correlate with the children's educational attainment. Some researchers who have done this (Jensen 1980; Mackintosh and Mascie-Taylor 1985) have found that this is in fact the case. This suggests that IQ tests are valid measures of intelligence.

Evaluation

Issues relating to the measurement of intelligence

One of the main issues with measuring intelligence is deciding what exactly it is that is being measured. There is a definite scarcity of precision in definitions of what is meant by intelligence. If a test is measuring 'innate general ability', then it matters greatly how this is defined in order to know what is being measured.

Another issue is that IQ tests tend to measure prior learning and miss non-academic thinking. The test scores are taken at face value without looking at other factors in a person's life. IQ tests in the past have expected those taking them to answer the questions quickly and accurately. They have been biased towards the middle class and western culture. The tests that are available now have far less bias and are reliable in that they are related to success in school in western society which is the culture

and institutions that use them. There is still a debate about the nature of intelligence and because of this the theories are not universally accepted. Therefore, until a consensus is reached as to what intelligence actually is, there will not be an agreement on what is being measured.

The role of genetic factors in the development of intelligence

What we need to consider is the extent to which the differences in IQ between individuals are genetically determined. Twin studies are important when looking at intelligence because identical (monozygotic or MZ) twins share the same genes and should show a high concordance rate if genetics play an important role in intelligence. Concordance rates are measured using correlations. Bouchard and McGue (1981) conducted a meta-analysis of 111 studies from around the world and found that average concordance rates for MZ twins raised together were 0.86, and for MZ twins raised apart 0.72, while for non-identical (dizygotic or DZ) twins raised together concordance rates were 0.60. This shows that genetics do have a role to play in intelligence, but for it to be purely genetics, the concordance rate would have to be 100 per cent; therefore, environment does play a part.

Children who are adopted share none of their genes with their adoptive parents. It can be assumed that if IQ differences are due to environmental factors, then IQs of adopted children should correlate with those of their adoptive parents. Scarr and Weinberg (1983) found that the IQ scores of adopted children showed they were more highly correlated with the IQ scores of their biological parents than with those of their adopted parents.

The study of intelligence from a genetic point of view was first investigated systematically in 1865 by Galton. He evaluated the spread of several traits in families and concluded that many traits, including mental ability, were passed on through genes. Studies show an increase in general ability over time in developed countries and this correlates with improvements in education, nutrition and health. Environmental conditions, such as high socio-economic status, demonstrate a significant role in intelligence.

Most studies on intelligence have shown that environmental factors are responsible for about 25 per cent of differences in IQ scores between people. Parents with high IQ scores tend to have children with high IQ scores. The human brain is divided into modules that perform separate tasks: the frontal lobes are involved in planning and risk assessment, while regions at the back of the brain are used for visual processing. Research using MRI scans has shown that the size of the brain's modules is under genetic control and the larger the module, the higher the person's intelligence. Studies of twins have shown that genetic effects vary regionally within the brain, with the frontal lobe being 90–95 per cent heritable and the hippocampus 40–69 per cent. Environmental factors influence several medial brain areas.

There is mounting evidence to suggest that brain structure is under genetic influence and at puberty changes in brain morphology happen that are

essential to optimal adult functioning. At the onset of puberty, grey matter volume starts to decrease and white matter volume increases. Research findings show that variations in total grey and white matter volume are genetically determined by 70–90 per cent in adult humans.

Over to you

If you had to investigate the role of genetics on intelligence, how would you do this? How would you make sure that it was not the environment that was exerting an influence?

Evaluation

The role of genetic factors in the development of intelligence

Research in this area suggests that genetic factors can account for about 50 per cent of intelligence. This suggests that evolutionary factors may be at work because thousands of years ago, there would have been many challenges for people to face such as finding food and shelter. Those who were intelligent enough to adapt to their environment survived to pass on their genes.

Evidence for the role of genes comes from family studies with the main evidence coming from twins that have been reared apart. Studies showing that the IQs of adopted twins have a closer relationship to their natural parents than their adoptive parents, help to add weight to genetic factors when it comes to intelligence. The nature of the genetic role and how it operates on intelligence is not well understood and needs more research before conclusions can be drawn.

A weakness of research using twins is that there are serious flaws. For example, early researchers did not have the benefit of DNA testing and had no way of knowing if twins were MZ or DZ. Therefore, decisions about whether twins were identical or not were usually decided on the basis of looks. This led to mistakes being made as it is not always possible to tell MZ from DZ without DNA tests and this has serious implications for the reliability of the findings.

Environmental factors also play a significant role on intelligence. Socio-economic status plays an important part in development, and research has found that children from a home with a low socio-economic status, if transferred to a home with high socio-economic status, improved their intelligence scores by up to 16 points.

The role of environmental factors in the development of intelligence

Before a baby is born, the environment of the womb is of paramount importance to how the baby develops. If the mother is healthy before conceiving, and continues to look after her health during pregnancy by eating a balanced diet and exercising, it is beneficial for the baby. The brain of a baby starts to develop as early as two weeks from conception. After four weeks, different parts of the brain develop. Babies in the womb can hear and recognise their mother's voice even before they are born.

A baby is born with very few neural connections, but as the child ages, neurons make connections with neighbouring neurons, which become more complex as the child grows. These connections continue to develop until the age of 16, when the process stops. A child who has been subjected to deprived or abnormal rearing conditions has arrested growth of dendrites, axons, synapses, inter-neurons, neurons and glia. The amygdala, cingulated and septal nuclei develop at different rates and are associated with the emergence of wariness, fear and play

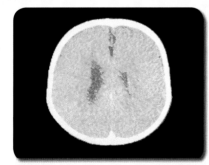
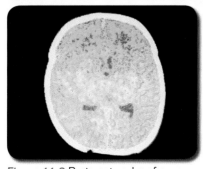

Figure 11.3 Brain networks of a newborn (top) and a 2-year-old (bottom)

behaviour. During the first three years of life, the medial amygdala, cingulated and septal nuclei are most vulnerable, and if there is not enough stimulation, these nuclei may waste away. The result leaves the child socially withdrawn, with pathological shyness and an inability to form normal emotional attachments.

Remember

There is evidence to suggest that it is a mixture between biology and environment that determines the development of intelligence.
The brain develops biologically, but through the stimulation of environmental factors, the neurons develop and become more complex. Without this interaction there would be no development.

Key Example

The environment a child is brought up in can also affect their performance. For example, in the 1960s the Headstart programme was initiated in the USA; it was originally intended to teach children from low-income homes what they needed to know in six weeks before they started kindergarten. It was apparent that six weeks was not long enough to make up for the five years of poverty the children had suffered. The Headstart programme was found to be so beneficial for the children in poverty that it was extended and still runs today. This shows that children who have parents that are unable to provide toys and books because of poverty are at a disadvantage when it comes to cognitive development. The programme has been reviewed over the years and has been shown to be effective in increasing the experience of children from low-income homes so that they are able to begin school ready to learn the appropriate lessons for their age group. Without Headstart this would not be possible.

There is also parental involvement to consider. There is evidence to suggest that children who are 'hot-housed' by parents who expect perfection have problems with trying to achieve perfect results. Those parents who are happy to help their child, without demanding excellence in every aspect, are more likely to have a child who succeeds academically.

Ablard, Karen, E., (1997), Parents' achievement goals and perfectionism in their academically talented children (*Journal of Youth and Adolescence*, 26 (6), pp. 651–67)

Aim: To find out whether parents of children who are 'hot-housed' demand perfectionism from their children and whether this causes future problems.

Method: 127 sets of parents and their academically talented children (56 per cent boys) were asked to complete a questionnaire to assess the achievement goals of parents and the level of perfectionism they expect.

Findings: Most parents reported learning goals for their talented children and did not emphasise meeting external standards. Children of parents who did emphasise performance goals were significantly more likely to be concerned about their mistakes, doubts about their actions, parental expectations and parental criticism. These children were also more likely to exhibit dysfunctional perfectionism.

Conclusions: Parents' achievement goals can help predict which students may be at risk of having problems with adjustment and underachievement in the future.

Evaluation

The role of environmental factors in the development of intelligence

The womb is an important environment for nurturing babies but research has shown that children who are breastfed during the first three to five months of life have higher scores on IQ tests at age six than children of the same age who were not breastfed. Studies have also shown that school attendance has an impact on IQ scores. Hot-housing, where children are intensively taught lessons and are pushed by their parents, does not have a major impact on IQ. There have been cases of children who have been reared in isolation and these children have difficulty in communicating and living in society and their IQ scores are way below average for their age. This shows that the role of environment is important in the development of intelligence. However, both heredity and environment contribute to intelligence and interact in various ways.

Summary

Theories of the nature of intelligence

Spearman's two-factor theory suggests that people's levels of intelligence are correlated with each other.

Thurstone's multifactor theory, on the other hand, suggests that people have seven independent primary mental abilities and may be good at one thing (e.g. language), but not others (e.g. numbers).

Gardner's multiple intelligences are represented in seven learning styles that represent the different ways that children learn.

Theories of cognitive development

Piaget's theory of cognitive development sees the child as a lone scientist who progresses through stages and can only complete the cognitive tasks that are appropriate for the stage they are at.

Vygotsky's theory, in contrast to Piaget's, sees the child as having a zone of proximal development, where the child can learn the next step from where they are with the help of other people.

Issues relating to the measurement of intelligence

IQ tests are measures of intelligence and have been found to be reliable. Some people do not believe that IQ tests do measure intelligence, but have difficulty explaining why an individual who scores highly on one test generally scores highly on other tests too

Intelligence

The role of genetic factors in the development of intelligence

Twin studies, family studies and adoption studies show that genetics do play a part in the role of intelligence, but there is not a 100 per cent concordance rate, so the environment does have a part to play.

The role of environmental factors in the development of intelligence

Pre- and post-natal factors are very important when considering the development of intelligence. The health of the mother and the environment of the womb is dependent on the food and drink she chooses to consume. Babies in the womb can hear and recognise their mother's voice.

Post-natal intelligence is related to the amount of stimulus a child is given. The connections in the neurons grow more complicated as the child grows. These connections fail to develop in children who do not receive much stimulation.

12 Adolescence and adulthood

There are transitional periods in early married life, when young adults begin their life together, and if children are born there is a further period of adjustment. Old age once again necessitates adjustment to a new period of life events.

OBJECTIVES

The specification requires you to have an awareness of the following:

- Lifespan theories of development (e.g. Erikson's 'eight ages of man'; Levinson's 'seasons of a man's life')

- Explanations of adolescent identity (e.g. Blos's psychoanalytic theory; Erikson's theory of psychosocial development; Marcia's theory)

- Conflict during adolescence, including storm and stress and alternative views

- Effects of events during middle adulthood (e.g. marriage, parenthood, divorce)

- Effects of events during late adulthood (e.g. retirement, adjustment to old age, bereavement).

INTRODUCTION

Individuals experience many changes through the various stages of life. There are changes to the physical body, along with cognitive changes and social and personality development. Adolescence is seen as a period of transition from childhood to adulthood, but middle age and late adulthood are also transitional.

The main question during adolescence is whether this is a time of storm and stress or whether it is merely a transitional period. Arguments are put down as being adolescent turmoil and this may exaggerate the reality.

Lifespan theories of development

Erikson's theory of development covers the whole lifespan, from birth to old age, in eight stages. According to Erikson, each stage is characterised by its own developmental 'task'. The task can be represented in terms of a particular crisis or conflict that has to be resolved for healthy development to continue. The term '**crisis**' does not necessarily mean catastrophe, but what Erikson called a 'normative crisis', which is a term he used it to indicate an expected and necessary part of development. In the first stage, infancy, the crisis is between trust and mistrust, and in all the stages, the crisis characteristics are dependent on each other: what happens in the earlier stages has an impact on the form the crisis takes in the later stages. Issues that have implications for the conflict between identity and identity diffusion (fifth stage) are encountered and dealt with in the earlier stages.

Erikson's developmental stages

Trust versus mistrust

This happens in the first year of life and the normative crisis is one of trust versus mistrust. This is the trust created through the parent's provision of life-sustaining care. The mutual recognition that this can generate forms the foundations of the sense of identity. Erikson states that the lack or impairment of trust and recognition 'can dangerously limit the capacity to feel *identical* when adolescent growth makes it incumbent on a person to abandon his childhood and to trust adulthood and, with it, the search for self-chosen loves and incentives' (Erikson 1968, p. 105).

Autonomy versus shame, doubt – 18 months to 3 years

In this stage, skills are mastered that help to build self-esteem and autonomy as the child gains control over his or her body and gains new skills. During this stage the child will learn to talk, feed him- or herself and be potty-trained. The child will learn right from wrong and, during the 'terrible twos', will develop autonomy. However, during this stage vulnerability also exists, and during toilet-training there is the potential to cause shame and doubt, and the child's self esteem may suffer as a result.

Initiative versus guilt – 3 to 5 years

The child loves to copy adults during this stage and to take the initiative in creating play situations. The emphasis is on playing roles in games where a blueprint is made for the adult world.

Industry versus inferiority – 6 to 12 years

This stage is important for learning, creating and accomplishing new skills and knowledge and, through this, developing a sense of industry. This is also a very social stage and unresolved feelings of inadequacy and inferiority may leave the child with problems with peers, which can lead to low self-esteem.

Identity versus identity confusion – 12 to 18 years

Until this stage, development mostly depends on what is done to the child, but from this stage onwards, development depends mostly on what the person does. As **adolescence** is a stage in which the person is no longer a child and not yet an adult, life becomes more complex and there is a struggle with social interactions and moral issues. The task during this stage is for the person to discover who he or she is as an individual and find his or her way in wider society. During this stage, the adolescent may go through a period of withdrawing from responsibilities; Erikson called this a **moratorium**. If the adolescent is unsuccessful in navigating this stage, they will experience role confusion and upheaval.

Figure 12.1 As a child becomes an adult, life becomes more complex

Intimacy versus isolation – 18 to 35 years

This stage can bring intimacy on a deep level, as it is during this stage that mutually satisfying relationships are formed, primarily through marriage and friendships. If negotiation through this stage is not successful, isolation and distance from others may occur.

Generativity versus stagnation – 35 to 55/65 years

During this stage, the significant task is to perpetuate culture, transmitting values of the culture through the family and establishing a stable environment. Strength at this stage comes through production of something that contributes to the betterment of society; Erikson calls this **generativity**. In this stage, inactivity and meaninglessness are to be avoided. If progression through this stage is not successful, stagnation and self-absorption may result.

Figure 12.2 Intimate relationships, such as marriage and friendships, are usually formed between 18 and 35 years

Integrity versus despair – 55/65 years to death

Integrity, according to Erikson, comes from the ability to look back on life with happiness and contentment, feeling fulfilled, with a sense of a contribution to the world and a detached concern for the whole of life, accepting death as the completion. However, some adults may reach this stage with a sense of despair at their experiences, and they may fear death as they struggle to find purpose in life.

> ## Over to you
>
> Is it only during the adolescent years that one searches for identity? Do the stages only appear within the age ranges that Erikson suggests? Is it always necessary to achieve industry before achieving identity?

Levinson's 'seasons of a man's life'

Levinson constructed a life theory that is shaped mainly by an individual's social and physical environment; it mainly involves work and family, with other things like religion, race and status also being important.

There are two key concepts in Levinson's theory:

- The stable period – a time when a person makes crucial life choices.

- The transitional period – at the end of one stage and the beginning of a new one, life can be either unsteady or smooth; the significance and quality of life commitments often change between the beginning and end of a period.

The six stages of adulthood in Levinson's theory of the seasons of a man's life are as follows:

1 Early adult transition – 17 to 22 years – a person makes initial choices for adult life and leaves adolescence.

2 Entering the adult world – 22 to 28 years – a person makes preliminary choices in love, occupation, friendships, values and lifestyle.

3 Age 30 transition – 28 to 30 years – changes in life structure occur, either moderate changes or, more often, a crisis of a severe and stressful nature.

4 Settling down – 33 to 40 years – the individual confronts demanding roles and expectations, as they are expected to think and behave like a parent. A niche is established in society, with progress in both family and career accomplishments.

5 Mid-life transition – 40 to 45 years – a time of crisis in the meaning, direction and value of each person's life, where parts of the self that have been neglected, such as talents, desires and aspirations, seek to find expression. At this time of life, men are increasingly aware of death and how short life is. Men at this age are seen more as parents than brothers to younger men, and this is a source of irritation at first.

6 Entering middle adulthood – 45 to 50 years – a new life structure is formed where a person commits to new tasks. Leaving a legacy becomes a main aim of this stage.

Over to you

Would the seasons be the same for women? What differences would there be, if any?

Levinson's model was based on biographical interviews with 40 American men between the ages of 35 and 45 years. The interviews lasted one or two hours and focused on topics such as the men's education, religion and political beliefs; he also asked about their life after their adolescent years. The men worked either as biology professors, novelists, business executives or industrial labourers. Levinson suggested that the life structure for each person evolves through the developmental stages as they age.

Evaluation

Lifespan theories of development

The stage of Erikson's psychosocial theory that has had the most psychological interest is the fifth stage of adolescence. Some psychologists dispute the idea that sameness and continuity during the adolescent stage is the main feature of a mature individual and have pointed out that a diffuse identity may be seen as adaptive in a culture where there is change and uncertainty. This means that Erikson's theory may not have cultural validity as it only applies to cultures that are relatively stable.

Feminists believe that Erikson does not account for the female processes of identity development as he did not consider sex differences when formulating his theory. Research suggests that females develop their identity through interpersonal relationships and males through preoccupation with solitary tasks. It could be said that men reach their identity and later develop intimacy, whereas women develop intimacy first in order to form their identity.

Explanations of adolescent identity

Adolescence can be described both biologically and culturally: biologically, through the profound physical changes that occur during puberty; and culturally, in the way that societies differ in the expectations, tasks and roles of young people in this period of their lives. In western society the social repercussions of puberty are not clearly defined, as children remain in school and continue in the care of their parents, and may remain financially dependent on them for even longer.

Blos's psychoanalytic theory

Blos provided a psychoanalytic interpretation of adolescence and suggested that just as a child goes through an individuation process in the third year of life, in adolescence there is a second individuation process. He argues that the adolescent has to disengage from loved ones within the family and needs to loosen ties in order to allow for new love objects in the world beyond the family. To achieve this disengagement, the adolescent needs to reactivate earlier patterns of behaviour and involvement, and this, according to Blos, involves regression. This disengagement can lead to feelings of separation and loss, and creates a 'hunger' that may be satisfied by delinquent behaviour, drugs and/or religion, which create intense emotional states.

Erikson's theory of psychosocial development

Blos had an influence on the early career of Erikson, as he went on to study identity formation throughout life and his contribution to identity formation in adolescence has been very influential.

In adolescence, the emphasis, according to Erikson, is on identity formation. His ideas differ from that of other psychoanalytic accounts by including more of a cultural element. According to Erikson, the roles and values of other people who are admired become incorporated; the individual retains some of his or her earlier childhood identifications and rejects others in line with developing abilities, interests and values. Erikson often used the term 'moratorium', by which he meant a breathing space within which identity can be incorporated without feeling under pressure.

Erikson suggested that in order to experience wholeness, the young person must feel a progressive continuity between the long years of childhood and the anticipation of what is to come, together with the person they perceive themselves to be and how they believe other people see them. Erikson suggested that one task for the adolescent in the fifth stage is to find a role in society and become committed to some ideological world view.

Identity confusion is the fifth stage of Erikson's stages of life, and he highlighted some key developmental issues that could become the focus of an identity crisis: the choices of political or religious commitments, decisions about career and sexual orientation, and the behaviour that is appropriate to a particular sex role. These problems can show themselves in a number of ways:

- Intimacy – this may be a problem, as the adolescent fears losing identity by becoming involved in close personal relationships or commitments, and this may lead the adolescent to desire isolation or even to establish relationships that are over-formal.

- Diffusion of time perspective – the adolescent may have anxieties about change and the idea of becoming an adult gives him or her a poor sense of timescales and leads to a reluctance to plan for the future.

- Diffusion of industry – there may be an inability to concentrate on work or study.

- Negative identity – the adolescent may reject the roles that are valued by parents or the community.

Marcia's theory

Marcia looked for evidence that young people do consider alternatives and make commitments during adolescence. To try to discover what he termed exploration, he used semi-structured interviews and focused on whether adolescents sought out information that could help them to make personal choices. Another thing that Marcia looked for was evidence of a genuine investment in a particular choice, which he called commitment. Table 12.1 shows the identity statuses related to the dimensions of exploration and commitment.

Table 12.1

		COMMITMENT	
		Yes	No
Exploration	Yes	Identity achievement	Moratorium
	No	Foreclosure	Identity diffusion

Marcia recorded the replies to his questionnaires and categorised them as follows.

Identity diffusion

Some of the young people interviewed had made no commitments and were not looking to make any in the near future. In some cases, there had been exploration in the past, but this had not resulted in commitment. Most of the young people in this category, however, had not actively explored alternatives.

Foreclosure

Some of the young people had made a commitment and were passionate about it, but it had been made without signs of exploration or questioning of alternatives. There seemed to have been little, if any, crisis experienced, but they seemed to have accepted the beliefs and values of parents or other influential people.

Moratorium

Marcia used Erikson's term to place those who were struggling with issues to do with employment choices or decisions about ideological issues, and who were trying to make a commitment. He argued that these adolescents were typically anxious in their search for identity.

Identity achievement

This is gained by having achieved a normative crisis and resolved it. After exploring alternatives, a commitment has been made which best fits their individuality. Marcia argues that these adolescents are thoughtful and reflective and open to new experiences and ideas, and are able to evaluate them according to their own beliefs and values.

Remember

Most research has tended to focus on Erikson's views on adolescence and the attempts to establish identity. Marcia investigated Erikson's ideas and found evidence to support the stages. Marcia found evidence that those people who form the most consistent self-identity in adolescence find it easier to form intimate relationships in adulthood. This supports Erikson's theory because it suggests that those who are better equipped to resolve the crisis of early adulthood are those who have successfully resolved the adolescent crisis.

Evaluation

Explanations of adolescent identity

Marcia's theory shows there can be a great deal of variation in determining an individual identity. It is difficult to separate identity development from personal values and beliefs, and emotional development is closely related to the development of morality. It is not only in adolescence that people search for factors that are tied to their identity; throughout life an individual might explore such things as faith and occupational preference.

Marcia conducted interviews with young people in order to form his theory. This approach is a good way of gathering in-depth, rich data. He asked participants whether they had established a commitment to an occupation and ideology and whether they were experiencing a decision-making period. Marcia then used their answers to develop a framework for thinking about identity. While interviews provide full accounts, there are problems with them in that they can affect the way participants answer and therefore make the data less reliable.

Conflict during adolescence, including storm and stress and alternative views

Stanley Hall, one of the founders of developmental psychology, portrayed adolescence as a time of personal storm and stress, and this was very influential in later psychological research and popular culture.

Rutter *et al.* (1976) conducted a study on the Isle of Wight and interviewed 14- to 15-year-olds. Their parents were also questioned about relationships with the adolescents, and were asked about the frequency and nature of any disagreements and difficulties they might have in 'getting through' to their children. The parents also answered questions about whether they felt their children could talk to them about their feelings and plans, and the extent to which the youngsters avoided interacting with the family.

Figure 12.3 Adolescence has been portrayed as a time of conflict

Table 12.2 Parent–child interactions reported by parents (Isle of Wight general population sample)

	BOYS	GIRLS
Arguments with parents	18%	19%
Communication difficulties	24%	9%
Physical withdrawal by child	12%	7%

Source: adapted from Rutter *et al.* (1976)

This study suggested that overall there was little evidence of serious alienation. Only one in six parents reported any altercations with their adolescent child, and only one in ten of the adolescents withdrew from family activities. There is a marked difference between the parents of boys and girls when it came to communication problems, with the parents of boys more likely to find communication difficult.

The other side of the story comes from the young people themselves. Their answers are shown in Table 12.3.

Table 12.3 Relationship with parents from teen viewpoint

	BOYS	GIRLS
Disagreement with parents	32%	27%
Argument with parents	42%	30%
Criticism of mother	27%	37%
Criticism of father	32%	31%
Rejection of mother	3%	2%
Rejection of father	5%	9%

Source: adapted from Rutter *et al.* (1976)

At first, these variations look as though they give a different story to that of the parents, but they are in fact less extraordinary than they might appear. Two-thirds of the adolescents made no criticism of their parents at all, while the criticisms of parents were instances of any critical remarks made during the interview. Arguments were not very frequent, and outright rejection was not very common at all.

Similar results come from the National Child Development Study reported by Ghodsian and Lambert (1978). Interviews with over 11,000 16-year-olds found that 89 per cent of boys and 87 per cent of girls said they got on well with their mothers, while 74 per cent of boys and 80 per cent of girls said they got on well with their fathers. These figures are similar to those found in large-scale surveys in the USA, where three-quarters of US families enjoy warm and pleasant relationships during the adolescent years. Steinberg (1990) reported that the majority of teenagers reported feeling loved and appreciated by their parents, and felt reassured that they could turn to them for advice.

Montemayor (1983) compared studies and found that disagreements were mostly based around household chores, times to be back home and completing homework, and this pattern has remained consistent since the 1920s. Montemayor suggests that parents and teenagers quarrel about twice a week, whereas husbands and wives quarrel once a week. The evidence appears to indicate that there is an increase in levels of conflict between parents and their adolescent children, but this is not great in the majority of households studied. Steinberg (1981) found that one in ten families suffer a dramatic deterioration in parent–child relationships during adolescence.

Remember

Holmes and Rahe (1967), looked at the medical records of over 5,000 navy personnel and asked them to fill in a questionnaire which assessed their level of stress against 43 life events. They used this questionnaire to determine whether stressful life events were correlated with illness. They found a positive correlation of 0.118 between the life events and illnesses.

Evaluation

Conflict during adolescence

Hall suggested the tendency of adolescence to be a time of storm and stress was biological in nature but that it was down to individual differences how far the storm and stress went. He suggested that conflict with parents was more likely to come from adolescents with what he termed 'ruder natures'. He also believed that culture influenced adolescence and suggested that storm and stress was more likely to occur in the USA with its growing urbanisation and all the temptations to vice which conflicted with the sedentary lifestyle. As Hall suggested, adolescents have an inherent need for activity and exploration.

Hall thought that storm and stress at this time was made worse by failure of parents, schools and religious organisations to recognise the potential hazards and make amendments accordingly. However, most of the early research in this area was made on adolescents whose behaviour was likely to gain attention and thus confirmed the view that most adolescents had a stormy and stressful time.

There is support for Hall's theory as there is a tendency toward conflict with parents, mood disruptions, various rates and types of risk behaviour and a higher degree of storm and stress than at other times in life. However, storm and stress is not inevitable and nearly all adolescents are satisfied with their life and are happy with most of their relationships and are hopeful about the future.

Recent research has shown that rebellion and moody behaviour is not typical adolescent behaviour and storm and stress is not seen as universal and inevitable. Many researchers believe that parent and adolescent conflicts are common, but they are usually over commonplace issues and hardly ever reach levels that could be considered severe.

Over to you

When it comes to the actual ceremony, marriage, according to Holmes and Rahe (1967), scores 50 and comes in seventh place on the social readjustment rating scale. Why do people find getting married so stressful?

Over to you

There is no doubt that becoming parents is a stressful time: pregnancy scores 40 on the Holmes and Rahe scale, and a new family member scores 39.

Figure 12.4 Some argue that the experience of love and commitment is essential for psychological health

Remember

Segraves (1985) argues that divorce will lead to ill health even when the stresses involved are excluded, because of the relationship between marriage and well-being. Adults who experience divorce are more likely to suffer mental health problems, such as depression, and increase their risk of earlier mortality.

Effects of events during middle adulthood

The task for 20- to 30-year-olds, according to Erikson, is 'intimacy versus isolation', which is the life crisis for young adults; the goal is to form a deep and lasting relationship. The experience of love and commitment is essential for psychological health, and without it comes isolation.

Burman and Margolin (1992) found that a stable and happy marriage is the best protector against illness and premature death. Chiriboga and Thurnher (1980) found that having separate interests greatly increases the happiness in a marriage.

Becoming parents brings lots of opportunities for socialising, and many people find that bringing up young children allows them to make friends with other parents. Another change that is usually, but not always, made by the mother is that of working hours. Most of the burden of care of young children is placed on the mother. Some women receive help from their own mother or the extended family, while other families can afford nursery care.

Abbey *et al.* (1994) studied the effects of becoming parents on 117 infertile couples and 74 presumed fertile couples. The infertile women who became parents had a greater overall feeling of well-being, but reduced marital satisfaction, compared to infertile women who had not become parents. Infertile men described the same negative effects as their wives, but the positive effects were not felt to the same extent. Becoming a parent had fewer positive and negative effects on the presumed fertile couples.

Divorce

The statistics are that one in three marriages end in divorce, usually in the first seven years. The effect of divorce on the partners was investigated by Kiecolt–Glaser and Glaser (1986), who found that those who experienced marital disruption had poorer immune function. This is not surprising, as divorce scores 73 and is second only to the death of a spouse on the social readjustment rating scale.

friends and family but do not feel the need to commit to a deeper relationship. Erikson sees this as important for progression to the next stage.

Individuals may develop a feeling of isolation but this is not inevitable as more and more people are leaving marriage until later (if they do marry), concentrating on education and career before settling down.

During middle adulthood the stage is generativity versus stagnation, according to Erikson, and the task is to contribute to society and pass on advice to the younger generation. Those who do not consider they have anything to contribute to society develop feelings of stagnation and dissatisfaction with their lack of productivity. Erikson later changed stagnation to self-absorption, which happens because individuals do not have the opportunity or an outlet for contributing to the younger generation and therefore have nothing but themselves to think about.

Erikson's theory is difficult to test scientifically because it would require all participants to fill in self-reports, clinical interviews and questionnaires over a lifetime. This would bring with it all the associated problems and difficulties. In addition to this, some of Erikson's ideas are not easy to put into a testable form and therefore empirical evidence for his theory is difficult to obtain.

There are many things that can happen during middle adulthood which may affect the individual and any of these have the potential to affect the way the individual progresses through to the old age stage.

Effects of events during late adulthood

Late adulthood (old age) is generally considered to begin at about age 65. The problems associated with old age were characterised by Erikson as integrity versus despair, a time in life when the individual reviews and evaluates their life. The result of the evaluation either brings satisfaction and acceptance of the inevitability of death, or a fear of death and feelings of regret. Although there are problems associated with old age, many people in their seventies are happy and engaged in a variety of activities. Studies of people in their seventies show that growing old is not necessarily synonymous with mental or physical deterioration.

Figure 12.5 Growing old can bring contentment or despair

Mein *et al.* (2003) investigated whether old age is associated with physical and mental improvement or deterioration when occupational grade and gender are considered. They used a self-report questionnaire method on a longitudinal study. They found that among those who continued to work, mental health functioning deteriorated, but it improved in those who retired. The mental health improvements were restricted to those who were in higher employment grades. Physical functioning declined in both working and retired people.

The impact of retirement and the adjustments made across time were investigated by Gall *et al.* (1997). They found that retirement had a positive impact on health and well-being during the first year. There was evidence for a retirement adjustment process in that aspects of well-being and psychological health changed from short to long term in those who had an internal locus of control.

Bereavement

Freud was the first person to focus attention on the pain of bereavement in a sensitive way. He called this time 'griefwork' and suggested that emotional attachments hold individuals together (cathexis) and griefwork is the process of releasing the attachment (decathexis). Freud suggested that people who are grieving work hard to separate themselves from the attachment to the dead person. There are five processes to go through, for the grieving person to establish a new identity without the deceased person.

- Grief is the response to loss and eases the reintegration into society and allows peace of mind.

- Griefwork is a difficult and time-consuming process.

- There is a long series of confrontations with the loss.

- The bereaved person instinctively resists 'letting go' of the attachment.

- If the griefwork is not completed properly, the result will be misery and dysfunction.

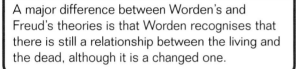

Remember

A major difference between Worden's and Freud's theories is that Worden recognises that there is still a relationship between the living and the dead, although it is a changed one.

Worden was influenced by Freud, but proposed that instead of the vague 'letting go' that Freud proposed, grieving people have specific tasks to complete in order to reconcile their grief. In Worden's theory, the bereaved are not just passive participants in the grief process, but active and self-determining.

Worden suggested there are four main tasks that have to be addressed by those who are grieving:

- To accept the reality of the loss.

- To work through to the pain of grief.

- To adjust to an environment in which the deceased is missing.

- To emotionally relocate the deceased and move on with life.

He proposed that those who are bereaved may go back and forth between two or three of the tasks while they are going through the grieving process, before they can work through the fourth and final task.

Accept the reality of the loss

Worden suggests that the grieving person accepts the reality of the loss; some evidence of this acceptance is found in the shift from 'is' to 'was' when talking about the dead person.

Work through the pain of grief

The expression of pain will differ from person to person, but all will experience some sort of pain. If the pain is suppressed or avoided, the grief pain is prolonged and the sense of mourning continues for longer.

Adjusting to a 'changed environment'

The bereaved person has to develop the skills they need to cope on their own, and very often this means taking on the tasks that the dead person used to do, especially in a marriage relationship. For example, if the dead partner used to deal with the financial management of the household, this now needs to be taken up by the grieving person. Withdrawing from the world or not facing up to the new demands prolongs the process and promotes the bereaved person's own helplessness.

Emotionally relocating the deceased and moving on with life

This final task is taking back the emotional energy that was invested in the relationship. Worden quotes Freud to demonstrate what he means by this: 'Mourning has a quite precise psychical task to perform: its function is to detach the survivors' memories and hopes from the dead' (Freud 1912–13, p. 65).

Evaluation

Effects of events during late adulthood

The effects of late adulthood (and any other stage) are difficult to test because each individual is unique. People would have to be willing to fill in the questionnaires and undergo the necessary clinical interviews in order to find out what was needed to detail the conflicts an individual was going through. This means that the views of those who were not willing, or able to do this, would not be considered.

The relationship between educational attainment and health has been shown by research to be important in old age. More highly educated people tend to live longer and in better health. Health disparities widen in middle age, but some research has found that these inequalities start to lessen in old age, while other studies have shown that these health discrepancies continue to widen in old age.

Research into life events in old age has tended to look at negative and undesirable events such as the death of loved ones. There are positive events that have been shown by research to moderate the impact of stressful events, things such as the beneficial effects of the birth of grandchildren, starting a new hobby or recreational activity.

Social involvement such as attending educational courses, doing voluntary or charity work, providing help to friends and family, participating in sports, social or other clubs or other activities has been shown by research to enhance cognitive functioning in old age. However, there are again differences in socio-economic status as people from lower socio-economic status tend not to take up or get involved in activities and so the benefits of this type of social involvement are not open to them. Research on depression in older adults has shown that these people have relatively few pleasant events and so treatments aimed at increasing social participation can reduce depression.

Summary

Explanations of adolescent identity

Blos's psychoanalytic theory is a concept of adolescence as a second individuation process.

Erikson's theory of psychosocial development states that to achieve a sense of wholeness, the young person must feel a sense of progression.

Marcia's theory looked for evidence of exploration and commitment.

Lifespan theories of development

Erikson's theory suggests that people go through eight psychosocial stages which affect the individual's development and personality. Erikson's theory is still relevant today.

Levinson's theory is important because it suggests that development and growth happen well into the adult years.

Adolescence and adulthood

Conflict during adolescence

According to Hall, this is normal and a time for personal storm and stress. Rutter, however, found little evidence of serious hostility. The National Child Development Study reported similar results to Rutter in interviews with over 11,000 16-year-olds.

Effects of events during late adulthood

Events such as retirement have a beneficial effect on well-being after a period of adjustment, especially with an internal locus of control. Bereavement is a time of adjustment and acceptance, and needs to be worked through in order to be able to move on with life.

Effects of events during middle adulthood

Events such as marriage are, according to the social readjustment rating scale, stressful times. Burman and Margolin found that a stable and happy marriage is the best protection against illness, while Chiriboga and Thurnher found that separate interests increased happiness. Parenthood was deemed to be beneficial to the well-being of those who had been infertile.

Divorce, number two on the social readjustment rating scale, had the effect of reducing the effect of the immune system in those who were experiencing marital disruption. Those who go through a divorce are more at risk of mental health problems and face an increased risk of earlier death.

13 Levels of consciousness

- Theories of sleep (e.g. restoration and ecological/evolutionary explanations)

- The role of endogenous and exogenous factors in bodily rhythms (e.g. circadian, infradian, ultradian rhythms, and disruption of these rhythms)

- Explanations for sleep disorders (e.g. narcolepsy, insomnia, hypersomnia).

INTRODUCTION

Consciousness is the awareness of unique thoughts, memories, feelings and sensations. Conscious experiences shift and change all the time – for example, while reading this book, your conscious awareness may be shifted by the smell of dinner coming from the kitchen, which reminds you how hungry you feel; you might then switch thoughts to a conversation you had with a friend on the way home from college. These thoughts can change dramatically from moment to moment, but your experience of them seems smooth and natural.

OBJECTIVES

The specification requires you to have an awareness of the following:

- Theories of **hypnosis**, including state and non-state explanations

- The nature of dreams (e.g. Freud's psychoanalytic theory, lucid dreaming, nightmares)

Key term

Hypnosis – this is a difficult concept to define, as the underlying mechanisms of hypnosis are not very well understood. The American Psychological Division of Psychological Hypnosis defines it as 'a procedure during which a health professional or researcher suggests that a client, patient or experimental participant experiences changes in sensations, perceptions, thoughts or behaviour'. While under hypnosis, people may become more receptive to suggestion, which causes changes in the way they think, feel and behave. Contrary to popular belief, when people are under hypnosis, they remain in control of their actions and are aware of what they are doing at any time.

Theories of hypnosis

There are two opposing views of hypnosis. One of these views, the state explanation, suggests that the hypnotic state is an altered conscious state and is different to the normal states of waking and sleeping. The debate about whether hypnosis is a state or a non-state is called the altered state debate.

Neo-dissociation theory

According to Hilgard (1986), the hypnotic state is one in which there is dissociation with the high control levels. This division allows those in the hypnotic state to split parts of their functioning into different levels of mental activity. Hilgard conducted experiments, called the cold-presser test, using the 'hidden observer' phenomenon, in which he placed a participant's arm in extremely cold water and the participant said out loud that they could not feel any pain. However, when they were asked to report what they felt by writing it down, they reported that they had felt a lot of pain. Hilgard suggested that the participant's consciousness was split into two parts, with the hidden observer writing; the hidden observer could reach thought channels that could recognise pain even when the hypnotised participant reported that they could not feel any pain.

Sarbin and Slagle (1979) argue that there is no way of differentiating between a hypnotic state and one that has not been hypnotised.

Non-state explanation

Other psychologists would not agree with the state explanation, arguing that hypnosis is not an altered state but a social response. Psychologists who argue that hypnosis does not involve an altered state of consciousness suggest that the effects of hypnosis can be produced without a hypnotic induction. They claim that differences in response to hypnotic suggestions are due to the individual's attitudes and motivations, and not to any special state. Spanos (1986) argued that people under hypnosis are acting in a socio-cognitive way – in other words, they are able to convince themselves that something is going to happen and this occurs cognitively and is not due to an altered state of consciousness.

Remember

Recent research has found a strong positive correlation between an individual who is easily put into a hypnotic state and his or her level of suggestibility. Some psychologists explain this by saying that hypnosis is a social construct, because the expectations that people have of how people behave when hypnotised leads them to behave in that way.

Key Example

Wagstaff *et al.* (2002): Is response expectancy sufficient to account for hypnotic negative hallucinations? (*Contemporary Hypnosis*, 19: 133–8)

Wagstaff suggests that hypnotic experiences may be explained by psychological concepts such as compliance, conformity, attitudes, beliefs, roles, expectations, attention and imagination.

Aim: To find out if the expectancy of participants can determine whether they see nothing (negative hallucinations) when hypnotised.

Method: Participants, under both hypnotic and non-hypnotic conditions, were led to believe they would see nothing (that is they would experience a negative hallucination), but they were in fact presented with a clear visual stimulus.

Findings: Although half the participants were 100 per cent confident that they would see nothing, they all reported seeing something. Expectancy was not correlated with the clarity of the image but it was with hypnotic depth.

Conclusions: Although the results did not support expectancy theory, they were compatible with both classic state theory and socio-cognitive approaches to hypnosis that stress the operation of strategic enactment and compliance.

Evaluation

Theories of hypnosis

Hypnosis is problematic and elusive because of difficulties in defining what it is and how it works, as well as its overall effectiveness. Psychologists differ in their opinions as to what it is and mainly fall into one of two camps: state and non-state. Those who believe it is an altered state of consciousness (state theorists), such as Hilgard, suggest that the hypnotic state is different to the normal (or non-state) conscious psychological functioning.

The psychologists who oppose the idea of an altered state of mind do not dispute the subjective reality of participants who claimed to be hypnotised. Nor do they believe the responses are faked or the result of compliance, but they do point to the fact that different participants have different abilities to obtain the 'state' and responses to suggestion by participants within the 'state' are also different. There have been various attempts to increase suggestibility of hypnotic participants with inconclusive results.

Non-state psychologists point to the fact that there have been no physiological changes found in the hypnotic state. Research has shown that the responses formed by suggestion following hypnosis can also be produced without hypnosis. Increases in suggestibility can also be reproduced and even exceeded by a variety of other techniques such as task motivation instructions, placebo pills and imagination training.

Those who use hypnosis suggest that the two central components of hypnosis are trance and suggestion. The trance state is a natural but distinct state of consciousness that everyone enters into on a daily basis when day dreaming or absorbed in concentration.

In reality, people experience hypnosis on a daily basis, never realising it is hypnosis. An example is when someone is reading a book, watching TV or playing on the computer and is so engrossed in what they are doing that they block out stimuli from outside their own thoughts, and then when someone tells them that they were calling them for five minutes they find it difficult to believe. These experiences show that hypnosis happens naturally without the need for a hypnotist but still leaves the question unanswered as to whether it is an altered state.

The nature of dreams

Most **dreams** are haphazard and vague, with flashes of randomness that seem to have little meaning. Freud proposed that dreams have meanings that manifest themselves through symbols in the content of the dream. He believed that the hidden meanings of dreams had a role in the health of the psyche, and saw dreams as being the channel for psychic/sexual energy, which he called 'libido'. This energy was like an electrical current in nature and was within all

the mental, emotional and sexual life of the person. Like electricity, the energy could build up and try to find release; if it was not released in a satisfactory way, mental or even physical pain would result. The latent content of dreams shows itself through symbols which are usually sexual in nature. So, for example, anything long, such as a baguette or rolling pin, would represent a penis, whereas opening a cupboard or going through a tunnel would represent the female genitalia.

Over to you

Do you always dream? What purpose do dreams serve?

Freud's aspects of dreams

Wish fulfilment

A dream may be seen as an expression of unconscious wishes. If the desire for something is socially or personally prohibited, it may present itself in a dream, either as it is or symbolically.

Dreamwork

Dreams often symbolically represent something that is prohibited; the real nature of the dream needs to be interpreted by a psychoanalyst to determine what the dream was about.

Manifest and latent content

The manifest content of the dream is what can be remembered and reported. The latent content is the hidden part of the dream and is often found in symbols. These are not immediately obvious to the dreamer and represent wishes and desires that are not always acceptable, either socially or personally.

Condensation

Two or more ideas may be represented by one object, word or situation. The dream is brief compared to the thoughts, feelings and emotions hidden in the content.

Displacement

In the dream, a person or object is replaced with another. This is done in order to take away the stress that is felt in connection with the actual object or person.

Representation

Thoughts are changed into images; to understand a dream, the images have to be translated back to thought processes.

Secondary revision

Events and scenes are linked together to make a comprehensible whole.

Transference

The feelings a person originally had for a parent are unconsciously transported to another person, such as the psychologist working with them.

Lucid dreaming

During lucid dreams the dreamer feels as though he or she is awake and able to influence the dream or even alter its course. Lucid dreams contain less imagery, and the dreamer can recall the dream more easily and in greater detail on waking. LeBerge (1985) devised a study to demonstrate that people who are having a lucid dream can change their eye movements at will, according to the instructions of the researcher. This is recorded on an EEG machine and shows that lucid dreamers do have some conscious control over their eye movements. The mechanisms behind lucid dreaming are still unknown.

Nightmares

Just about everyone has a nightmare at some point in their lives. A nightmare is a particularly distressing dream that can cause a strong, negative emotion in the dreamer. The dreamer usually feels a sense of fear or horror, and may encounter situations of danger or discomfort. The dreamer usually wakens in a state of terror and may find it difficult to go back to sleep for a long time.

Sometimes the cause of a nightmare is physical, such as sleeping in an uncomfortable position, having a fever or eating before going to bed. This can trigger a nightmare because an increase in the body's metabolism and brain activity is triggered, and with nothing to do but sleep, the result is a nightmare.

Figure 13.1 Nightmares cause strong, negative emotions in the dreamer (John Henry Fuseli's *The Nightmare*)

Sometimes the cause of a nightmare is psychological and can occur after a traumatic event, such as an assault or a severe accident. The nightmares of those suffering from post-traumatic stress disorder (PTSD) come into this category. The content of these nightmares is usually directly related to the trauma, and the nightmares repeat themselves over and over. Other psychological causes of nightmares include things like stress in a person's waking life, such as trouble at work or with a partner, or worry over finance.

Some people are subject to frequent nightmares, which do not seem related to happenings in their waking lives; these people tend to be more sensitive, creative and emotional than other people.

The cognitive view of dreams

The cognitive view of dreams is that they are useful in learning and play a cognitive role in children who have more REM sleep than adults. This theory suggests that dreams are a way of sorting out problems that have occurred during the day. This view of dreaming may show how dreams can provide solutions and insight into problems which explains why things may seem clearer in the

morning after a good night's sleep. Dreams may also be effective learning tools and improve and consolidate cognitive abilities. This is also closely related to the idea that dreams help 'tidy up' the clutter in the mind and so refresh and prepare for the next day.

Hall explored the cognitive dimensions of dreaming and his was one of the first theories of dream interpretation based on quantitative analysis. His work is still relevant today, mostly because of the system of dream content analysis that he developed with Van De Castle. Known as the Hall Van De Castle scale, it is a quantitative system which scores a dream report with 16 empirical scales. Some of the scales are: settings, objects, people, animals and mythological creatures.

He studied thousands of dreams collected from his students and from all around the world which was a huge milestone in the scientific study of dreams. This research, started in the 1960s, is still being added to and used by psychologists, sociologists and anthropologists. This means that researchers can easily get a picture of dreaming cognition that is measurable, quantitative and statistically significant.

According to Hall, dreams reveal the structure of how we think about our lives. Hall suggested that dreams reveal cognitive structures including:

- Conceptions of self (how we appear to ourselves and the roles we play in life).
- Conceptions of others (the people in our lives and our reaction to their needs).
- Conceptions of the world (our environment could be a barren wasteland or a nurturing place).
- Conceptions of penalties (how we view what is allowed and what is forbidden).
- Conceptions of conflict (inner discord and how we solve it).

Hall suggested that dream content has coherent meaning and the conceptions are like maps to our actions and reveal the reason why we select one way rather than another.

Evaluation

The nature of dreams

Freud's theory of dreams has been very influential and is still used today to explain dreams. However, other researchers have suggested different reasons for dreaming. The discovery of the association between rapid eye movement (REM) sleep and dreaming, and the development of sleep laboratory techniques led to the activation-synthesis model which suggests that dreams are a subjective interpretation of brain signals generated during sleep. During REM sleep, according to this theory, circuits in the brain are activated to cause areas of the limbic system involved in memories, emotions and sensations to become active. In response to this activity, the brain tries to find meaning and the result is dreaming.

The adaptive function of dreams, although not extensively studied, suggests that dreams help the individual to adapt to surroundings, to learn and defend themselves through dreams. The evolutionary advantage of dreaming remains unclear. However, the adaptive function of dreams makes it an important function of life as it is physiologically advantageous because it helps to restore mental and physical balance. This remains a controversial viewpoint as there has not been enough research into this theory to show the complete psychological and physiological advantages of dreaming from an evolutionary standpoint.

The research into dreams is still continuing and the implications that can be drawn from the findings for the psychology of dreaming are controversial. The most recent theories emphasise the adaptive function of dreams related to emotion and learning.

Theories of sleep

The discovery of REM sleep

The discovery of REM sleep led to the association with dreaming. REM sleep was also found in cats and was shown in that species to be controlled by the pontine brainstem. It became clear that the brain produces two activation states: waking and REM sleep. Each has its own distinctive state of consciousness.

Restoration

Adam and Oswald (1983) suggest that the wear and tear on our bodies that occurs during the day is repaired during sleep. This is a biological theory and evidence in favour of this is the fact that when we are ill, sleep helps to restore the body to health. Research into this area suggests that non-REM sleep is involved in restoration. Harmann (1973) showed that there is an increase in the non-REM sleep of people who have undergone intense periods of exercise. One way that the body restores itself is by producing growth hormone, which has an important part to play in the metabolism of proteins. The restoration of body tissue needs protein synthesis, which is renewed and replaced during sleep. The highest concentration of growth hormone in the bloodstream is found during sleep.

The restorative theory of sleep suggests that body tissues heal and regenerate during non-REM sleep, but some researchers believe that rather than tissue restoration, sleep acts as an enforced immobiliser in order for the body to rest, and that it is this rest that acts as the restorative factor. It is generally accepted that brain tissue heals during REM sleep because the cerebral cortex cannot rest during the waking state.

> ### Remember
>
> Most people in the western world suffer from sleep deprivation. Hundreds of years ago, people had to rise and go to bed with the rising and setting of the sun, but nowadays, with electric light and TV, most people sleep 500 hours less per year on average than people in the past. Sleep deprivation can have a profound effect on an individual's quality of life.

Ecological and evolutionary explanations

The reason we sleep, according to this theory, is to protect us from predators. Sleeping at night promotes survival by reducing the risk of accident, because humans have poor night vision. Nocturnal activity would be dangerous and by sleeping at night, we avoid such dangers. Therefore, this gives those who sleep during the time of darkness an advantage. As a result, sleeping at night is a behaviour that is passed on from one generation to the next.

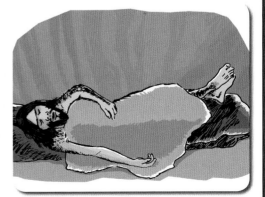

Figure 13.2 The evolutionary theory of sleep

Evaluation

Theories of sleep

Research into sleep deprivation has shown that lack of sleep impairs speech, memory and problem-solving skills. There is therefore more to the functions of sleep than bodily repair and the underlying reason for sleep may be in brain development. Studies into sleep deprivation have shown that without sleep people are more likely to lose control of their planning, sense of time and language skills. Being awake from 7am until midnight, a 17 hour day, is the same as having a blood alcohol level of 0.05 per cent which is the legal driving limit.

Restoration theories and ecological theories agree in that they suggest that because it is common in so many animals, sleep must serve some useful purpose. However, the ecological theory uses an evolutionary perspective and suggests that sleep must serve a necessary function for survival. Mammals use energy in keeping their body temperature constant and more energy is used while looking for food, avoiding predators and so on. Therefore the evolutionary approach to sleep suggests that one of the main reasons for sleep is to force mammal's activity levels to drop and reduce their body temperature in order for energy conservation. This theory has some face validity as the percentage of sleep needed by a species is affected by food requirements, predator avoidance and the size of the species.

There is, however, a difference between REM and NREM sleep in the amount of energy used. In REM sleep it is almost as much as being awake as the brain waves remain very similar to those of a fully active and functional brain. This means that the theory does not fully explain the REM function of sleep though, as energy use drops significantly during NREM sleep, the theory could possibly explain this type of sleep.

Conversely, it has been found that there is not a great deal more energy conserved while asleep than while resting. In fact, sleep only reduces energy rates by five to ten per cent and therefore rest would definitely be more advantageous from an evolutionary perspective as rest would reduce the dangers that sleeping has with its loss of consciousness. This therefore means that the idea of energy conservation is not an adequate explanation to explain the function of sleep.

The restoration theory of the function of sleep suggests that the purpose of sleep is to recover resources after using them all day and REM sleep is said to be important for growth and repair of brain tissue. Slow-wave sleep is said to be important for bodily growth and repair.

Support for the restoration theory comes from patients recovering from injuries to their central nervous system (CNS), who show a significant increase in the amount of REM sleep. This shows that in a time of recovery, the brain allows more REM sleep to occur to speed recovery. As support for the theory is based on patients with brain injuries, it raises questions why there is an increase in REM sleep. It is unclear whether the REM increase was because the brain needed to recover or if the extra REM was caused by the injury to the CNS. Therefore, the restoration theory may not apply to healthy people without brain injuries.

Research has shown, however, that tissue growth of new cells in the skin happens faster when asleep. This underlies the restoration theory as it shows that restoration does occur during sleep. Another replenishment that happens during sleep is the replacement of neurotransmitters and hormones which deplete during the course of the day, but REM sleep enables neurons to synthesize with new neurotransmitters for release when waking up. This is again support for the restoration theory as it means that key brain chemicals are replaced while asleep in order to function properly upon waking.

The role of endogenous and exogenous factors in bodily rhythms

A rhythm is something that is repeated at periodic intervals. All biological systems have these rhythms which are called biorhythms or bodily rhythms. Endogenous rhythms are internal rhythms (biological clocks). Kleitman and Armitage (1979) suggested there is a basic rest/activity cycle that goes on throughout the day and night. They found that participants' performance on verbal and spatial tasks throughout the day had a 96-minute cycle.

Figure 13.3 The sleep/wake cycle

Infradian rhythms last longer than a day; these include such things as the menstrual cycle, seasonal mating, migration or hibernation. McClintock (1971) found that women who spend large amounts of time together synchronise their menstrual cycle, and women who spend a large amount of time in the company of men have shorter cycles.

A cycle that lasts about 24 hours, such as the sleep/wake cycle, is called a circadian rhythm. Shorter rhythms, such as sleep stages, heartbeat, breathing, and so on, are called ultradian rhythms. A blind person who receives no light input still experiences circadian rhythms. Miles, Raynal and Wilson (1977) found that a blind man had circadian rhythms of 24.9, which indicates that the working of an internal clock is closer to 25 hours, which suggests that we have to adjust our clocks each day.

A number of studies have investigated cycles of more than 24 hours by putting participants in caves where circadian cycles can be controlled with artificial light. Kleitman (1963) found that participants could not adjust to a 28-hour day. Folkard et al. (1985) found that participants could cope well on a 23-hour cycle, but on a 22-hour cycle the participants' bodies reverted to a natural cycle.

Rhythms are set off by external stimuli or other features in the environment such as light; these are known as exogenous factors. Day length is the most dominant zeitgeber (time giver), but the seasons are also important, as are the phases of the moon, the availability of food, pheromones and social environment.

Shift work disrupts the cycle, and on average it takes about three days to adjust to a 12-hour shift in time. The most difficult pattern to cope with is one week on nights and the next week on days. This pattern could affect the performance of the worker and lead to tiredness, poor performance and accidents. Gold et al. (1992) found more errors and sleepiness among nurses on rotating shifts than those who worked permanent days or nights. Novak et al. (1990) recorded more injury rates for shift workers in a chemical plant.

Jet lag can cause tiredness and headaches, along with minor adjustment problems similar to those experienced by people on shift work. Webb and Agnew (1971) found that regular travellers who stuck to a rigid pattern of meals and exercise found adjustment easier, even if it meant that they had to eat at different times to everyone else.

The role of endogenous and exogenous factors in bodily rhythms

The pituitary gland controls menstruation and is therefore an internal rhythm. External factors can, however, influence it as research found that when women live together their periods occur at the same time. A study was conducted that collected samples of sweat from a group of women and rubbed it on the upper lips of other women. This synchronised their periods, due to pheromones and shows that internal rhythms can adapt to changing environmental conditions to a certain extent.

There may be evolutionary benefits of females menstruating at the same time as it may be that women will ovulate and conceive at the same time. Therefore, the children of a group of women would grow up together which would aid hunting and foraging.

The women may also share the burden of child rearing and infant survival may be increased as the women could share breastfeeding and infants of mothers who died in childbirth would therefore survive.

There seem to be a number of biological clocks in the brain that govern internal rhythms. These clocks are thought to be co-ordinated by a 'master' clock located in the hypothalamus.

The rhythm of endogenous cycles has to be adapted to external events, such as nighttime or winter so that the onset of sleep, hibernation and leaf opening occurs at the right time. Where external or exogenous factors have a role in the pattern of rhythmic activities, they are called 'zeitgebers' which means 'time givers'. Zeitgebers include light and dark, temperature, noise, eating and social patterns.

Eskimos have regular sleep/wake cycles, even though they have continuous darkness in winter. The dominant zeitgeber for Eskimos is probably social patterns.

Research was conducted on second generation squirrels raised in a laboratory where temperature and light were controlled and so remained the same all year. It was found that in the Autumn the squirrels would start to hoard food. This shows that this infradian rhythm is very difficult to modify.

An unborn embryo has regular rhythms of activity and rest which suggests that endogenous pacemakers arise from inherited, genetic mechanisms. It also suggests that these rhythms can be largely maintained without any external cues of time (zeitgebers).

All the research suggests there is at least one internal exogenous clock or pacemaker and zeitgebers can reset this internal clock to some extent.

Explanations for sleep disorders

Narcolepsy

Remember

Those with narcolepsy do not spend more time asleep in a 24-hour period than normal sleepers. In addition to the daytime involuntary sleep episodes, most people with the disorder also experience long periods of wakefulness during the night.

Narcolepsy is a neurological disorder that is caused by the brain's failure to regulate normal sleep/wake cycles. People with narcolepsy experience fleeting urges to sleep throughout the day. They sometimes fall asleep for anything from a few seconds to several minutes, and in rare cases some people remain asleep for an hour or even longer.

The sleep episodes of narcolepsy can occur at any time and the condition is very disabling. People have been known to fall asleep at work or school, during a conversation, playing games or even when driving a car. In addition to daytime sleeping, three other symptoms are frequently found in narcolepsy: cataplexy

(the sudden loss of voluntary muscle tone); hallucinations that are vivid during sleep; and brief episodes of total paralysis at the beginning and end of sleep.

For most adults, sleep lasts about eight hours and has four to six separate sleep cycles. Sleep cycles are characterised by a section of non-rapid eye movement (NREM) sleep, which is followed by rapid eye movement (REM) sleep. The NREM sleep can be divided into stages, according to the size and frequency of brainwaves. REM sleep is accompanied by heightened brain activity and temporary paralysis of the muscles that control body movement. When people are woken from sleep, they say they have been dreaming more often if they were in REM sleep when they were woken than if they were in NREM sleep. Transitions between NREM and REM sleep are managed by interactions among groups of neurons in certain parts of the brain.

It is believed that narcolepsy is the result of disease processes affecting the brain mechanisms that regulate REM sleep. For normal sleep patterns, a typical sleep cycle is about 100–110 minutes long, beginning with NREM and moving to REM sleep after about 80–100 minutes. People with narcolepsy, however, enter REM sleep within minutes of falling asleep.

Insomnia

Insomnia is characterised by difficulty getting to sleep or staying asleep long enough to wake feeling refreshed, despite having enough opportunity to sleep. A person with insomnia may have problems with waking in the night; this is most common in older people. Another problem is not feeling refreshed after sleeping, and feeling irritable and tired during the day. This leaves people unable to function normally, with difficulty concentrating. The least common type of sleep disturbance is waking early in the morning.

Psychological causes of insomnia

There are a number of possible causes for insomnia. Psychological causes include anxiety or a disrupted sleeping environment. Anxiety keeps the person awake because of the increased tension, apprehension and feelings of helplessness that induce worry and uncertainty. The individual has difficulty sleeping because of the worries that are brought on by the anxiety.

Biological causes of insomnia

Insomnia can also be caused by biological factors, such as an underlying physical condition or mental health problem. Hormonal changes in women can cause insomnia through premenstrual syndrome, menstruation, pregnancy and menopause. Medical conditions such as allergies, arthritis, asthma, heart disease, high blood pressure, hyperthyroidism and Parkinson's disease may also be responsible for insomnia. Melatonin, the hormone that helps control sleep, decreases with age; by the age of 60, the body produces very little melatonin.

Hypersomnia

People with hypersomnia have prolonged night-time sleep and excessive daytime sleepiness. People with this disorder often feel compelled to nap during the

Remember

Hypersomnia may be caused by narcolepsy, dysfunction of the autonomic nervous system or drug or alcohol abuse. In some cases there is a physical problem, such as a tumour or head injury.

day, often at inappropriate times, and these daytime naps do not provide relief from the symptoms. They often experience difficulty waking up from a long sleep and are sometimes disoriented. Other symptoms include anxiety, increased irritation, a decrease in energy, slow thought processes, loss of appetite, hallucinations and memory difficulties.

Evaluation

Explanations for sleep disorders

The cause of narcolepsy may be genetic as the genes that control the production of chemicals in the brain that may signal sleep and wake cycles have been strongly associated with the disorder. There is reason to believe that narcolepsy may be due to a deficiency in the production of hypocretin which is a chemical in the brain. However, researchers have also found abnormalities in various parts of the brain involved in regulating REM sleep. These abnormalities apparently contribute to the development of symptoms of narcolepsy. It is likely that a number of factors interact to cause neurological dysfunction and REM sleep disturbances, causing narcolepsy.

Insomnia sometimes only lasts a few days and goes away on its own. This is especially true if the individual is having problems sleeping because of temporary stress brought on by external stimuli. At other times, however, insomnia is more persistent and chronic insomnia is usually caused by an underlying mental or physical issue.

Insomnia is merely a label for poor sleep but the cause is sometimes more serious than the symptoms of insomnia. Psychological problems, such as depression, anxiety or chronic stress, may cause insomnia. Other causes of insomnia could be medical problems such as asthma, hyperthyroidism, acid reflux, allergies, or chronic pain, to name but a few.

There are some sleep disorders that can cause insomnia including narcolepsy, restless legs syndrome and sleep apnea. Sleep apnea is a serious sleep disorder that occurs when a person's breathing is interrupted during sleep. It is a disorder in which the breathing stops during sleep due to a blockage of the upper airways. These pauses in breathing interrupt the individual's sleep making them wake up many times each hour. Many people with sleep apnea do not remember that they have woken up many times during the night but they feel the effects in other ways, such as being exhausted, irritable or depressed the next day. There are many possible causes of sleep apnea but people who develop the disorder basically do not get enough oxygen into their lungs during sleep. Some of the main causes in adults include obesity, having a large tongue and/or tonsils, throat or tongue muscles that relax too much during sleep and having an unusual head shape.

Summary

The nature of dreams

Freud's psychoanalytic theory suggests that the dream state is one that allows the hidden unconscious thought into the conscious mind. The manifest content hides the latent content through symbols, and the real meaning of the dream is not apparent to the dreamer.

Lucid dreaming is when the individual feels as though they are awake and able to influence their dreams. EEG recordings show that lucid dreamers have control over their eye movements.

The cause of nightmares is sometimes physical, such as sleeping in an uncomfortable position, and sometimes psychological, such as after a traumatic event. Stress has been known to cause nightmares.

Theories of hypnosis, including state and non-state explanations

These are two opposing views of hypnosis; the debate about whether the hypnotic state is an altered state of consciousness or a non-state is called the altered state debate. Those who think it is an altered state suggest that the consciousness is split into two parts. Other psychologists argue that hypnosis is a social response.

Levels of consciousness

Theories of sleep

Some people believe the reason we sleep is for restoration of the body. This is mainly evident when illness strikes, as sleep then helps to restore the body to health.

Ecological/evolutionary explanations of sleep suggest that it is to keep people safe from predators.

The role of endogenous and exogenous factors in bodily rhythms

Circadian rhythms last about 24 hours (e.g. the sleep/wake cycle), whereas ultradian rhythms last for shorter amounts of time (e.g. heartbeat, breathing).

Jet lag can cause tiredness and headaches in the same way that shift work can, due to the interruption of natural rhythms.

Explanations for sleep disorders

Narcolepsy is a sleep disorder that is caused by the failure of the brain to regulate normal sleep/wake cycles. People with this disorder feel the need to sleep throughout the day.

People with insomnia have difficulty going to sleep or staying asleep long enough to feel refreshed when they wake. Possible causes include anxiety, disrupted sleep environment or an underlying physical or mental health problem.

People with hypersomnia feel compelled to nap during the day and have difficulty waking up from a long sleep.

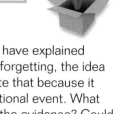

Exam focus ▶

Exam structure: Chapters 9–13

The material covered in chapters 9 to 13 relates to section B on the PY 4 paper.

Candidates are expected to answer at least one question from this section.

The focus in these topics is for candidates to be able to describe, analyse and evaluate, as appropriate, theories/explanations, research methods, findings, conclusions, usefulness and impact on society.

The question is marked out of 25: AO1 = 10, AO2 = 15.

AO1: Knowledge and understanding of science and how science works

AO1 requires you to show knowledge and understanding by providing detailed information about theories, studies and explanations of the psychological aspect the particular question is asking about.

AO2: Application of knowledge and understanding of science and how science works

AO2 requires you to demonstrate an ability to analyse and evaluate psychological theories, concepts and studies. Ensure you can build a good argument around the topic in question in order to demonstrate AO2 skills.

Basically, AO1 is describing theories and/or research, while AO2 is evaluating any theories and/or research by referring to research evidence. The question is clearly weighted more towards AO2, evaluating said theories and/or studies, so candidates should not spend too long describing studies and/or research; the bulk of the essay should be evaluating these topics.

Example questions

AO1: Knowledge and understanding – 10 marks
AO2: Evaluation – 15 marks

Example question: Describe and evaulate explanations of forgetting.

AO1: You could receive credit for explanations such as decay, displacement, interference, processing depth, amnesia, ageing, state dependency, environmental cues, denial or repression.

AO2: Evaluation points include making a balanced, reasoned and sustained evaluation of the evidence – use the research findings relating to the explanations you have used to back up your explanation. For example, if you have explained repression as an explanation of forgetting, the idea of flashbulb memory would refute that because it is a vivid memory of a very emotional event. What conclusions can be drawn from the evidence? Could there be another explanation? If there are other explanations, use them either to confirm what you have said or suggest that there could be a different explanation. Use research findings as evidence.

Example question: Discuss explanations of relationship formation.

AO1: You could receive credit for explanations of relationship formation, such as the early stages of attraction, the sociobiological explanation and social exchange theory.

AO2: Evaluation points include the fact that research tends to neglect friendship formation and this is a very important part of relationships. Theories do not reflect the dynamic, interactive nature of relationships in everyday life. Most of the research has focused on the assumption of heterosexual romantic relationships as representative of other types of relationship when this may not be the case. Research into relationships is usually based in western societies and assumes that this can be applied to all relationships, showing the ethnocentric nature of the research.

Example question: Describe and evaluate theories of cognitive development.

AO1: You could receive credit for an explanation of cognitive theories (e.g. Piaget) or interactive theories (e.g. Vygotsky).

AO2: Evaluation points include the fact that Piaget saw the child as a lone scientist and did not account for the social side of cognitive development. Vygotsky, on the other hand, strongly argued for the social constructivist view of cognitive development, suggesting that all thought arises first in actions between people, and only then becomes internalised.

Exam tips

1 Read the question carefully.
2 Clearly describe and evaluate the topic.
3 Refer to evidence that supports the topic – analyse and criticise this evidence.
4 Watch the time – spend about 40 minutes on each question.

14 Health psychology

The way health is promoted through health programmes is important in making up-to-date information on healthy living accessible to the public.

Chapters 14 to 18 relate to part C of the PY 4 exam, and at the end of Chapter 18 on page 242 you will find an examination focus feature with details about this part of the examination and tips about how to tackle it.

INTRODUCTION

Health psychology is a field of applied psychology that promotes personal and public health, using psychological theory and knowledge. Those in the health psychology area are concerned with how habits and behaviour interact with biology and have an impact on health, illness and physical well-being.

Addiction may be viewed as a continued involvement with an activity or substance even though there are negative consequences associated with it. The way addiction is treated depends on what the cause is believed to be. For example, if it is believed to have a biological basis, the treatment will be a physical one.

Stress management is very important as stress can cause severe health problems and in extreme cases death. Personality can have an impact on an individual's health as it dictates the way they react with their environment.

OBJECTIVES

The specification requires you to have an awareness of the following:

● Theories of addiction, including biological and social/psychological explanations

● Treatment of addiction (e.g. biological and social/psychological treatments)

● Management of stress, including physiologically based and psychologically based techniques

● Issues in health promotion (e.g. the health belief model, theory of reasoned action, health education programmes)

● Factors affecting health behaviour (e.g. personality type, age, social class).

Theories of addiction

Most people when they think of addiction assume the taking of drugs. However, there is a growing movement which views a number of behaviours as addictive. This includes behaviours such as gambling, overeating, sex, exercise, videogame playing, love, internet use and work.

Griffiths suggests that all addictions have a number of distinct components in common and these core components are salience, mood modification, tolerance, withdrawal, conflict and relapse.

Salience

This means that the addictive behaviour takes up the largest part of the person's life and overshadows other priorities and thoughts.

Mood modification

This occurs when the addictive activity becomes the most important interest in the person's life as they experience a 'high' or 'buzz'. Their thoughts become totally preoccupied and craving for the addictive activity dominates their thinking and feelings and socialised behaviour deteriorates. For example, if they are not actually engaged in the addictive behaviour, they will be thinking about the next time they will be engaged in that behaviour.

Tolerance

This is the process whereby increasing amounts of activity related to the addiction are needed to get mood modifying effects. This basically means that if they were engaged in activities related to the addictive behaviour, they would gradually build up the amount of time spent engaged in those activities.

Withdrawal symptoms

These are the unpleasant mental states and/or physical effects that occur when they are prevented from carrying out the addictive activities. For example, restlessness, irritability, moodiness and an inability to focus.

Conflict

This refers to the conflicts between the addictive behaviour and interpersonal conflict, conflicts with other activities (i.e. job, school, socialising, hobbies and interests) or even personal conflict upon the realisation that they are doing too much of the activity. This could typically originate from subjective feelings of a loss of control.

Relapse

This is the tendency to revert back to earlier patterns of behaviour after a period of abstinence. In the most extreme of cases, the compulsive behaviour can be quickly reinstated after cycles of abstinence or control.

According to Griffiths, the main difference between a healthy excessive enthusiasm and an addiction is that healthy enthusiasms add to life and addictions take away from it.

Biological explanations

The biological approach is concerned with physical addiction in which the body has become dependent on a substance to the extent that the person becomes tolerant and has to take more and more to achieve the same effects. A person who is dependent on a substance will suffer withdrawal symptoms, such as diarrhoea, nausea and shaking, if they suddenly stop taking the substance. Although addiction begins with the voluntary act of taking the substance, it changes into an involuntary, compulsive craving for the substance. This compulsion leads to dramatic changes in brain function, brought about by prolonged substance misuse.

There is no clear reason why people become addicted. Koob and Le Moal (1997) suggest that an important challenge for neurobiological research is to understand the neuroadaptive differences between controlled drug use, loss of control and the processes in the body that lead to **addiction**.

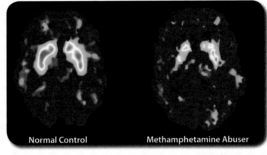

Normal Control   Methamphetamine Abuser

Figure 14.1 Brain scans of an addict and a non-addict

Neurobiology is affected by substance dependence because it alters brain function and these substances affect normal perceptions, emotions and motivational processes in the brain. Nicotine can affect a number of systems simultaneously, including memory and learning, and pain control, according to Ashton and Golding (1989).

Some people may find it harder to quit once they start, or may experience more severe withdrawal symptoms if they try to quit. Factors that make it difficult to quit may be genetic. Twin studies have shown a possible genetic influence – if one twin is an alcoholic, the other twin is twice as likely to become an alcoholic too. Adopted children whose biological parents are alcoholics are four times as likely to become alcohol-dependent than other children who are adopted.

Key terms

Addiction – a psychological or physical dependency on a natural or synthetic substance, to such an extent that stopping taking the substance causes severe trauma.

Neurotransmitters – chemicals that transmit signals from a neuron to a target cell across the synapse. Neurotransmitters are essential for memory, mood, learning, behaviour, sleep, pain perception and sexual urge.

Remember

The changes in brain function lead the medical profession to view addiction as an illness that needs to be treated. The individual is the problem, and stopping the individual from taking the substance that they are addicted to is seen as the cure for the addiction. However, once someone is addicted it is difficult for them to change their behaviour without treatment.

Evaluation

Theories of addiction – biological

The evidence for addiction being biological needs further investigation as there is no clear reason why, from a biological point of view, people become addicted. When the biological view looks at whether addiction could be genetic in nature, there is again no research that has identified genes as a

cause. This is because, when monozygotic twins are studied, the concordance rate for addiction is not 100 per cent which it should be if genes were the only factor involved in addiction. This means that environmental conditions must be important.

Though it seems likely that there is a genetic element, exactly what the gene codes are has not yet been found. The main question is whether addictive behaviour is encoded in the genes or whether a biological mechanism drives addictive behaviour. One genetic factor, found in Eskimos, Asians and the American Indians, is that they are all genetically inclined to have a deficiency in the production of acetaldehyde, an enzyme important for alcohol degradation. These groups of people are hypersensitive to the effects of alcohol in their system, with Eskimos and American Indians having a higher rate of alcoholism than Asians. Eskimos and American Indians are more likely to be addicted to gambling, a behaviour not seen in Asians. This raises the question as to whether a single gene can be responsible for addictive behaviour.

The strongest argument for addiction and genetics comes from the pattern of inheritance. All studies conducted in this area show that it is sons, not daughters, who are more likely to inherit the risk of alcoholism. It is still unclear how much of this has its basis in genetics. It could be that the sons model themselves on their fathers. As research continues in this area, the role played by genetics in addiction will become clearer. As of this moment, it is suspected to be a major component of most addictions and at the very least predisposes individuals to indulge in addictive behaviour.

Figure 14.2 Alcohol is often used as a social tool

Remember

Alcohol is a socially accepted way of unwinding after a long, hard day at work, or as an enjoyable aspect of socialising with others. Alcohol is more affordable than in the past, and although drinking has been part of British culture for hundreds of years, in recent times there has been concern that binge drinking is causing problems.

Social/psychological explanations

Han *et al.* (1999) conducted research into identical (monozygotic or MZ) twins and same-sex non-identical (dizygotic or DZ) twins, to investigate the genetic and environmental factors in substance abuse in adolescents. They found that the major influences on the decision to use substances were mostly environmental.

The Department of Health guidelines recommend a maximum alcohol intake of three to four units per day for men and two to three units for women. However, 5.9 million people in the UK admit to drinking more than twice the recommended amount. The Institute of Alcohol Studies points out that there is a growing culture of intoxication in young people, and research has shown that 36 per cent of men and 27 per cent of women aged 16 to 24 said they had been binge drinking at least once in the previous week. Binge drinking in young people may persist and become a problem of addiction.

Evaluation

Theories of addiction – social/psychological

Environmental factors may be to blame for addictive behaviour as can be seen in the studies carried out on twins. Cognitive explanations of addiction can show how individual differences can account for addictive behaviour. For example, millions of people all over the world gamble but not all of them are addicted. Those that do become addicted may have developed faulty cognitive biases or irrational thinking patterns.

The patterns of drinking, explained through social learning theory, are developed through perceptions of other people and, having started drinking for social reasons, the individual's biology may be affected. Then the withdrawal symptoms they suffer will encourage them to keep on with the habit in order to keep them from experiencing the drop in mood that would occur through lack of use.

The main challenge for any theory about addiction is to explain how it occurs in order to develop a better understanding of prevention and recovery from it. A successful theory should be able to show when addiction is likely to occur and give insights into the prevention and treatment of addiction. Addiction is not easily explained by psychological or biological factors on their own, but rather involves a number of factors that intertwine. These factors can be psychological, genetic and socio-cultural, all working together in the environment of the addict.

Treatment of addiction

Biological treatment

There is not, as yet, a magic pill that will cure alcoholism. Some drugs have been developed that will reduce cravings for those who are sincerely trying to stop drinking and want treatment for alcoholism or addiction.

There are nicotine patches for those who want to give up smoking, and research by West and Zhou (2007) concluded that nicotine replacement therapy is associated with improved long-term abstinence rates.

Heroin addicts are often prescribed methadone (a synthetic analgesic similar to morphine) to help reduce the withdrawal symptoms of the addiction. By using methadone, the individual can stabilise and start to rehabilitate; this is best done with the help of psychological treatments alongside the methadone.

Key Example

Brewer *et al*. (1998): A meta-analysis of predictors of continued drug use during and after treatment for opiate addiction (*Addiction*, 93, 73–92)

Aim: To review research with a view to find out if it would be possible to improve outcomes by addressing patient characteristics that predict continued drug use.

Method: A review of 69 studies that reported information on the variables that are associated with continued illicit drug use during and after treatment for opiate addiction.

Findings: There were behaviours that were statistically significant as predictors of continued use, including: high level of opiate drug use before treatment; prior treatment for opiate addiction; no previous abstinence from opiates; abstinence from or light use of alcohol; depression; high stress levels;

unemployment or employment problems; socialising with others who are substance abusing; short length of treatment and leaving treatment before completion.

Conclusions: To address relapse, treatment interventions should address numerous areas of the addict's life because no single variable predicts continued drug use.

Social/psychological treatment

Cognitive behaviour therapy has been found to be valuable in treating alcoholism and drug addiction. This is especially true as part of an overall programme of recovery. The therapy is a short-term, focused approach and works by using the same learning processes the individual used to develop the dependency in the first place. The treatment involves teaching the individual to recognise situations in which they are most likely to drink or use drugs. The treatment consists of two parts.

Functional analysis

The individual gains an insight into why he or she drinks or uses drugs. The individual works together with the therapist to identify the thoughts, feelings and circumstances experienced before and after taking a drink or using drugs. They also work to identify situations in which they have difficulties coping. This helps the individual to determine the risks that are likely to lead to relapse.

Skills training

This part of the treatment is necessary, as an individual who has used alcohol or drugs as a means of coping with his or her problems needs to learn or relearn coping strategies. The main aim of cognitive behaviour therapy is to educate the addict to change the way that he or she thinks about the substance abuse, and to learn new ways of coping with the circumstances that led to the addiction in the past. The therapist helps the individual to develop healthier skills and habits, while unlearning old habits.

Research has had mixed results on cognitive behaviour therapy. More than 24 controlled trials have been conducted among users of tobacco, alcohol, cocaine, marijuana, opiates and other sorts of substances, making cognitive behaviour therapy one of the most frequently evaluated psychosocial approaches to treating substance abuse. The findings of these studies show that cognitive behaviour therapy is more effective than no treatment at all. When it is compared with other treatments, some show cognitive behaviour therapy to be more effective, while others show it to have equal effectiveness.

Evaluation

Treatment of addiction

The way addiction is viewed has an immense impact on the strategy for dealing with the problem. For example, if it is viewed as a lifestyle choice, then the way to counteract the addiction would be through education and deterrence. If it is viewed as a mental disorder, then the way to

counteract addiction would be treatment. If, however, addiction is viewed as being a choice of a disordered life, then it should be counteracted through deterrence, education and treatment.

Research has shown that treatment can help people who are addicted to successfully regain their lives. The key principle that has emerged from this research, that is needed to form the basis of any effective treatment programme, is the need to acknowledge that addiction is a complex but treatable disease that affects brain function and behaviour. There is no single treatment that is appropriate for everyone. Effective treatments have to be readily available and attend to the many needs the individual has, not just the addiction.

Continuing in treatment and attending counselling sessions is essential. Behavioural therapies are the most common form of drug abuse treatment. Medication is an important part of treatment for many individuals but needs to be combined with counselling or other behavioural treatment.

Management of stress

Stress is a state of psychological tension caused by certain pressures or forces, which can be either physical or psychological, which place a strain on the individual. Sources of stress, or stressors, are different for different people, because people differ in terms of their behaviour, gender, social class, ethnicity and culture – something that one person finds stressful may not even be noticed by another person. Sometimes anxiety and depression accompany stress, and drugs are often used to treat these disorders. The stress response involves increased levels of some neurotransmitters (e.g. adrenaline) and increased activity in the limbic system and the sympathetic nervous system.

Physiological treatments

Anti-anxiety, or anxiolytics, come from a group of drugs known as benzodiazepines and are the most commonly prescribed drugs for stress management. They are minor tranquillisers and decrease arousal by affecting hormone levels and the activity in the limbic system. Since the stress response produces high arousal, tranquillisers reduce the arousal and may reduce the stress, but they have no direct effect on the stressor. They may, however, relax the individual enough to be able to cope more effectively with the stressor.

Remember

Tranquillisers may relax the individual enough to enable him or her to cope more effectively with the stressor.

Beta blockers are used to slow the heart rate and reduce the strength of its contraction to reduce blood pressure. These are used because long-term stress often goes together with hypertension (high blood pressure), which can lead to strokes. Beta blockers have the effect of decreasing sympathetic nervous system activity, which helps the individual to feel calm and relaxed.

Psychological treatments

Biofeedback is a behavioural treatment of stress. Biofeedback is a method of stress reduction which uses equipment to feedback to the individual information about bodily processes, such as their heart rate and blood pressure. People are not often aware of these processes and biofeedback allows the

Figure 14.3 Biofeedback helps people to reduce stress levels through an awareness of bodily processes

individual to 'see' or 'hear' what is going on. Electrodes are attached to the individual's skin and measure blood pressure, muscle tension and skin temperature; these are displayed on a monitor. With the help of a therapist, the individual learns to change his or her heart rate or blood pressure, while taking note of the progress through the feedback on the monitor. Eventually, the individual will be able to achieve this without the feedback from the monitor.

There are three common forms of biofeedback: electromyography (EMG), which measures muscle tension; thermal biofeedback, which measures skin temperature; and electroencephalography (EEG), which measures brainwave activity.

Relaxation appears to provide the basis for successful biofeedback therapy. When the body is under chronic stress, internal processes like blood pressure and heart rate become overactive and the biofeedback process allows the individual to reduce blood pressure and heart rate through relaxation techniques and mental exercises. They then see the results on the monitor, which encourages them to carry on and reap the benefits of a calmer body.

Remember

Some psychologists suggest that it is learning the relaxation technique that reduces stress in the individual rather than the biofeedback process.

Stress inoculation therapy (SIT)

This is based on the idea that just as a person can be inoculated against tetanus to become resistant to it, so they can be 'inoculated' or prepared to become resistant to stress. SIT has three phases, at the end of which the person is better equipped to cope with the stressors in his or her life.

Phase 1

The therapist explains important concepts, such as how people often make their stress worse by unconsciously using bad coping habits. The person then identifies the sources of stress in his or her life and examines how he or she copes with stressful situations; the person is encouraged to think of alternative ways of coping. The main aim at this point is to put across the idea that stressors are puzzles to be solved, rather than obstacles. Coping strategies are worked through for the stressors that have been identified. Those stressors that are unable to change should be accepted, so that coping strategies can be adjusted accordingly. This process gives the person a sense of control.

Phase 2

In this phase, skills for dealing with stressors are learnt, including a list of positive, reassuring and encouraging coping statements. At the same time, negative statements that are self-critical must be identified and discarded. The coping strategies taught in this phase are individual to the person and his or her particular strengths and vulnerabilities, in order for the treatment to be effective.

Phase 3

In the final phase, opportunity to practise coping skills is provided, and a variety of methods are used to simulate stressful situations, to make the situation realistic. The person may be encouraged to role-play a stressful situation and practise using the coping strategies until they become natural and easy to act out.

> ## Remember
> SIT is useful for individuals, couples and groups.

SIT consists of 8 to 15 sessions, with booster and follow-up sessions over a 3- to 12-month period.

Evaluation

Management of stress

Biofeedback has advantages as it can be used in isolation or in combination with other techniques. There is evidence to show that it is particularly effective with children. However, there are disadvantages with biofeedback as studies have shown that individuals may learn to relax some muscles but this may not always lead to a feeling of relaxation. There are also problems with time, expense and location as the equipment used makes using the apparatus at home quite difficult. Some psychologists suggest that there is no advantage to biofeedback over ordinary relaxation techniques.

The advantages of stress inoculation training (SIT) are that it provides practical skills that are applicable to real life. However, compared to other stress management techniques there has not been a great amount of research conducted into its effectiveness. The few studies that have been carried out indicate that SIT is effective as a technique and is particularly useful for long-term change. The benefits of SIT can last for years if the individual continues to practise the techniques.

Issues in health promotion

An important question in health promotion is why some people adopt particular health behaviours and other people do not. The models of health behaviour try to answer this question.

Health belief model

The health belief model (HBM) was originally developed by psychologists working in the public health service in the USA. They wanted to understand and explain why people failed to use the free service of a tuberculosis (TB) screening programme. Since then, the HBM has been amended to predict more general behaviours, including sexual risk behaviours and the transmission of HIV/AIDS. It is a psychological model that tries to predict and explain health behaviours.

The HBM looks at a person's reasons for taking health-related action and describes the thoughts behind why he or she takes the action, and the reason for taking the action at that particular moment. People's motivation and interest in their health varies enormously. The HBM is based on the understanding that people will take health-related action if they think they are at high risk

of developing a disease. For example, a person who thinks he or she has a high risk of developing lung cancer is more likely to follow advice to give up smoking.

Table 14.1 The health belief model for health promotion practice

CONCEPT	EXPLANATION CONSIDERATIONS	APPLICATION OF HOW TO HELP PEOPLE MAKE HEALTHY CHOICES
Perceived susceptibility	When considering specific health problems, people think very differently about how likely they are to be affected.	Identify the population at risk and the risk levels. Personalise the risk based on a person's behaviour. Heighten perceived susceptibility if person's perceived susceptibility is too low.
Perceived severity	The assessment an individual makes of the seriousness of the condition, and its potential consequences.	Identify the consequences of the risk.
Perceived benefits	The belief a person has in the effectiveness of the advised action to reduce the risk or seriousness of the condition.	State the action needed and describe the positive effects to be expected.
Perceived barriers	The assessment an individual makes of the tangible and psychological costs of the advised action.	Recognise and reduce barriers through reassurance, incentives and assistance.
Cues to action	The strategies a person activates to prepare for the action.	Give information on how to achieve goals, promote awareness and give reminders.
Self-efficacy	The confidence the person has to take action.	Provide training and guidance in taking action.

Theory of reasoned action

The theory of reasoned action (TRA) describes intention as the best predictor of whether or not behaviour is performed. According to the TRA, things that determine behavioural intention are attitudes towards the behaviour and subjective norms associated with the behaviour.

Attitudes towards the behaviour refers to the beliefs held by an individual about the positive or negative value associated with the particular health behaviour and its outcomes.

Subjective norm refers to an individual's value, either positive or negative, that is associated with the particular behaviour.

Health behaviours can be promoted by designing interventions to change behavioural intention, by affecting attitude and subjective norm.

Attitude ⟹ Intention ⟹ Behaviour

> ## Evaluation
>
> ### Issues in health promotion
>
> One of the main issues in health promotion is to identify what people believe in order to understand their underlying thought processes. Research is carried out to try to understand why some people are healthy and others are not and then how to improve health. As this research relies on self-reporting there is always the problem of validity because this method is open to social desirability bias and therefore calls the validity into question.
>
> If the research is conducted properly, it has the practical application of creating strategies to promote a healthier lifestyle, and if successful, the nation's health will improve and put less strain on the NHS. Health promotion is a powerful strategy for social development as it addresses the factors that influence inequalities in health.
>
> There is also the problem of ethics as health changes may be forced through legislation and this may pose problems for some social groups. For example, vaccinating babies against diseases is acceptable but if there is a doubt about possible dangers with the vaccine, it leaves parents in a dilemma whether to have their child vaccinated. They may be unsure which is worse – the dangers of the vaccine or the dangers of the disease.

Factors affecting health behaviour

Personality type

Personality is a difficult concept to define. A typical definition views the individual's personality as their characteristic way of acting, feeling, reacting and perceiving the world. There is reason to believe that personality type is related to an individual's health. Research has identified that the lifestyle of an individual has a significant effect on their health. Health is affected by many things, such as smoking, the kinds of foods we eat, and exercise. Individuals who take part in dangerous activities put themselves at risk of broken bones or head injury.

Cloninger (1986) described three personality types, based on novelty seeking, harm avoidance and reward dependence. The individual who is high in novelty seeking is impulsive, exploratory and eager to take up new interests. They neglect details and quickly get distracted and bored. The person who is low in novelty seeking is slow to make decisions, focuses on details, likes order and is slow to become angry. People high in harm avoidance are cautious, tense, inhibited, easily fatigued, shy and apprehensive. People with low harm avoidance are optimistic, outgoing, energetic and relaxed. Reward-dependent people love being rewarded, particularly with verbal signals of social approval, and they seek to maintain behaviour that has been associated with rewards.

Figure 14.4 The novelty seeker may take part in risky activities

The novelty seeker may take part in risky activities, such as skydiving or motorbike racing. Choices of this nature may lead to accident and injury. The individual with low novelty-seeking trait will prefer a daily routine and will avoid taking risks.

Some personality types are more susceptible to disease and stress. It is known that bodily response to stress produces cortisol; if cortisol remains in the system too long it can trigger a build-up of fatty deposits in the arteries going to the heart. This would eventually lead to heart disease. Type A personality was first identified by two heart specialists, Friedman and Rosenman, during the 1950s. They noticed that people who tended to have heart attacks had certain characteristic ways of behaving, which they called Type A personalities. Type A people are highly competitive, impatient, hostile, aggressive, impulsive and find it difficult to relax. Type B people are the opposite of Type A: they are not competitive, find it easy to relax and are easygoing.

Friedman and Rosenman (1974) conducted a longitudinal study of over 3,500 men, who were middle-aged and healthy at the start of the study. Eight and a half years later, they found that those with a Type A personality were twice as likely to have heart disease as those with Type B.

Schiffer *et al.* (2005) investigated whether Type D personality is associated with impaired health and increased depressive symptoms. Individuals with a Type D personality tend to have increased negative emotions across time and situations, and they are inclined not to share these emotions with others, because of fear of rejection or disapproval. Eighty-four patients completed questionnaires to assess their personality type, health status and mood status. They found that Type D patients were more likely to experience impaired health when compared with non-Type Ds. Type Ds also reported symptoms of depression more often.

Remember

Studies have shown that men and women handle stress differently. This may be due to the oestrogen hormone, as women are three times more likely to develop depression in response to stress in their lives.

Over to you

Why do you think that people in lower social classes are more likely to suffer from cancer, heart disease and respiratory disease?

Social class

There are differences in the occurrence of illness by social class. People in lower social classes are more likely to suffer from cancer, heart disease and respiratory disease. Children and adults in lower social classes are more likely to suffer from infective and parasitic diseases, pneumonia, poisonings and violence. There are differences in the diet and fitness of different social classes, and also in their habits — for example, smoking. Those in lower social classes are more likely to suffer from poor nutrition, bad housing and underprivileged neighbourhoods.

Evaluation

Factors affecting health behaviour

While personality factors may play a part in health, gender may also be one of the factors worth looking at. There is contrasting evidence when it comes to which of the sexes are healthier as men tend to be faster during aerobic exercise due to their greater muscle strength. Women only possess two-thirds of the overall physical strength of men but their abdominal muscles are as strong as those of men.

Cancer affects both genders and all ages but the level of cancers which affect women are declining or remaining stable, particularly breast cancer. This is probably because women's groups have campaigned

for awareness of such cancers as breast cancer and ovarian cancer. However, the cancers that affect men are remaining level or increasing. This could be due to the funding situation. More money is spent on breast cancer research than on prostate cancer although the mortality rates for both genders are nearly the same. Men are more likely to be victims of cancer than women.

Women have larger stomachs, kidneys and livers than men and women's hearts beat more rapidly at 80 beats per minute while men's heart beat is 72 beats per minute, but women are less likely to develop high blood pressure. On average, women live longer than men by about five years and although women are more likely to react to pain more quickly than men, they have a higher pain threshold, which means they have a higher tolerance for pain.

Summary

Theories of addiction

Biological factors that make it difficult to stop addictive behaviour may be genetic.

Social/psychological explanations could be that addiction starts with socialising with people who drink/take drugs and doing the same to be 'sociable'. Binge drinking is a social problem and this may lead to addiction.

Management of stress

Physiologically based management of stress includes anti-anxiety drugs that help to relax the individual and allow them time to cope more effectively with the stressor.

Psychologically based techniques include biofeedback, which is a behavioural treatment, and stress inoculation therapy, which aims to prepare the individual to be able to resist the stress response to a stressor.

Treatment of addiction

Biological treatments include drugs that help reduce withdrawal symptoms and reduce cravings for those who are sincerely trying to give up drinking.

Psychological treatments such as cognitive behavioural therapy are useful in treating alcoholism and drug addiction. Cognitive behaviour therapy works best when combined with other treatments.

Health psychology

Issues in health promotion

The health belief model looks at an individual's reason for taking health-related action and describes the thoughts that lie behind the action – for example, people will take action if they believe they are at high risk of developing a disease.

Theory of reasoned action suggests that the best predictor of behaviour is intention.

Factors affecting health behaviour

Personality type may be an indicator of the type of illness that an individual is likely to get – for example, a Type A personality is likely to have heart disease, whereas a Type D personality is likely to suffer from impaired health.

Social class has a bearing on health, as those from the lower classes are more likely to suffer illnesses such as cancer, heart disease and respiratory problems.

15

INTRODUCTION

Educational psychology is concerned with how people learn and how effective educational institutions are in enabling **learning**. Many factors have been identified that assist in the process of learning and these have been applied to classroom teaching. The way that children develop cognitively has also been taken into account when devising learning programmes for effective teaching and learning in the classroom. Special educational needs are also part of the discipline of educational psychology, and programmes have been developed to help students overcome a variety of needs in order for them to learn effectively.

OBJECTIVES

The specification requires you to have an awareness of the following:

- Behaviourist learning theory applied to education, including classical and operant conditioning

- Cognitive developmental theories applied to education (e.g. Piaget, Vygotsky, Bruner)

- Individual differences in learning styles (e.g. Curry's onion model, Grasha's six learning styles, gender and cultural differences)

- Motivating factors in the classroom (e.g. teaching styles, attribution theory, Maslow's hierarchy of needs)

- Special educational needs, including assessment, categorisation and strategies for education of at least one special educational need (e.g. dyslexia, autism).

Key term

Learning – a change in behaviour through **practice, training or experience**. Evidence for this is found in observable behaviour changes and the acquisition of skills. There may also be unobservable changes in knowledge.

Behaviourist theory of learning

Behaviourists believe that the only appropriate way of studying material is through scientific investigation of observable behaviour. There is no room for introspection in behaviourist theory, as behaviourists argue that we cannot know what we cannot see. Internal processes such as memory, attention and all thought processes are unnecessary concepts that confuse attempts to explain behaviour; these can be thought of as a 'black box'.

The main mechanism of behaviour is stimulus–response; through conditioning, stimulus–response can be turned into complex behaviour. Reinforcing the behaviour increases the likelihood of the behaviour being repeated.

Remember

Behaviourists believe that people are born as 'blank slates' and have to learn everything. This learning process occurs either through classical conditioning or operant conditioning.

Classical conditioning

Classical conditioning was first demonstrated by Pavlov, who showed that learning is a process that occurs through associations between an environmental stimulus and a naturally occurring stimulus. The basic principles of classical conditioning are outlined below.

Unconditioned stimulus

This is a stimulus that naturally and automatically triggers a response – for example, in Pavlov's experiment, the sight of food elicited a salivation response in dogs. The food was the unconditioned stimulus.

Unconditioned response

This is the unlearned response that naturally occurs in reaction to the unconditioned stimulus. The salivation of the dogs in response to the sight of food was the unconditioned response.

Conditioned stimulus

This is a previously neutral stimulus that becomes associated with the unconditioned stimulus and, after conditioning, triggers the conditioned response. For Pavlov's dogs, the ringing of a bell each time they were being fed eventually led to the dogs salivating at the sound of the bell. In this case, the conditioned stimulus is the sound of the bell.

Conditioned response

This is the learned response to a previously neutral stimulus. In Pavlov's dogs, the conditioned response was the salivation of the dogs when they heard the sound of the bell.

Classical conditioning in the classroom

Teachers can apply classical conditioning in class by creating a positive environment to help students overcome fear or anxiety. In situations where a student may become anxious, such as performing in front of a group, pleasant surroundings can allow the student to learn new associations, so that instead of feeling anxious and tense in these situations, they learn to stay calm and relaxed.

Figure 15.1 Creating a positive classroom environment

Operant conditioning

Positive reinforcement

Skinner's theory of operant conditioning is based on the idea that learning is a function of change in observable behaviour. He investigated operant conditioning by using rats in a 'Skinner box', and discovered that the rat's behaviour was conditioned by positive reinforcement. He found that the rats in the Skinner box learned to press a lever to obtain the reward of food. The food was a positive reinforcer and increased the frequency of the response.

Negative reinforcement

Skinner subjected the rats to a loud noise that they could stop by pressing a lever and found that they would press the lever to stop the noise. This was negative reinforcement. The term 'negative' refers to something that is reinforcing behaviour by ending the objectionable stimulus. So removal of something objectionable, such as a loud noise or an electric shock, increased the frequency of the behaviour.

Operant conditioning in the classroom

Operant conditioning has been used in education in all sorts of ways, from giving out merit marks and stickers for good behaviour, to expressions of praise from the teacher. Teachers can apply positive reinforcement in the classroom by praising the performance of those students who do well. For example, a teacher gave her class a weekly quiz and the result of the first weekly test was low, so she began praising the performance of those students who answered the questions correctly; as a result of the praise, the performance of all the students on the weekly quiz improved as the weeks went by.

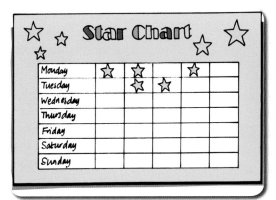

Figure 15.2 Applying positive reinforcement in the classroom

Negative reinforcement works by reinforcing behaviour by taking away or preventing something unpleasant. For example, if a teacher had a problem with the attendance of some students, she could apply negative reinforcement by giving a 'homework pass' for 100 per cent attendance in class. This would improve the attendance of the students in order for them to avoid having homework.

Cognitive developmental theories

Piaget

Jean Piaget was the first person to propose a theory of cognitive development based on the way children of different ages behave. He suggested that the mind of a young child works in a different way to that of an adult. Children's thinking, according to Piaget, goes through a series of distinct and consecutive stages on the way to adulthood. Their progress is not entirely smooth; instead there are stages in which they move into completely new ways of thought. These transitions, according to Piaget, happen at about 18 months, 7 years and 12 years. He pointed out that children cannot complete certain tasks, no matter how bright they are, until they are psychologically mature enough to do so.

Piaget argued that children have to construct their own knowledge and they do this through experimentation. Experience allows children to create schemas or mental models, which may be altered through assimilation, accommodation and equilibrium.

- **Assimilation** – the process of a child taking in and absorbing new information or a new experience through the use of existing schemas.

- **Accommodation** – where the child changes the schema as a result of new information. The schema adapts to match the special characteristics of objects and situations.

- **Equilibrium** – the child reaches a balance of the information collected.

Piaget's learning theory is based on stages that children go through in order to learn. In each stage, the learning process is different and a little more complex.

Vygotsky

A major criticism of Piaget's theory is that it did not allow for the effects of the social environment. Vygotsky, however, emphasised the role of society, as he believed this was essential to human cognitive development. He argued that Piaget had neglected the impact of cultural systems on development by concentrating on the child as a solitary thinker. Vygotsky argued that Piaget viewed development as if it came from within the child, either as maturation or as the child's own discoveries. While he agreed that this was probably true of cognitive development up to the age of 2 years, after this, cognitive growth is heavily influenced by the social aspect of sign systems. Vygotsky believed that thinking would be impossible without speech and other sign systems. Language, voluntary attention and memory are all mental functions that come from the culture and begin with interaction between the child and another person. What begins as a social function becomes internalised and occurs within the child.

Development happens through reconstruction, according to Vygotsky; children come across the same situation over and over again, but each time they deal with it at a higher level and reconstruct the situation. Abstract or theoretical thinking is the highest level of thinking; children need instruction in abstract concepts, such as writing or mathematics. While children may develop some concepts on their own, Vygotsky argued that they would not develop abstract forms of thought without instruction in abstract sign systems.

The child, according to Vygotsky, has a zone of proximal development (ZPD) – that is, the next step in development – and this is only attainable through the help and support of an adult or more competent peer.

> ## Remember
>
> Vygotsky agreed with Piaget to a certain extent, but felt that Piaget had left out the social side of learning that was, to Vygotsky, very important in the way the child acquires new information.

Cognitive theory in the classroom

Piaget in the classroom

As children experiment with something new, they mentally categorise it according to the information they have previously processed. In order for children to encode the new thing into their brains, teachers should base their instructions on schemas that the children already know. This means that a teacher should assess the current stage of a child's cognitive development and set tasks that are compatible with the stage the child is in. This allows the child to approach tasks that are tailored to his or her needs, and which are likely to be motivating.

Piaget's theory would say that teachers must give children learning opportunities that enable them to advance to the next developmental step by creating disequilibrium. This would enable the child to assimilate and accommodate the new information. The child should be allowed opportunities to explore things by themselves and learn through discovery. Piaget believed that teachers are guides to

Figure 15.3 Learning through discovery

children's learning and the curriculum should be adapted to each individual child's needs and intellectual levels.

Vygotsky in the classroom

The concept of the zone of proximal development is founded on the notion that development is defined by what a child can do independently and what the child can do with help from either an adult or a more competent peer. A teacher would need to know both levels of the ZPD in order to know where the child is at the time and what the child is capable of achieving. This means that the teacher must plan activities that include not only what children in the class are capable of doing on their own, but also what they can learn with other people's help.

Tasks shouldn't be too advanced, as only instructions and activities that are within the ZPD support development. Instructions should be provided that enable practice in the ZPD for individual children or groups of children. Cooperative learning activities with groups of children at different levels could be beneficial, as the more adept ones could help the others by bringing them up to the level they are capable of reaching.

Evaluation

Cognitive developmental theories

The developmental theory put forward by Piaget has been very influential and given psychologists insights into the quality and limitation of children's thinking. However, replications and alterations to Piaget's methods have demonstrated that Piaget underestimated the cognitive abilities of children. Some psychologists argue that Piaget's findings were a result of how his tests were structured rather than the limitation of children's thought processes.

Piaget suggested that children's thought processes go through distinct stages as they mature which meant that he saw cognitive development as genetic and largely unaffected by environmental factors. In support of this, studies have shown that older children do better at the tasks Piaget used.

With Vygotsky's theory there is little scientific evidence to support the theory. The emphasis on social interaction does not stipulate the exact nature of the help needed to achieve the zone of proximal development and nor does it state the age of the 'older other' who may help. In fact it has been shown that someone of the same age may help bring an individual on if they have greater knowledge and can communicate well.

Vygotsky's theory does bridge the gap between social and cognitive approaches and helps psychologists to understand how to help learners reach their potential. This means that there is more potential for the classroom than with Piaget's theory.

Individual differences in learning styles

It is commonly believed that most students have a particular method, or style, of taking in and processing information; from this belief, the notion of individualised learning styles originated in the 1970s, and has grown in popularity in recent years. Therefore, learning styles are different ways of learning and comprise educating methods geared towards each individual that are supposed to allow the individual learner to learn to the best of his or her ability.

Curry's onion model

Curry proposed a model of learning that could be compared to the layers of an onion. The innermost layer is composed of measures of personality as found in psychometric personality tests. These measures represent the cognitive personality style of the individual learner and reveal the way the learner prefers to adapt and assimilate information. Curry suggested that cognitive personality styles of individuals are relatively permanent and are the motivating factors for the learner.

The middle layer of the onion represents the information-processing style. This is assessed using style measures, such as Kolb's (1976) learning style inventory, Tamir and Cohen's (1980) cognitive preference inventory (CPI), and Shmeck, Ribich and Ramania's (1977) inventory of learning processes (ILP); it shows the way the learner takes in information and the way that new learning is used.

The outer layer is the way the learner prefers to gain knowledge and is the instructional preference. This includes measures from Friedman and Stritter's (1976) instructional preference questionnaire, Rezler and Rezmovich's (1981) instructional preference inventory, and Riechmann and Grasha's (1974) Grasha-Riechmann student learning style scales. Instructional preference is defined as an individual's preferred learning environment. Curry suggested that students' instructional preferences were modified by environmental influences. The educational environment has the biggest influence on the outer layer, less on the middle layer and none on the inner core.

Grasha's six learning styles

Some students like individual instruction, while others prefer group work. Some students are more independent than other students. Grasha developed the student learning styles scale to measure the preferences of students when they were interacting with teachers and peers. The Grasha-Riechmann student learning style scale was made to assess the individual learning styles of students in school and college. There are six learning styles and most students have all of them to a greater or lesser extent.

Independent learners

These are confident students who prefer to work alone, without conferring with others.

Dependent learners

These students need structure and guidance and prefer to have someone tell them precisely what to do. They like feedback from teachers or from peers.

Competitive learners

Competitive learners always want to do better than anyone else in the class. They view the classroom as a win-or-lose situation and they compete to win. They need recognition for their achievements.

Figure 15.4 Some students work best with structure and guidance

Collaborative learners

These students learn through cooperating with others in the class and with their teachers. They prefer group work and small group discussions.

Avoidant learners

Students in this category are reluctant to learn and are uninterested in classroom activities. They do not enjoy learning and may not even want to attend class.

Participant learners

These students enjoy classroom activities and discussion. They are highly motivated, eager to learn and take responsibility for their learning.

Evaluation

Individual differences in learning styles

There has been over 30 years of educational research into learning styles and there is no evidence to support any one theory of learning styles. This means there is a danger of labelling a student as a particular type of learner as there are limitations to any learning styles model and any theory or model of learning styles is a simplification of how students learn. If too much emphasis is put on one of the areas of learning, say, visual, then students may miss out on developing other areas.

Environment, culture, teaching methods and curriculum requirements are all part of the learning process and learning style is only one of a variety of factors affecting the way a student learns. The presentation of the material to be learned in multiple formats does appear to result in learning gains but this may be because of the times the student views the material rather than individual learning style.

No matter what style the student has, the examination system is clearly geared towards the written word.

Gender and cultural differences

There have always been significant differences in the educational success of boys and girls. However, there have been changes over the years. Boys in the 1960s achieved results that were on average 5 per cent better than girls at all levels of the education system, with the exception of the 11+ examination. This was true until the mid 1980s, when both genders began to improve their school performance, but girls improved more than boys.

In 2007 girls outperformed boys at GCSE by 9.1 per cent, and at every key stage, except in maths at key stage 2. Girls outperformed boys in English at all the key stages, and in 2007 the gender gap for GCSE results in English was 13.9 per cent, with 69.2 per cent of girls achieving grades A★ to C, compared with only 55.3 per cent of boys. This gap in English is mirrored throughout the rest of the GCSEs, as English underpins all the other subjects with the exception of maths. The gender gap in maths and science is still present, but is not nearly so striking.

Nosek *et al.* (2009) investigated international school science test scores for gender differences. The researchers looked at whether cultural beliefs about gender and

science could negatively affect the science performance of girls. They had data from half a million people in 34 countries and found that if a culture has the belief that females are not usually scientists, this can actually harm the science performance of girls.

Research conducted by Allcock and Hulme (2010) found that learning styles are only one part of effective teaching and learning. For student achievement, planning lessons around students' learning styles was no more effective than planning lessons around student ability differences. The conclusions were that learning styles should be included as part of the teaching and learning process, as part of a varied and personalised approach.

Evaluation

Gender and cultural differences

Children in various cultures learn different rules for communicating with adults through facial expressions, body language and physical gestures. A classroom teacher could misinterpret these unless they know about these differences. Although most teachers are concerned to treat all students equally, research findings have shown that Asians gain less teacher attention and are often spoken to in simplistic language. In spite of this, a higher number of Asian students gain GCSE English language than white students.

Teachers in general have low expectations of black pupils because of stereotyped views that black children are not academic but are good at sport. Afro-Caribbean girls were found to be determined to succeed and did well despite their disadvantage.

The home life of some ethnic minorities plays a part in determining educational achievement as ethnic minorities are more likely to be working class. Among Afro-Caribbeans there are a large number of one-parent families, where there might be a lack of knowledge of the importance of play and parent–child interaction. Families who lack a father figure also lack a secure sense of identity and this can have a detrimental effect on the children's education.

West Indian family life is often busy and family orientated, giving children a rich verbal culture but a lack of space to carry out homework tasks. This means that while children may learn many complex lessons about life in general, the education system with its rules and regulations may not be as easy to grasp for this group of students.

Motivating factors in the classroom

Motivation can be said to be the activation of goal-oriented behaviour and is either intrinsic or extrinsic.

Intrinsic motivation is driven by interest or enjoyment in the task to be carried out. Research shows that students who are intrinsically motivated enjoy their studies and have high levels of educational achievement. These students attribute their educational results to internal factors under their control, such as the amount of effort they choose to put into a task. They want to do the best they can because they see themselves as the main reason behind successful mastery of the topic.

A student who is driven by extrinsic motivation is looking for rewards for their efforts. They work at a subject because they want to avoid punishment for not doing the work. At the same time, they do the task because they are looking for rewards such as money or good grades.

Key Example

Diseth, Å., and Kobbeltvedt, T., (2010): A mediation analysis of achievement motives, goals, learning strategies and academic achievement (*British Journal of Educational Psychology*, 80, 671–87)

Aim: To investigate the relationship between achievement motives, achievement goals, learning strategies and academic achievement.

Method: 229 student participants were used. As a measure the researchers used items from the achievement motives scale (AMS), the approaches and study skills inventory for students and an achievement goal scale.

Findings: Academic achievement was measured by examination grade and was positively correlated with performance approach goal, strategic learning strategies and mastery goal. There was a negative correlation with performance avoidance and surface learning strategy.

Conclusions: This study provided evidence for the direct effect of different types of motivation and learning strategies as predictors of academic achievement.

Teaching styles

Heimlich and Norland (2002) suggest that the belief teachers have about students' role in learning is reflected in their teaching style. Most teachers have a preferred teaching style that they use in the classroom.

Teachers who are friendly, considerate of their students' needs and have a leadership style are effective teachers, according to Bass (1990).

Formal authority

The formal authority style of teaching is where the teacher is responsible for providing the content of the lesson and the student is expected to take delivery of the content. The main concern of teachers with this style of teaching is passing on knowledge. They are not concerned with building relationships with their students and they do not usually call for much student participation in class.

Demonstrator or personal model

A teacher who has this style of teaching likes to demonstrate skills and then act as a guide to students while they develop and apply the skills and knowledge. They show the students how to do a task properly and then help them master the task or problem to be solved.

Teachers with this teaching style expect students to take some responsibility for learning what they need to know. They encourage students to participate and change their lessons to include various learning styles. They expect students to ask for help when they find something difficult.

Facilitator

Teachers with this type of teaching style focus on activities. They expect students to take responsibility for their own learning and show initiative for meeting the demands of the learning tasks set. These teachers design group tasks that require students to collaborate and solve problems together.

Delegator

Teachers with this style have a student-centred approach, and put the emphasis for learning on individual students. These teachers will act as consultants as they set tasks for their students, to design and put into operation complex projects. Students are expected to work independently, with or without other members of the class.

Attribution theory in the classroom

People try to explain what is going on around them, and the explanations they make to describe success or failure are based on the following three reasons.

1   The cause of success or failure is attributed to either internal or external factors. For example, success or failure is believed to be due to something within the individual (e.g. natural ability) or something outside of the individual's control (e.g. poor lighting).

2   The cause of success or failure is attributed to stable or unstable factors. For example, if the cause is seen as stable, the result is likely to be the same if repeated. If, however, the cause is seen as unstable, the outcome may be different each time.

3   The cause of success or failure is attributed to controllable or uncontrollable factors. Controllable factors are those that the individual believes he or she can alter, while uncontrollable factors are believed to be out of the individual's ability to alter.

People interpret their environment in a way that allows them to maintain a positive self-image. Attribution theory suggests that people will attribute their success or failure in ways that allow them to feel as good as possible about themselves. This means that when they get good results from a test or exam, they are likely to attribute the success to their own abilities or efforts. If they get poor results, however, they are likely to attribute their failure to things that they have no control over, such as bad teaching, too much to learn or bad luck.

If a person attributes success or failure to internal factors, then he or she is more likely to be motivated to put in lots of effort to ensure success. If someone attributes success or failure to external factors, however, he or she would not see any point in being motivated to put in lots of effort, as the result is perceived as being out of the person's control. According to attribution theory, there are four motivational factors to education.

- **Ability** – an internal and stable factor that is not under the control of the student.

- **Task difficulty** – an external and stable factor that is beyond the control of the student.

- **Effort** – an internal and unstable factor that is under the control of the student.

- **Luck** – an external and unstable factor that is beyond the control of the student.

The main idea behind attribution theory is that an individual's own perceptions for success or failure determine the amount of effort they put into the task.

For example, a student may believe that a task was difficult when in fact it was objectively easy, or that they put in a great deal of effort to complete a task when in reality they put in very little. The way the individual makes attributions for success or failure is determined by his or her perceptions; this, in turn, determines the amount of effort the person puts into the task.

Maslow's hierarchy of needs

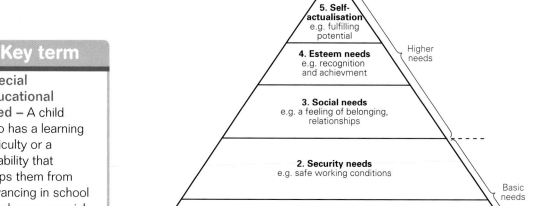

Figure 15.5 Maslow's hierarchy of needs

Key term

Special educational need – A child who has a learning difficulty or a disability that stops them from advancing in school may have a special educational need (SEN). Students who have SEN have significantly greater difficulty learning than most students of their age, or they have a disability which means they have problems using the general educational facilities provided for students of their age.

The basic needs, according to Maslow, are food, breathing, water, sex, sleep, homeostasis (stable equilibrium) and excretion. The basic need for water and food must be met before students can begin to learn. For example, if a student does not have breakfast before going to school, it will be difficult to concentrate on learning, as the student will be preoccupied with the need for food.

The most important educational goal is gaining knowledge and retaining the new knowledge. Teachers can create a sense of belonging in the classroom so the students' needs for security and friendship can be met. If the students are given enough praise, this should also raise their self-esteem and confidence.

Evaluation

Motivating factors in the classroom

A number of studies have shown that students perform better if they expect their work to be evaluated by the teacher. This is true if the students are intrinsically or extrinsically motivated. Other research shows that the difficulty of the task makes a difference to intrinsically motivated students. For example, an individual's intrinsic motivation to spend time on an interesting task is less likely if the goal is difficult than if there is no specific goal. There is also evidence that those who expected their task to be evaluated showed less intrinsic motivation than those who did not expect their task to be evaluated.

Diseth and Kobbeltvedt (2010) considered previous research to be inconclusive regarding learning strategies, motivation and achievement goals and academic achievement and set out to examine the effects of different types of motivation and learning strategies on exam results.

Research has found that high motivation in students is linked to reduced dropout rates and increased levels of student success. Those students who are highly engaged and active while learning and have choice and control over the learning process with a curriculum that is individualised, authentic and related to their interests do very well in the education system.

Intrinsically motivated students retain information for longer and are less likely to need special attention during revision. They are also more likely to be lifelong learners and continue to educate themselves even when they are not in a formal school setting.

Special educational needs

Children with SEN are entitled to full-time education that is suitable for their needs. The Code of Practice is a guide for schools and local authorities on how they should identify, assess and provide help for children with SEN. The Code of Practice says that an individual education plan (IEP) should be produced for each child with SEN, and must include details of the help the student needs which is different or additional to that required by those children who do not have SEN. A statement of special educational needs is drawn up after assessment and is reviewed each year, to ensure the support the child is receiving is meeting their needs and that they are progressing.

Assessment

In the past, schools would label those students working below level 1 in the National Curriculum with the code W at the end of the key stage test results. However, the code W did not measure progress; nor did it state how far below level 1 a student was. This was rectified in 1998 by the publication of P (performance) scales. The P scales are descriptions of attainment levels below the National Curriculum level 1. Since September 2007, the use of P scales for all students with SEN is a statutory part of National Curriculum assessment.

The P scales are not a full description of all that students might achieve, but are intended as a framework to map the progress of students. The main benefit of using P scales for students with SEN is the ability to track their progress and recognise their attainment. The P scales also offer a shared language and focus across all school settings, to portray attainment below level 1 of the National Curriculum. The P scales also allow parents/carers of students to see progress and attainment on a regular basis. The scales also provide information for targets to be set.

A statutory assessment

The local education authority (LEA) carries out any assessment that is necessary. They ask advice from the child's school, an educational psychologist, a doctor, social services (who will only give advice if they know the child) and anyone else the LEA considers suitable.

Key terms

Statutory assessment – a detailed investigation to explore what special educational needs a child has and what help should be provided for the child to advance in school. A statutory assessment is only needed if the school is unable to provide all the help the child needs.

Dyslexia – a learning disorder which makes it very difficult for an individual to learn to read and write; there are often problems with spoken language too. There is a difficulty with the skills involved in accurate and fluent word reading and spelling, along with difficulties in phonological awareness, verbal memory and verbal processing.

Evaluation

On 14 September 2010, Ofsted published a review of schools and early years provision of special educational needs. It pointed out that in the best examples of assessment, the non-statutory Common Assessment Framework was being used together with the Special Educational Needs Code of Practice. Ofsted stated in the report that this would provide a better assessment by coordinating the work of a number of different organisations.

Children with obvious and severe needs were assessed at an early age and relatively quickly. However, the assessment of children with needs that are not so obvious was inconsistent, with children with similar needs being assessed as needing different levels of support, depending on the area they lived in.

Remember

Ofsted claimed that more than one-fifth of all children at school in England are classified as having a special educational need (SEN).

Dyslexia

There are many different theories of dyslexia and making sense of the competing theories is not easy. There are some that suggest biological reasons for dyslexia, including language areas of the brain with a difference or dysfunction in the cerebellum affecting speech processing. Other theories suggest that cognitive factors such as phonological processing deficits, visual and temporal timing difficulties may be at fault and problems with working memory. Social interactive theory suggests that society's reaction to dyslexia make a difference to the person with dyslexia.

A good indication of the severity and persistence of dyslexic difficulties can be gained by examining how the individual responds or has responded to well-founded intervention (Rose Review 2009).

Remember

It has been estimated that 4 per cent of the UK population has dyslexia and that 10 per cent show some of the symptoms of dyslexia.

Assessment

Assessment for dyslexia involves a series of psychometric tests to compare reading and spelling in a standardised way with a normal range of specific measures.

Strategies for education of children with dyslexia

Studies have shown that children who have difficulties learning to read benefit from a multi-sensory method of teaching. A multi-sensory teaching approach means the child learns through more than one sense. Most teaching in schools is conducted through sight or hearing, and a dyslexic child might have difficulties with either or both of these senses.

The Orton-Gillingham multi-sensory method differs from other methods in how it is taught and what is taught. Phonemic awareness is taught as the first step,

Figure 15.6 Children who have difficulty learning to read benefit from a multi-sensory approach

breaking down a word into individual phonemes. Students are taught to take individual sounds and blend them into a word, delete sounds and compare sounds, all in their heads. These are skills that it is easiest to learn before attempting printed letters.

The next step is to teach which sounds are represented by which letters. Next to be taught are the six types of syllables that compose English words. If students know the type of syllable they are looking at, they will know the sound the vowel will make.

The probabilities and rules of the English language are taught next, as there are several ways to spell the same sounds – for example, the sound SHUN can be spelled 'tion', 'sion' or 'cion'. Dyslexic students should be taught these rules and probabilities.

Research has shown that people with dyslexia learn better when they use all of their senses. A student with dyslexia who is beginning to read may see the letter A, say it aloud and draw it in the air, all at the same time. They would be given lots of practice and direct, explicit instructions. The rules of the English language should be taught one at a time, and practice should be maintained until the student is able to recognise the rule and spell the word or words, before teaching another rule.

By the time a student is identified as dyslexic, he or she is usually quite confused about the written language; therefore, the lessons must start at the very beginning and continue until a solid foundation is built. Teachers must continually monitor the student's understanding and progress.

Below is a list of other strategies that have proved useful with dyslexic students.

- Handouts on coloured paper in the student's preferred colour.

- Fonts that are clearest – Arial, Comic Sans, Tahoma.

- Text should be enlarged if necessary.

- New vocabulary should be identified and explained as it arises.

Most teachers are aware of dyslexia and are adjusting their teaching methods to meet the needs of these students. Staff development programmes are available for teachers, and some LEAs offer help to students with dyslexia in mainstream education. The city and county of Swansea is leading the way in this area; it has asked schools to sign up to 'dyslexia-friendly status' and organises awareness training for teachers and support assistants.

Over to you

Oakland *et al.* (1998) conducted research into the development of reading and spelling skills of students with dyslexia. They found that students on a two-year programme demonstrated significantly higher reading recognition and comprehension than a control group who had not been on the programme. What does this show about dyslexia? How can this research be evaluated?

Evaluation

Special educational needs

Different types of dyslexia can be found which can affect a child's ability to spell as well as read. One sort of dyslexia usually occurs after a brain injury or trauma to the area of the brain that controls reading and writing and is called 'trauma dyslexia'. This is very rare and hardly ever seen in school-age children.

Another type of dyslexia is 'primary dyslexia', a type of dysfunction of the left side of the cerebral cortex which does not change with age. The individual with this type of dyslexia may struggle with reading and writing even as an adult as they are rarely able to advance past a primary level of reading. This type of dyslexia is found more in boys than girls.

Yet another type of dyslexia is referred to as 'secondary' or 'developmental dyslexia' and is thought to be caused by hormonal development during the early stages of foetal development. This type of dyslexia diminishes as the child matures and again is more common in boys than girls.

Summary

Behaviourist learning theory

Behaviourist learning theory has been applied to education in the classroom through classical conditioning, where the teacher provides a positive environment in which students can feel safe and learn in a relaxed manner. Operant conditioning has been used in the form of a token economy, giving merit marks or stickers/gold stars to students who have done well, to encourage the students to keep up the good work.

Cognitive developmental theories

Piaget viewed the child as a 'lone scientist' going through stages of intellectual development, only capable of learning the information that was suitable for the stage of development he or she was going through.

Vygotsky said the child had a zone of proximal development, which was the next step in the child's development and could only be achieved through the help of a more capable peer or an adult.

Motivating factors in the classroom

A teaching style is the style that a teacher adopts to teach the class. Research findings show that a teacher who is friendly and cares for the students, but is also authoritative, is more likely to be an effective teacher.

Attribution style is a good indicator of student performance in exams. If students have an internal style of attribution, they will take control of their own learning and make sure they know all the material that needs to be covered for the exams. Those who have an external attribution style expect the teacher and others to provide them with what they need.

Maslow's hierarchy of needs suggests that for learning to take place, the physiological, safety, belonging and esteem needs of the student need to be met in order for them to be able to focus on the higher levels needed for learning.

Educational psychology

Individual differences in learning styles

Curry's onion is based on the idea that learning can be compared to layers of an onion, with the inner layer being the individual's personality, the middle layer representing the learning style and the outer layer being the individual's preferred way of gaining the instruction.

Grasha's six learning styles are based on the way that individual students prefer to learn. There are six styles and most students have them all to a greater or lesser extent.

Gender differences in learning have always been present, with girls outperforming boys in 2007 in all subjects at GCSE and at every key stage except maths at key stage 2.

Special educational needs

A special educational needs statement is provided for students who have need of support in order for them to progress in their education.

Assessment is a detailed investigation to discover the needs of the child; advice is sought from a variety of people.

Dyslexia affects the skills involved in reading and spelling. There are strategies that help students with dyslexia, including a multi-sensory approach to teaching.

16 Forensic psychology

OBJECTIVES

The specification requires you to have an awareness of the following:

- Approaches to profiling (e.g. the US top-down approach, the British bottom-up approach, geographical profiling)

- Decision-making of juries (e.g. minority influence, majority influence, characteristics of the defendant)

- Theories of crime (biological, social, psychological)

- Factors affecting the accuracy of eyewitness testimony (e.g. reconstructive memory, face recognition, attributional biases, the role of emotion)

- Treatment and punishment of crime (e.g. cognitive therapies, behavioural therapies, zero tolerance).

INTRODUCTION

Forensic psychology deals with the psychological aspects of the legal processes in courts. This covers the decision-making of juries and the influences that affect those decisions, including eyewitness testimony and the social pressure that juries are under. The term is also used to refer to the investigation of criminal activity, profiling of criminal behaviour and the treatment and punishment of crime.

Remember

Forensic psychologists often implement programmes for modifying offender behaviour and carry out research to provide up-to-date knowledge of behaviour pertaining to any aspect of the criminal justice system, which could include witnesses or criminals or both.

Approaches to profiling

Offender profiling is the creation of a sketch of a criminal based on the analysis of a crime scene. This gives the police a good idea of important facts about a criminal, such as their profession, where they are likely to live and whether they are likely to commit an offence again or not. Offender profiling is more likely to be used in cases such as rape, paedophilia, ritualistic crime and murder. The goals of profiling are to make an assessment of the crime scene in order to give the police an idea of the criminal and the way in which they are likely to be caught. Some of the approaches to offender profiling are the top-down approach, the bottom-up approach and geographical profiling.

The top-down approach to profiling is used by the FBI in the USA and is based on in-depth interviews with a number of convicted murderers. It is a technique that attempts to identify a criminal by analysis of the type of crime committed. The information collected from the crime scene, the nature of the attack, information about the victim and forensic evidence are then used to provide information about the perpetrator of the crime.

Figure 16.1 Analysing a crime scene gives the police a lot of information about criminals

The information gathered leads the investigators to categorise offenders, depending on whether they are 'organised' or 'disorganised'. Organised means a murderer planned the crime, had complete control at the scene and left few or no clues as to his or her identity. Disorganised, on the other hand, means a murder was not planned and the crime scene shows evidence of haphazard behaviour.

This approach means that not all crimes are suitable for profiling, as crimes such as destruction of property or murder during a robbery do not reveal the personality of the offender.

The bottom-up approach, which is used in Britain, takes evidence and data from the crime scene and builds up a profile bit by bit, until a reasonable conclusion is reached. A profile of an offender is built by finding an association with the characteristics of the offence and the type of offender. The focus of the bottom-up approach is on the offence committed, and the profile is constructed using evidence from the crime scene to find behaviour that would fit the evidence. Canter, the first person to introduce offender profiling to the UK, suggested that the behaviour shown when committing a crime is reflected in daily life. What he meant by that is the style of speech, victim choice and how the criminal plans will all be present in their day-to-day life and will be left as tell-tale signs at the crime scene.

Evaluation

- The US system is based on interviews with known offenders which may not be of any help in crimes that are different to those committed by the interviewees.

- Profilers have only been slightly more effective at profiling than detectives.

- The variety of crimes the top-down system can be used for is limited.

- The British system is more scientific and can be used in a range of crimes.

Questionnaires were sent out to the CID by Britton (1992) to find out how effective offender profiling had been. He found that most cases where a victim was profiled had not led to an arrest; however, the respondents commented that they knew profiling could have a lot of potential.

Kocsis (2003) conducted research into profiling and compared the profile of a probable offender prepared by professional profilers, police officers, psychologists, college students and self-declared psychics. To write the profile they were all given information from a solved murder investigation. It was found that professional profilers gave more information about the behaviour before, during and after the crime, as well as non-physical attributes of the offender. They also wrote more information about the crime scene.

Snook (2008) suggests that the belief that criminal profilers can predict a criminal's characteristics from crime scene evidence may be an illusion and there is no sound empirical evidence to support the possibility. He goes on to say that criminal profilers should not be used as an investigative tool, because of the lack of scientific support.

Decision-making of juries

Figure 16.2 Trial by jury

The evidence in a trial is presented by both the plaintiff (petitioner) and the defendant for the jury to decide on a verdict. There are usually 12 jurors in England and Wales, while in Scotland there are 15. After hearing the evidence, the jury leaves the courtroom to consider a verdict. The way that juries make decisions has been the subject of psychological study for decades. The problem with most research in this area is that real juries in court are not allowed to discuss the trial with anyone other than those on the jury; therefore, simulations of court cases have been used for research. The legal system assumes that jurors are 'blank slates' who can objectively decide the facts of a case and reach a reasonable verdict. However, that is not always the case, and sometimes bias creeps in.

One way that psychologists suggest jurors make decisions is through changing the information presented into a story. Pennington and Hastie (1986) demonstrated that the order in which the evidence is presented affected the verdict judgments and credibility. They found that the story constructed by the juror led them to select the verdict that fit the story best, based on the evidence as they understood it.

Kalven and Zeisel (1966) showed that trial judges agreed with juries in criminal cases nearly 80 per cent of the time. They also found that fewer disagreements arose in straightforward cases where the evidence was clear, and in these cases the juries were more lenient.

Pre-trial publicity is a factor which may affect the way the jury perceives the

defendant; the belief the jury holds before a trial can influence their decision. There have been trials in America where people selected for jury service were not allowed to sit on the jury if they did not believe in the death penalty.

Majority influence

Research into majority influence shows that people want to be liked; in a jury situation they may not want to go against what the majority think because they are worried about what the rest of the jurors would think of them. Evaluation apprehension makes people become self-conscious and anxious; people in a jury may think their views are being evaluated, so they go along with the majority in order not to be seen as different.

Discussion of an issue often causes individuals to change their opinions. Explanations for these changes suggest that what has taken place is a result of either **informational** or **normative influence** processes.

Normative influence was proposed by Deutsch and Gerard (1955), who argued that humans have a need for social acceptance and approval. When individuals are in a potentially embarrassing situation, such as disagreeing with the majority, they are more likely to comply with the group. This is because they are faced with a conflict between their own and other people's opinions and the majority have coercive power.

Deutsch and Gerard (1955) suggested that informational influence is based on the need that people have for certainty. When individuals are in uncertain situations, they are more likely to refer to others to know how to react.

As it is not allowed to conduct research on real-life juries, Kaplan and Miller (1987) investigated the conditions in which either informative or normative influence was used during discussion. Groups discussed and made decisions while attempting to discover the true or correct answer, or a made a judgement on a moral issue. The groups were asked to reach either a majority or a unanimous decision. The findings were that more informational than normative influence was apparent in the true or correct answer group, and was stronger when a unanimous verdict was required. Kaplan and Miller concluded that the mode of influence that predominates in group discussion depends on the type of issue and on the decision that needs to be made at the end of the deliberation.

Minority influence

Minority influence takes place when either an individual or a small number of people influence a large number of people to change their minds. Moscovici (1980) suggests that this happens if the minority is consistent, without being too pushy.

For minorities to influence the majority, Moscovici (1980) noted that they must be consistent in their opinion and put across their views with confidence. They should also appear to be unbiased. Consistency is important because it gives the impression that the minority are convinced that they are correct and

Over to you

How do you think that pre-trial publicity might affect a jury? Would it make a difference to the way the jury viewed the witness or the accused? What could be done to ensure the jury members were not affected by pre-trial publicity?

Key terms

Conformity – yielding to group pressure. This occurs when a person adopts the attitudes, beliefs and behaviour of people in a group in response to real or imagined group pressure.
Normative social influence – the desire to be liked and to fit in with the group.
Informational social influence – the desire to be right. When we are unsure, we look to others for guidance, especially if we think they have more knowledge than us.

are committed to their view. This makes the majority take notice and rethink their position. If a member of the jury shows consistency with self-confidence and creates uncertainty and doubt, the rest of the jurors will question their own views and consider what has been put before them by the minority. Mugny and Papasamou (1980) point out that if the minority appear flexible and willing to compromise, they are more likely to be listened to and therefore have a better chance of changing the majority view.

Over to you

Do you think majority influence or minority influence would affect a jury most?

Nemeth (1977) conducted research into juries where the trial required unanimous decisions and where a two-thirds majority was required. The findings were that the unanimous groups were more likely to reach full consensus. Their deliberations were characterised by more arguments, and more opinions were changed as a result of the deliberation process. They had more confidence in the verdict as a result and tended to feel that justice had been done.

Figure 16.3 The characteristics of the defendant can affect the decision of the jury

Characteristics of the defendant

Another factor that affects the decision of the jury is the appearance of the defendant. If the defendant is good-looking, the jury is less likely to return a guilty verdict. Psychologists have demonstrated that attractive people are more liked and that can be applied in the courtroom too. Attractive defendants are seen as more credible, receive lighter sentences if they are convicted and are acquitted more often than those who are considered unattractive.

Stewart (1985) found a correlation between the attractiveness of a defendant and the severity of the punishment given. The least attractive defendants were dealt the most severe punishments, while those who were deemed to be attractive had negative correlation with punishment.

Squire and Newhouse (2003) investigated the effects of facial features and skin tone on perceived likelihood of guilt and length of sentencing. Surprisingly, they found that those people with European skin tone were sentenced to more years in prison and found to be guiltier than African American people. They also found that attractiveness did not have an effect on perceived likelihood of guilt. However, Sigall and Ostrove (1975) found that if attractiveness was part of the crime, more attractive defendants received harsher sentences.

The clothing defendants wear is also important, as is their hairstyle, and even the jewellery they wear can make a difference to the way the jurors think about a defendant.

Ackerman *et al.* (1984) conducted research into the characteristics of the defendant by holding fictitious court cases involving child abuse. They used male undergraduate students and male high school students to determine if the tendency to deal harshly with alleged criminals is due to defendant characteristics. They found that male defendants receive longer sentences than female defendants. No significant effects for case content were found; younger jurors gave longer sentences to a parent who beat a child, and older jurors attributed more responsibility and gave longer sentences to a parent who burnt a child.

Another factor that could influence the decision of a jury is the age of the defendant. Pozzulo *et al.* (2010) used a mock jury and found that higher guilt ratings were found for a male versus a female defendant. Female jurors thought the victim was more accurate, truthful and believable than male jurors.

Bergeron and Mckelvie (2004) presented participants with a sketch to read of either a murder or a theft, in which the perpetrator was a 20-, 40- or 60-year-old man; the participants were asked to give sentences and parole recommendations. They found that punishment was harsher for the murder than for the theft. For murder, participants punished the 40-year-old man more harshly than the 20- or 60-year-old. This inverted U shape was for murder only.

Evaluation

Decision-making of juries

There has been a great deal of research into juries and juror decision-making. While there are still many gaps in understanding how factors, such as publicity before a trial, scientific evidence, inadmissible evidence and jury instructions, influence juries, there has been some headway made on other factors.

Pennington and Hastie found that story evidence was most persuasive and more effective for the prosecution, as the argument for the defence was less plausible. They suggest that this was due to the nature of the case that they used in the study, one which was adapted from a real case. They used a laboratory experiment for their research which could have produced results that were not on a par with real-life jury decision-making.

The research by Kalven and Zeisel showing that judges agreed with the decision of the jury 80 per cent of the time may be due to the way that the judge summed up the case before the jury retired to make their verdict. The judge may not have meant to sway the jury one way or another, but research has shown that the way the judge sums up has an effect on the decision of a jury.

Research by Nemeth showed that if the jury had deliberated long and hard, it was more likely to be confident that justice had been done and was happier with the verdict.

A major problem with research into jury decision-making is that it has to be conducted outside the courtroom. This is because the courts do not allow juries to discuss their deliberations, or any part of the trial, with others. This means that the way juries are researched has, by necessity, been done in artificial conditions. This means that most of the research conducted into jury decision-making lacks ecological validity.

Theories of crime

Theories of crime look at the reasons for criminal behaviour. Biological theories look at the biological make-up of a person; psychological theories suggest that the reason for committing crime is psychological. These arguments should

Figure 16.4 Lombroso's criminal types

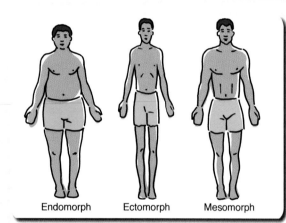

Figure 16.5 Sheldon's body types

be weighed against each other to determine which has the better description of why people commit crime.

Biological theories of crime

Biological theories of crime look at the link between certain biological traits and an increased tendency to commit crimes. These theories look at the physical body of criminals, including genes, brain and body types, and are based on the idea that biological features determine criminal behaviour.

Physiological

Lombroso (1876) was an Italian doctor who suggested that criminals showed atavism. He used this term for people who were not fully evolved, and considered them 'throwbacks' to earlier primates. Criminals, according to Lombroso, have traits that are different to modern humans that are easily identifiable. The body and head of a 'born criminal' are different, he claimed, because the skulls, brains and other parts of the skeletons of criminals showed peculiarities in their anatomical composition: they have large, forward-projecting jaws, low, sloping foreheads, high cheekbones, flattened or hawk-like noses or fleshy lips and hard, shifty eyes; they also showed insensitivity to pain.

Sheldon (1940) developed a classification system that connected the human physique to crime. He classified people into three body shapes, which he suggested correspond with three different personality types:

- **Endomorph** – these people are fat and soft; they tend to be sociable and relaxed. They have wide hips and quite a lot of fat spread across the body, including the upper arms and thighs, but they have quite slim ankles and wrists, which contrast with the rest of the body.

- **Ectomorph** – people of this type are thin and fragile, introverted and restrained. They are physically thin and narrow, with narrow shoulders and hips, a thin narrow face and high forehead. They have a thin, narrow chest and abdomen and very little body fat. Psychologically they are self-conscious, private people, emotionally restrained and thoughtful.

- **Mesomorph** – these people are muscular and hard, aggressive and adventurous. They are broad-shouldered, with narrow waists. They are muscular, with strong forearms and thighs and have very little body fat. Psychologically they are courageous and adventurous, with an enthusiasm for physical activity. They are indifferent to what others think and have a desire to dominate.

Remember

Sheldon's theory can be criticised on the grounds that other studies have failed to produce consistent results to show that mesomorphs are more likely to commit crime. It could be that mesomorphs who commit crime are muscular as a result of manual labour.

Genetic

Jacobs *et al.* (1965) investigated chromosomes in males in Corstairs hospital in Scotland, an institution that cares for prisoners who are mentally ill, and found that XYY men are overrepresented in the prison hospital population. Seven out of 196 males had this syndrome, and in the general population the figure is one in 1,000. This led Jacobs to suggest that men with the XYY syndrome were more aggressive than normal XY men. Studies of the inmates of similar institutions in England, Australia, Denmark and the USA have shown similar findings.

Family studies

Family studies may be used as evidence for nature or nurture because families share both genetics and environment. This means that we cannot be certain which of the two has the most influence.

Farrington (2002) investigated the concentration of offending in families by studying three generations of relatives, including fathers, mothers, sons, daughters, uncles, aunts and grandparents. It was found that if one relative had been arrested, there was a high probability that another relative had also been arrested. The most important relative was the father; if the father had been arrested, there was a high chance of sons being arrested too. Another finding of this study was that having a young mother

> ### Remember
>
> Farrington *et al.*'s (2001) study suggests that antisocial behaviour runs in families, but that the neighbourhood is also a contributing factor. This means that criminal behaviour could be an interaction between genetic factors and environmental factors.

and living in a bad neighbourhood added to the probability of fathers and sons being arrested. Farrington concluded that antisocial behaviour is carried on within families both between generations and within generations.

Twin studies compare the rate of criminal behaviour of identical or monozygotic (MZ) twins with those non-identical or dizygotic (DZ) twins. MZ twins are those with exactly the same genetic make-up, while dizygotic twins are those who share only half of their genetic make-up. Twin studies compare MZ twins and their rates of criminal behaviour with the rates of DZ twins. These studies are used to measure the roles of genetic and environmental influence; if the outcome shows that there is a higher concordance rate for criminal behaviour for MZ twins than for DZ twins, it can be assumed there is a genetic influence.

A study conducted by Grove *et al.* (1990) looked at 32 sets of MZ twins who were separated shortly after birth and reared apart. They found that there was sufficient evidence to suggest that drug-related problems and antisocial behaviour were inherited. Other studies also support the contention that genetics increase the risk for criminal behaviour. This particular study looked at twins reared apart, who therefore did not share the same environment as those reared together.

Brain damage

Damage to the prefrontal cortex in seriously violent offenders was found by Raine *et al.* (1997) through the use of PET scans to study the brains of living impulsive killers. They compared the murderers'

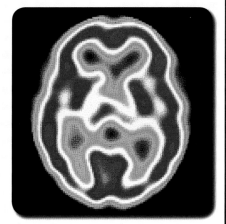

Figure 16.6 A PET scan of someone's brain

brains with age-matched and gender-matched controls. The prefrontal cortex controls impulsive behaviour. The task involved sustained attention, watching a screen for 32 minutes and responding each time a zero appeared. The individuals who were impulsive missed many of the zeros. The conclusion drawn by Raine *et al.* was that deficits in the prefrontal cortex may be related to violence.

Social theories of crime

Social disorganisation theory suggests that urban conditions affect crime rates. Unemployment rates, high school drop-out rates and high numbers of single-parent households all contribute to low income levels and crime.

Strain theory proposes that people in a low-income group have fewer opportunities to reach their goals, so will commit crime in an effort to reach them. The goals that people aspire to are usually wealth, power, prestige and material possessions, and an individual from a low social class has less opportunity to achieve these goals than someone from a higher class.

Self-fulfilling prophecy

This theory is based on the idea that if individuals are treated as though they were clever or stupid, they would behave that way and even become that way. The individual would therefore have his or her prophecy fulfilled. Rosenthal and Jacobson (1968) gave all the children in an elementary school a test and then told the teacher that some of the children were above average intelligence when in actual fact they were not. At the end of the year, those children whom the teachers believed were above average had improved faster than the rest of the class, showed better social skills and were more capable than other students. Rosenthal and Jacobson suggested that this was because the 'prophecy' came true because the teachers responded differently to them, giving them more feedback, having higher expectations of them, and so on.

Psychological theories of crime

Social learning theory states that crime is a learned behaviour that is influenced by an individual's family members, peer groups and other groups within the community. The individual may have peers or family members who commit crimes, and they have learnt from them that crime has its rewards.

Cognitive development

This theory proposes that the thoughts people have about morality and the law may lead to criminal activity. Kohlberg (1958) suggested that there are three levels of moral reasoning, each having two stages. During middle childhood, children are in the first stage of moral development. At this time, the pre-conventional level, moral reasoning is based on obedience and punishment avoidance. The second stage, the conventional level, is reached at the end of middle childhood; moral reasoning is based on the expectations that their family and other people they look up to have for them. The final stage is the post-conventional level, which usually occurs during early adulthood. Individuals at this level go beyond social conventions and are open to acting as agents of social change to improve existing law and order, although, according to Kohlberg, they do value the laws of the social system.

Those who do not progress through the stages may not have adequate morals and, as a consequence, may become delinquents.

Psychodynamic

The psychodynamic theory holds that the structure of personality has three parts: the id, the ego and the superego. The id, which is the primitive, instinctive part and is governed by the pleasure principle, needs immediate satisfaction. The ego, which is the conscious and intellectual part, is governed by the reality principle and the need to behave in socially accepted ways. The superego is the ethical and moral part, which is learnt from parents/carers and teachers, and provokes feelings of guilt. These three parts of the personality are in conflict with each other, with the ego trying to balance the demands of the id with the constraints of the superego.

Freud argued that moral behaviour was controlled by the superego, which is divided into the conscience and the ego ideal. Conscience is the source of feeling guilty and is composed of rules imposed by parents. The conscience represents the punishing parent. The ego ideal is the source of feelings of pride and represents the rewarding parent. The ego ideal rewards when behaviour follows moral values.

Psychoanalytic theory suggests that the superego is either underdeveloped or overdeveloped. For example, if an individual commits a violent sex crime, it is thought that this is due to an underdeveloped superego because the urges could not be controlled. On the other hand, a person who has an overdeveloped superego would suffer from guilt and anxiety. This person may commit a crime to reduce the guilt because they know that punishment will follow. These people unconsciously leave clues at the scene in order to be arrested. Regoli and Hewitt (1994) suggested this happened in the famous case in 1924 when Bobby Franks was murdered.

Maternal deprivation

Bowlby (1951) suggested that early separation from the primary caregiver, usually the mother (maternal deprivation), would lead to delinquency and a lack of social conscience. He investigated the effects of maternal deprivation to look at the possible causes of habitual delinquency.

The participants were children, with an age range of 5–16 years, who were attending a child guidance clinic. They and their parents were interviewed about the children's early experiences. The group consisted of 44 'thieves' or delinquents who had been involved in stealing. There was a control group of 44 emotionally disturbed teenagers. The findings were that some of the delinquents displayed an affectionless character, with a lack of normal affection, shame or responsibility. Before the age of 2 years, 86 per cent of the children had been in foster homes or hospital and were not often visited by their families. Bowlby concluded that this disaffected state, which he termed affectionless psychopathy, was due to the attachment bonds being disturbed in early life.

Remember

Bowlby's control group were also attending the child guidance clinic and were emotionally disturbed, and therefore not a good comparison group. Also, the data gathered from the parents were retrospective, and the memory of events when the child was young could have been distorted.

Personality and crime

A theory of criminal behaviour based on a theory of personality was put forward by Hans Eysenck (1964). He proposed that people's behaviour is consistent over time and that behavioural consistency is due to the underlying tendencies to behave in particular ways.

Eysenck assumed that human beings were hedonistic, seeking pleasure and avoiding pain. Delinquent acts such as theft or violence were, according to Eysenck, pleasurable or beneficial to the offender. Eysenck proposed that offending is a natural and even rational thing to do in the search for pleasure; to explain why everyone was not a criminal, Eysenck suggested that the conscience opposed the hedonistic tendency. Eysenck viewed the conscience as a conditioned fear response, and claimed that those who commit crimes have not built up strong consciences because they have an inherently poor ability to be conditioned.

Over to you

Out of the theories of crime listed, which do you think is most likely to be the cause of criminal behaviour? Do you think it is an adequate theory on its own or do you think that it lacks something? If two theories were to be used together, which two would you use? Taken together, would these two theories be an adequate explanation for criminal activity?

There are three dimensions of personality: extraversion (E), neuroticism (N) and psychoticism (P). People who rate highly on E build up conditioned responses less well than others because they have low levels of cortical arousal; people who rate highly on N also build up conditioned responses less well because their high level of anxiety interferes with the conditioning. The people most likely to be criminal would be those people who have a high rating on N who are extroverts. Eysenck also predicted that those who rate highly on P would also tend to be offenders, because the traits related to P – emotional coldness, low empathy, high hostility and inhumanity – are typical of criminals.

Evaluation

Theories of crime

Lombroso's theory of crime was that criminals look different to other people and behave in a different way. The different behaviours of a criminal, according to Lombroso, was that they have an inability to adjust to social and moral norms and to tell between right and wrong. They have an inability to form friendships or show any kind of guilt or remorse or feelings towards other people.

However, there is no psychological evidence to show that these behaviours are only true for criminals. Lombroso's theory has been criticised because he did not use a control group and the sample he used contained mostly mentally disturbed people.

His theory was useful, however, as he challenged the idea that criminals are wicked by showing that there may be a genetic factor involved rather than individual choice.

Sheldon's theory has been criticised because he used subjective criteria to allocate normal and delinquent sub-types into conditions. Follow-up studies have produced inconsistent results and are therefore unreliable. The theory underestimates the environmental influences on behaviour. The reason for the mesomorphs being muscular may be that they are employed in manual labour as a result of poverty. Muscular people may realise that they can use their strength to control other people and achieve what they want. There may be a different response by the police to people who look tough when compared with people who look weak and this may lead to a negative judgement of tough-looking people.

The main problem with twin studies is that it is difficult to separate environmental causes from genetic ones. This is because as well as sharing genes, twins also share environments. This is true even when twins are separated as the environment for each twin is likely to remain similar even though they are not together.

Freud's theory is very difficult to test empirically and evidence that has been gathered is not favourable. The id, ego and superego are not observable and there is no way to measure them or show if one is ruling the others. There is a long time between the childhood stage and the events that are said to be affected by this.

Factors affecting the accuracy of eyewitness testimony

Key term

Eyewitness testimony – a legal term referring to the account given by people who have witnessed an event. These people may be required to give a description of the sequence of events in a robbery or road accident, and their witness accounts may include identification of suspects, details of the crime scene and the timing of the incident. Eyewitness testimony is an important research area because juries pay close attention to eyewitness testimony and rely on it as a valuable source of information.

Reconstructive memory

Memory involves active reconstruction and is not simply a matter of accessing information and watching it like a video. Schemas and past experiences lead to distortions in memory during storage and recall.

Past experience influences what is seen. For example, Cohen (1981) showed a video tape to participants and described the woman in it as either a waitress or a librarian. After watching the video, participants were asked questions about the woman, such as, 'What was she doing?' Participants tended to remember the features that were consistent with the stereotype for the job they had been told about.

When considering eyewitness testimony, it is important to bear in mind that when people try to recall what they witnessed, their recall is likely to be affected by previous experience.

Leading questions

Loftus and Palmer (1974) conducted research into how reliable eyewitness testimony is by conducting two experiments. Participants were shown films of car accidents and then had to answer questions about the events that occurred in the films. The researchers found that the question, 'About how fast were the cars going when they smashed into each other?' received higher estimates of speed than questions which used the verbs 'collided', 'bumped', 'contacted' or 'hit' in place of 'smashed'. In addition to this, one week later, the participants

who had been asked the question with the verb 'smashed' were more likely to say yes when asked if they had seen broken glass in the film. (There was in fact no broken glass present in the film.) This shows that the questions asked after an event may cause a reconstruction of that event in memory.

Face recognition

There are problems with face recognition in eyewitness testimony because using the face to identify individuals is probably one of the most demanding tasks the visual system has to deal with. Errors in face recognition can have catastrophic consequences. The Devlin Report (1976) recommended that prosecutions that were based on eyewitness testimony were weak and unsound and should be stopped, because of the likelihood of wrong identification. Davies (1996) reviewed criminal convictions in England and Wales and concluded that until Devlin's recommendations are carried into law, there will continue to be miscarriages of justice based on mistaken identity.

Research conducted by Wells *et al.* (1979) investigated face recognition in participants who were not expecting to have to recall the face. Individual participants were left in an office in which there was a calculator on the desk. A confederate appeared and put the calculator in her handbag. When the participants were asked to identify the 'thief' from six pictures, only 58 per cent were correct. In a follow-up mock trial, 80 per cent of the witnesses were believed.

Attributional biases

Figure 16.7 Attributional biases can affect how we view things

Attributions people make with regard to why someone did something depends on situational factors and the disposition or character of the actor. Hedonic relevance occurs when it concerns the individual personally.

If something is of relevance to an individual, he or she is more likely to attribute the cause of behaviour to dispositional factors. However, if the individual did not consider it of importance, he or she would be more likely to attribute the cause to situational factors. For example, if an individual was driving a car and another car smashed into him or her, the individual would be likely to attribute to the other car driver that he or she was driving too fast. This would be attributing the cause of the crash to the other driver's character because he or she was driving too fast.

However, if someone witnessed two other cars crashing, he or she would be more likely to say there was ice on the road. This would be attributing the cause to situational factors.

The fundamental attribution error happens when an individual attributes causes to the disposition of others but to situational factors for themselves. This is a common type of cognitive bias and places an emphasis on the internal personality characteristics on someone's behaviour in a situation, rather than looking at external situational factors. In cases of eyewitness testimony, there may be a

tendency for the witness to overemphasise the level of violence used, or the speed of the getaway car, and the lack of care the villains used.

The role of emotion

The threat of personal injury is likely to produce an emotional response in a witness; however, the amount of anxiety felt will vary from person to person. Some people will respond with anger and others with anxiety. Many studies have shown that the effect of arousal levels on performance show that performance is poor when arousal is low, when relaxed, or high, when anxious, and that performance is best at medium levels of arousal. The Yerkes Dodson law expresses this rule.

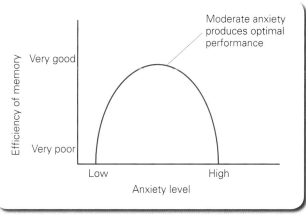

Figure 16.8 The Yerkes Dodson curve

Witnessing a crime involves high levels of arousal; therefore, the witness recall of events is likely to be poor. MacLeod *et al.* (1986) investigated 379 eyewitness reports of physical assault and compared them to crimes in which no physical injury occurred. They found that there was no overall difference in accuracy.

A study conducted by Clifford and Scott (1978) found that participants who watched a film of a violent attack remembered fewer of the 40 items of information about the event than a control group who saw a less stressful version. Witnessing a real crime is probably more stressful than taking part in a memory experiment, so memory accuracy could be even more affected in real life.

Remember

Freud's repression theory would indicate that the high emotional impact of a physical assault would be repressed and therefore forgotten.

Brown and Kulik (1977) describe flashbulb memory as something that has a huge emotional impact on the individual. They believe that this type of memory is qualitatively different to other memories and leaves a long-lasting, clear memory trace. Neisser and Harsch (1992) researched this using a group of Americans, who completed a questionnaire concerning the circumstances in which they heard of the *Challenger* space shuttle disaster the day after the explosion. They repeated the questionnaire three years later and found that the accounts had changed considerably over time.

In a study that looked into the accuracy of 14 witnesses of an armed robbery, Odinot *et al.* (2009) used security camera recordings of the event to assess the accuracy of the witness accounts. Of all of the information that was remembered, 84 per cent was correct. Those who reported a high level of emotional impact had a higher level of accuracy.

Remember

These studies show that there is disagreement about the effect of emotion on memory.

Treatment and punishment of crime

Punishment of crime through the judicial system may include such things as a fine, term of imprisonment, probation or community service. The penalties for crime reflect the policy decisions made by parliament and the interpretation of the law made by the court.

When deciding an appropriate punishment, a judge may take into account the offender's age, prior criminal record and other circumstances surrounding the crime or the offender's personal circumstances. Punishment of crime may be for retribution or rehabilitation. If, for example, the reason for punishment is rehabilitation, then the idea is to reform the wrongdoer and change their attitude to what they have done so that they know what they did was wrong in order for them not to offend again. Retribution is the idea of getting the offender to suffer for what they have done in order to give them what they deserve.

Key Example

Buikhuisen (1974): General deterrence: Research and theory (*Abstracts on Criminology and Penology*, 14(3), 285–98)

Aim: To test whether the awareness that an action is illegal and will be punished would act as a deterrent.

Method: A field experiment was used in a city in the Netherlands. A publicity campaign informed motorists of an intensive enforcement drive in which police would be checking for worn tyres. The percentage of motorists replacing worn tyres in the experimental city was compared to a control city.

Findings: A significantly higher number of people replaced worn tyres when the threat of detection and punishment was high.

Conclusions: If the threat of detection and punishment is high, people are less likely to commit crime.

Behaviour modification

The idea of behaviour modification is to change the undesirable behaviour, such as aggression, to a more appropriate behaviour. Token economy programmes use operant conditioning to replace aggression with more appropriate behaviour. Individuals are given tokens for approved behaviour and these tokens can be used for a reward, such as watching the TV. Token economies are effective in institutions like prison, but the change in behaviour may only be temporary in order to reap the rewards.

Remember

Token economy – a system designed to reinforce a particular behaviour by giving tokens, which can be saved up and exchanged for a treat. To be successful, the individual must be reinforced with the tokens for behaviour that meets the required standard.

For a token economy to work effectively, consistency needs to be high among all the people administering the tokens as rewards. The tokens also have to have a value to those receiving them, so that they see the reward as something desirable. The results of a token economy are not transferred to the outside world, when the tokens are not administered.

Anger management

On anger management programmes people are taught to control the feelings of anger and to replace inappropriate behaviour, such as aggression, with more adaptive responses. Anger management is based on the idea that people can learn to control their aggression, and they are given help to recognise thoughts that lead to an aggressive attack. Once the thoughts are recognised, they are then helped to change those thoughts. Towards the end of the programme, situations are set up to give the individual a chance to apply these new techniques, and progress is monitored.

McDougall *et al.* (1987) investigated the impact of an anger management programme on 18 young offenders in prison. They found that after the programme, offences were reduced. Research conducted by Goldstein *et al.* (1989) found that anger management programmes, together with social skills training, were effective in stopping young offenders from reoffending. They compared the reoffending rates of a control group, who had no intervention, and found that those who had undergone anger management and social skills training were less likely to reoffend.

Evaluation

Treatment and punishment of crime

The problem with the judicial system is that the sentence is likely to reflect the outlook of the judge and political views showing the need to be tough on crime. This means that tougher sentences will be given in times when the government are showing that they mean to be harsh on criminals.

Treatment of crime is likely to reflect the idea that the criminal is not to blame for the crime committed, or, if they are to blame, they can be rehabilitated so that they do not commit more crimes. Treatments tend to be aimed at those who are addicted to a substance or those who are mentally ill. Rehabilitation programmes concentrate on getting the offender off drugs or alcohol dependence in the hope that if they are not addicted, they will not need to commit crimes to pay for their habit.

Another way of rehabilitating criminals is through education. Prisoners are given opportunities to increase their knowledge and gain qualifications. The idea behind this is to ensure that they are employable when they leave prison as many inmates of prisons have difficulty reading and writing. If they make a success of their studies and gain qualifications when they are in prison, they are more likely to find employment when they leave prison and this may help them to stay away from committing crimes.

Buikhuisen (1974) was convinced that people would rather not commit a crime if they were aware that they may be caught and punished. He argued that the perception of the seriousness of the offence, the risk of detection and awareness of the severity of punishment all combine to act as a disincentive to commit crime. He conducted research into the idea that the threat of punishment would act as a deterrent.

Summary

Decision-making of juries

This area has been investigated from a minority and a majority angle. The characteristics of the defendant are very important to the jury, as those who are attractive or dress well are more likely to be found not guilty, or, if they are found guilty, they tend to receive lighter sentences.

Approaches to profiling

The main approaches to profiling are the US top-down approach and the British bottom-up approach. The top-down approach uses case studies and information from the crime scene to determine whether the offender is 'organised' or 'disorganised'. The bottom-up approach takes evidence from the crime scene and builds up the profile bit by bit, until a reasonable conclusion is reached and a profile is made by finding an association with the characteristics of the crime and the type of offender.

Theories of crime

These are based on biological factors, such as body type, genetics and neurology. Psychological theories of crime, such as that of Freud, have suggested that the early development of the individual is very important.

Forensic psychology

Factors affecting the accuracy of eyewitness testimony

These include emotional factors, such as those found in flashbulb memories or repression, meaning that the incident will be either remembered extremely well (flashbulb) or forgotten due to protection of the ego (repression). Reconstructive memory and leading questions may also affect the accuracy of eyewitness testimony.

Treatment and punishment of crime

This includes behaviour modification treatments, which aim to change behaviour through token economies and are based on operant conditioning. Anger management programmes, together with social skills programmes, are more effective at reducing reoffending rates than no intervention.

17 Sport psychology

INTRODUCTION

Psychology is used in sport because it can provide information on how to keep motivated, what to do when under stress, how to cope in team situations and the effects an audience may have on performance. Sport psychology is also useful for promoting sport and showing the benefits of exercise on well-being and the overall effect of physical exercise on mental health.

OBJECTIVES

The specification requires you to have an awareness of the following:

- Improving motivation in sport (e.g. explanations of motivation and ways of improving motivation)

- Internal factors affecting sporting performance (e.g. arousal, anxiety, attribution theory)

- External factors affecting sporting performance (e.g. team membership, audience effects)

- Effects of exercise on well-being (e.g. effects of physical and mental health)

- Theories of aggression in sport (e.g. frustration–aggression hypothesis, ethological (behavioural) theory, social-learning theory).

Improving motivation in sport

Motivation is the psychological feature that stimulates a person towards a desired goal. It is the fulfilling of a need and gives purpose and direction to behaviour. It also impacts on how we feel, think and interact with others. It is for this reason that motivation is so important in sport. The motivation of an individual is also related to their arousal, anxiety and stress levels. Arousal will benefit an athlete by improving performance, but the optimal threshold is different for every individual and for different situations.

Intrinsic motivation

Intrinsic motivation is the internal satisfaction felt when an individual carries out an activity either because they feel it is the right thing to do or because they get pleasure out of doing it. A person who is intrinsically motivated will go to the gym or play a game of football for the enjoyment they get from doing the activity.

Extrinsic motivation

External motivating factors come from outside the individual. External factors could be rewards, such as praise from the team or coach, or winning prize money or a medal. These rewards give the individual satisfaction and pleasure that might not be felt from the task alone. An extrinsically motivated person will work for the reward they will get even if they have little interest in the task itself.

Research conducted by Koka and Hein (2003) concluded that teachers should provide positive feedback and create a learning environment that is non-threatening and challenging. This shows that intrinsic motivation is tied in with external challenges and rewards. For example, a boy may like to play football, but if his coach and teammates are always negative about his performance, he may lose his liking for playing the game. In the same way, if he is praised for his performance by his coach and teammates, he will gain more enjoyment from it than just his satisfaction from playing the game.

Woods (1998) suggested that extrinsic motivation should be geared to the individual – for example, some individuals thrive on public praise while others are content with a quiet 'well done'. The praise should be given as soon as possible and should be directed to a particular skill, in order for the extrinsic motivation (in this case, praise) to improve intrinsic motivation and lead the individual to want to achieve the goals for themselves.

Key term

Motivation – the desire to do something, and the process that arouses, sustains and regulates behaviour.

Remember

Most people are motivated by a combination of factors, some internal and some external.

Remember

The more skills a person has, the more likely he or she is to be successful, and this will increase motivation.

Over to you

Would praise alone be enough to keep someone motivated?

Achievement motivation is an individual's motivation to succeed and encourages the individual to direct behaviour towards goals. An athlete who is motivated to win a race would engage in behaviour that would give him or her the best chance of winning, even if it meant spending most of the time training. Achievement motivation may be affected by how much the individual desires success and also the fear of failure. The individual has a choice of possible actions – for example, whether to approach or avoid achievement situations, how much effort is applied and whether to continue to try to win. These actions all affect the outcome and have an impact on future performances.

Figure 17.1 Athletes who are motivated do everything they can to improve their chances of winning

Evaluation

Improving motivation in sport

When measuring achievement motivation, one of the causes for concern is the way that assessments are carried out as the participants are asked to report their attitudes or use an anxiety scale. The reason for the concern is that these have been shown to be unreliable measures. This is because when it comes to analysing the results, it is unclear how the scores for motives should be interpreted. For example, sometimes a score is ignored if the motivation of the participant does not seem strong.

Research findings on the level of relationship between achievement motivation and success have been contradictory. As the term achievement motivation has been used to describe achievement in general, some psychologists have suggested it would be more useful to break it down in order to describe sports-specific motivation. For example, an individual may be motivated to achieve success at football but not at piano playing and a measure of their motivation could be competitiveness.

Competitors in sport tend to be more intrinsically motivated than extrinsically although sometimes a trainer will use an extrinsic motivator to boost intrinsic motivation. However, this is not well supported because, for example, there are many athletes whose performance has declined as soon as lucrative contracts have been offered.

Internal factors affecting sporting performance

Attribution theory

Attribution theory describes how people explain why things happen. The information that individuals use to explain what causes events can be either internal or external. For example, in situations where there are definite outcomes, such as win or lose, individuals tend to explain the outcome from either an internal or external attribution viewpoint. Internal attributions are those where the individual places the responsibility for the outcome within themselves. For example, if an individual wins, he or she would say it was due to running well or training hard (or both). The person would explain the fact

that he or she won by saying it was something within him or herself or was due to something he or she had done. If an individual with internal attribution loses, he or she would probably say that it was due to not training hard enough.

Over to you

If you got something wrong when playing a game, being able to blame someone else would make you feel better. However, accepting responsibility yourself would mean that you could see what the problem was and learn how to overcome it. Which of these would be most beneficial in the long run?

People with external attribution give the reason for outcomes as something outside of themselves. For example, athletes with external attribution would explain a win by saying that luck was on their side and the competition had not performed as well as they had expected. If an individual with external attribution loses, he or she would explain it by saying that something out of his or her control had contributed to the outcome, such as the referee being biased or the opposition being used to the home ground.

Rees *et al.* (2005) argue that the attributions people make have important consequences for their self-esteem, and the feelings of pride or shame affect their future performance and effort. Zajonc (1965) explained this phenomenon through drive theory. According to this theory, the presence of an audience increases the psychological arousal of performers. The increased drive reduces performance on difficult tasks that are unlearnt or unpractised, and improves performance on well-learnt tasks.

Key term

Arousal – the state of being prepared for action. The term is often used interchangeably with alertness.

Arousal

Arousal is the state of being prepared for action; the term is often used interchangeably with alertness. Arousal activates the organs in the body under the control of the autonomic nervous system and can be gauged by physiological indicators such as blood pressure, galvanic skin reaction, heart rate, respiration rate and muscle tension (Weinberg and Hunt 1976).

If the arousal level of an athlete is too high, they may become anxious and distracted, which would prevent them from being able to perform at their best. If their arousal level were too low, however, they would lack energy and motivation. In order to maximise their ability, athletes must be in the right state of arousal for optimum performance.

There are several theories to show how arousal may affect performance, including the following:

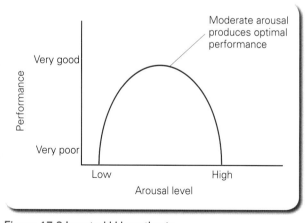

Figure 17.2 Inverted U hypothesis

- **Drive theory** – this states that as an athlete's arousal state or state of anxiety increases, the higher their performance will be. Sports psychologists tend not to support drive theory, because, as mentioned earlier, over-arousal may reduce the quality of performance.

- **Inverted U hypothesis** – this asserts that maximum performance is achieved when moderate arousal is reached. Poor performance is the result of under- or over-arousal.

- **Individual zones of optimal functioning** – this maintains that there are individual differences in levels of anxiety and arousal for individuals to perform at their best. There are different levels of optimal functioning for each sport too – for example, weightlifters generate maximum power during the lift and perform best at high levels of arousal, whereas a bowler in cricket benefits from low levels because of the need to perform controlled movements.

A study investigating the reasons given by children for taking part in sporting activities was conducted by Daley and O'Gara (1998). They found that age and gender made a difference to the reasons given – for example, girls were more motivated by achievement than boys.

Evaluation

Internal factors affecting sporting performance

Motivation from within is characterised by interest and enjoyment from participation in sport. Intrinsic motivation is considered to be the healthiest type of motivation because it reflects the athlete's enthusiasm to perform an activity merely for the reward of taking part.

Research into athlete's goal orientation and their level of intrinsic motivation provided support for the idea that focusing on personal mastery and self-referenced goals promotes intrinsic motivation to a greater degree than focusing on winning. This research provides evidence to support the idea that enjoyment provides the most positive type of intrinsic motivation and outcomes.

Research has demonstrated that during competitions considered important, intrinsically motivated athletes developed positive, task-orientated coping strategies whereas extrinsically motivated athletes were far less likely to achieve their goals and tended to avoid dealing with key issues.

External factors affecting sporting performance

Team membership

Remember

Questionnaires rely on the participants understanding the questions and answering honestly.

There is more to making a team than putting a group of individuals together. For a group of people to become a team, they need to be able to communicate with each other, have trust in each other and have a clear goal that they are all aiming towards. One way that teams assess their cohesion is by getting the team members to fill in a Group Environment Questionnaire (GEQ), which measures how well individuals in the group view the task, their place in the group and the way they perceive other members of the group. A number of studies have found that the GEQ has high validity and reliability. Brawley *et al.* (1987) reported three studies which inspected the GEQ and found that it was able to successfully predict the difference in self-responsibility attributions between high task and low task cohesive athletes of team sports. A team that has good communication, where all the members get on well together, has high task cohesion; these teams tend to appraise the team's performance more favourably than those with low task

Over to you

How do you think an audience that was silent or booed the participants would affect the performance?

Figure 17.3 An audience can bring about a change in the performance of an athelete

cohesion. Team success can increase the communication and sense of ability, which can also contribute to the development of the team's cohesion.

Audience effect

Audience effect refers to a change in performance by an athlete which is brought about by the presence of others. An audience may be reactive or inactive. An inactive audience is passive: it sits and watches what happens; while a reactive audience responds enthusiastically, clapping and shouting encouragement in support of their team.

Social facilitation

The effect of a group of people watching and judging athletes sometimes intensifies performance, although at other times performance may suffer because of the presence of other people. This tendency for an audience to affect the performance is called social facilitation, and the effect may be either positive or negative. A positive effect is one that increases the athletes' performance, while a negative effect decreases the performance. The mere presence of others facilitates performance when the task is easy or well known and practised, but inhibits performance when the task is difficult or challenging. Research into social facilitation has focused on two areas: first, when people are working side by side but on individual tasks, and second, when a group of people are watching an individual performing a task.

Research on the audience effect was investigated by Michaels *et al.* (1982), who found that when watched by an audience good pool players increased their shot accuracy by 9 per cent, but poor players decreased their shot accuracy by 11 per cent. Those athletes at the top of their game are often lifted by the crowd and give their best performances, but the less confident often find the crowds intimidating and because of this, may not perform at their best.

The home effect

Research shows that teams win more games playing at home than away. Schwartz and Barsky (1977) suggest that this is true even when fatigue from travelling and lack of familiarity with the home playing area is taken out of the equation. They argue that it is the support of the home crowd that gives the team the advantage. Schwartz and Barsky note that successful performance is not only affected by an athlete's skill and abilities, but also by the enthusiasm, passion and number of their well-wishers. This is shown to be true in the Olympic Games, where the host country wins more medals than they have done in previous games, and more than in subsequent games when they are not the hosts.

Key Example

Macphail *et al.* (2003): Young people's socialisation into sport: A case study of an athletics club (*Sport, Education and Society*, 8(2), 251–67)

The role of parents in children's sports may be as a driver to and from practices and games, or something more complex like being a coach or an official at the game.

Aim: To investigate young people's socialisation into sport.

Method: Young people (nine to fifteen years old) were used in an 18-month long investigation of the junior section of an athletics club in England. Field notes, interviews and a psychometric questionnaire were used to gather data.

Findings: There is a trend towards increasing numbers of younger children participating in adult-organised, community-based sport. Most of the young people participating in the introductory groups at the club began their socialisation into sport by sampling a range of sports. Friendships were an important consideration when it came to choice of sports undertaken.

Conclusions: Community-based programmes are a good way to involve young people in sport.

Parents may also shape a child's psychological development through their involvement as they play an important role in affecting the young person's motivation, competence and emotional responses. The feedback from a parent can affect how a child perceives their own performance and also determines how long that child stays involved in a sport.

Evaluation

External factors affecting sporting performance

Those athletes who are motivated by extrinsic factors tend to suffer more anxiety before or during a match or game and also feel more guilt when they do not perform at their best. Research has found that when extrinsic motivation is the only reason for athletic participation, athletes lose interest and do not enjoy playing and practising their sport. Extrinsic motivation can also give the athlete a negative self-perception because if they fail to achieve a particular extrinsic reward, they may feel they are not as good as they thought they were.

An athlete may have intrinsic and extrinsic motivations at the same time. However, extrinsic motivation may strengthen or weaken an athlete's original intrinsic reasons for playing. If an athlete is rewarded extrinsically for a positive performance, for example, by crowd admiration or winning a cup or money, they often feel more intrinsically motivated to play.

Effects of exercise on well-being

Exercise has been shown by research to have positive effects on people's psychological and physical well-being. Stubbe *et al.* (2007) investigated the association between leisure time exercise participation and life satisfaction and happiness. They found that those who took part in exercise were more satisfied with their lives and happier than those who did not exercise; this effect was found across all age ranges. They concluded that exercise participation is associated with higher levels of life satisfaction and happiness.

There is also evidence to suggest that regular exercise decreases the chance of suffering from various illnesses. Penedo and Dahn (2005) reviewed many

studies (cross-sectional, longitudinal and randomised clinical trials), evaluating the relationship between exercise and physical and mental health. They paid particular attention to physical conditions such as obesity, cancer, cardiovascular disease and sexual dysfunction; in addition, they examined studies relating physical activity and depression and other mood states. The results supported other studies that suggest that exercise has beneficial effects for physical and mental health.

The physical effects of regular exercise include the reduction of the risk of premature death due to heart disease. Physical activity also reduces high blood pressure or the risk of developing high blood pressure. The risk of certain cancers, such as colon cancer and breast cancer, are also reduced with regular exercise. There is evidence to suggest that exercise reduces the risk of developing diabetes and can reduce or maintain body weight or body fat. Another advantage of regular exercise is that it builds and maintains healthy muscles, bones and joints. Sporting performance is enhanced as is the ability to concentrate and therefore work at a task.

High levels of physical activity have a positive effect on mental health, according to Stephens (1988), who suggests that physical activity boosts mood and feelings of well-being, as well as reducing symptoms of anxiety and depression. Landers and Petruzzello (1994) conducted a meta-analysis of 27 studies carried out between 1960 and 1992 and found that physical exercise reduces anxiety.

The psychological benefits of physical activity, in addition to boosting mood and reducing the symptoms of anxiety, also apply to depression. Research into depression and exercise has found that the beneficial effects of exercise lift the depressed mood state and also improve mental functioning. Studies have been conducted on many types of exercise, including cycling, walking, jogging and sporting activities such as racket ball, weightlifting, softball and football, and all have been found to be beneficial. Some studies have also looked at yoga and Taekwondo and found participants had less depression, less confusion, less anxiety, less anger and less fatigue. So it appears that no matter what the exercise there are psychological benefits.

The benefits on social life are also enhanced through exercise. Exercising with another person can help to motivate and make workouts more interesting. Physical exercise with another person can be much more fun than exercising alone. Running, cycling and other activities are often run for charity and the opportunity to meet people and make friends while raising funds for a good cause is a great way of having fun with like-minded people. There is also the team spirit that accompanies such activities which builds bonds that tie the team together by showing appreciation and respect to others for their accomplishments. Team sports provide the opportunity for children to develop and strengthen their social skills by teaching them how to cooperate with their team mates, how to follow rules and be a good team member.

Evaluation

Effects of exercise on well-being

Regular exercise has been shown to be essential for health and physical activity is regarded as one of the most effective ways of preventing disease. However, there are many individuals who do not like the idea of regular physical exercise and are placing themselves in a position where, because of their sedentary lifestyle, they may develop heart disease. This is because physical idleness is one of the biggest causes of heart disease. The heart is the most essential muscle in the body and needs exercise in order to stay in good shape so that it can effectively pump blood around the body.

Research has shown that exercise and physical activity have beneficial effects on physical and mental health. People who engage in regular physical activity display more desirable health outcomes across a variety of physical conditions. Exercise has been shown to be effective in preventing coronary heart disease, stroke and type two diabetes. Researchers have found that 30 minutes of moderate physical activity on five or more days a week is enough to reap the health benefits. Children and young people need to be active for at least an hour each day to benefit from exercise. Exercise leads to stronger bones and muscles, more energy and a better social life. There is a vast amount of evidence which shows that physical activity can indirectly improve subjective well-being and life quality by reducing the risk of disease and premature death. There is also evidence to show that exercise has a direct role in the prevention and treatment of mental health problems.

The impact of exercise on health was at first researched for the benefits on diseases such as coronary heart disease, obesity and diabetes. However, there has been over 25 years of research into the benefits of exercise in the treatment of mental health and improving mental well-being in the general population. This field of research is so vast that over 30 meta-analyses have reviewed more than 500 studies which have pointed to the benefits for exercise as a therapy for clinical or sub-clinical depression or anxiety.

There is now sufficient evidence to show that exercise is effective in treating clinical depression. In addition, exercise can improve self-perception and self-esteem, enhance mood and reduce stress. There is weaker evidence that exercise can improve cognitive function in older adults and give more independence in later life.

Theories of aggression in sport

Dollard *et al.* (1939) describe aggression as a sequence of behaviours in which the goal is to injure another person, while Berkowitz suggests that it is behaviour that is carried out with the intention of harming someone. Both of these definitions emphasise that it is a deliberate act on the part of the aggressor. There is some debate as to the origin of aggression in sport: some theories suggest it is innate, while others suggest that aggression is learnt.

Instinct theories

As the name implies, **instinct** theory suggests that aggression is innate. Frustration is also thought to be innate, and Dollard *et al.* (1939) argue that frustration plays a key role in aggression. Frustration can be caused by many different circumstances, such as having a point disallowed, being fouled by an opponent or not achieving personal goals or targets.

Psychologists have distinguished between two types of aggression:

- **Hostile aggression** – where the sole purpose of the behaviour is to harm someone. This would include deliberately kicking someone or head-butting them to cause them harm. This is also called reactive aggression and is driven by anger.

> ### Key term
>
> **Instinct** – the inborn capacity of an individual to respond to a stimulus in a relatively fixed way.

- **Instrumental aggression** – where aggression is used as a means to obtain something. Someone who tackles hard to gain possession of the ball would fall into this category. This sort of aggression is not accompanied by anger and is called channelled aggression.

Freud believed that we have instincts that need to be satisfied and aggression is part of our death instincts, which are destructive parts of our personality. These death instincts conflict with life instincts, which are creative and positive. Exercise is one method of managing the aggressive drive in a positive way, and it is cathartic because exercise allows the release of pent-up aggression. Another way Freud claimed aggression is shown is through the ego defence mechanism of displacement. If an individual has had a frustrating day at work or school, he or she could go and play sport in the evening, where there is an opportunity to release the aggression in a more acceptable way than shouting at a boss or teacher. The theory allows for individuals to release their aggressive feelings in a safe and controlled environment.

Figure 17.4 Hostile aggression in sport is driven by anger

Remember

Freud's theory is difficult to test and therefore difficult to prove right or wrong. So although the ideas he put forward may seem feasible, there is no way of knowing if they are correct.

Remember

The frustration-aggression hypothesis was questioned because it failed to account for justified frustration. Doob and Sears (1939) repeated their experiment with justified frustration and found that anger decreased significantly.

Frustration-aggression hypothesis

When people think they are being stopped from reaching a goal, their frustration may turn to aggression. Dollard *et al.* (1939) proposed the frustration-aggression hypothesis when they suggested that occurrence of aggression is brought about by frustration. Doob and Sears (1939) investigated this hypothesis, asking participants to imagine frustrating and non-frustrating situations. The participants reported feeling angry in the frustrating situations.

Berkowitz (1993) argued that aggression is a response to unpleasant stimuli and negative effect (unpleasant emotions and feelings, such as anxiety, anger, annoyance or pain). Negative effect can trigger a 'fight or flight' response and associated thoughts and reactions that are connected to such experiences. The factors that need to be taken into account for a fight or flight response are: how the individual examines and controls feelings and how they analyse the situation.

Social learning theory

Social learning theory, as the name implies, asserts that aggression is learnt. The way that aggression is learnt is by watching someone being rewarded for their behaviour; this is known as vicarious reinforcement. Bandura believed that aggressive behaviour can be learnt by watching a role model being aggressive. An observer is more likely to reproduce the behaviour of someone they admire. Therefore, in well-publicised sports, such as football, the aggressive behaviour of someone's favourite football player is seen on the television and this could lead to replication of this behaviour in other matches.

Evaluation

Theories of aggression in sport

Reducing aggression in sport, while still leaving room for the athletes to be competitive, is a goal worth aiming for. Results of psychological assessment and personality profile of athletes conducted by sports psychologists can help coaches and management in the selection process and team-building. This is because some personality types have a greater tendency to impulsive and aggressive behaviours than others.

It is difficult to establish a non-aggressive stance in some sports such as football as the sporting arena is the only place where violence and aggression are not only tolerated but encouraged and rewarded by members of society. Violence in sport has become a special problem and should be treated as such. If some of the fouls made on the football pitch were carried on in the outside world there would be some players that would be in jail for quite a long time.

Summary

Improving motivation in sport

Explanations of motivation include intrinsic motivation, which comes from within, and extrinsic motivation, which are motivating factors that come from outside the individual.

Ways of improving motivation include goal setting and gearing the extrinsic motivating factors to the individual in order to make them personal.

Internal factors affecting sporting performance

Arousal is the state of being prepared for action, with the arousal level reaching maximum at the time of the performance for the athlete to perform at his or her best.

Attribution theory explains how athletes account for their performance. If they have an internal attribution, they will think the responsibility for winning is down to themselves, whereas those with an external attribution will look to outside forces, including luck, to explain why they have won.

Effects of exercise on well-being

The effects of exercise on physical and mental health have been shown by research to be positive. Research has shown that regular exercise has beneficial effects on health and well-being and happiness ratings.

Sport psychology

External factors affecting sporting performance

A team needs good communication and cohesion to be successful. Audience effects are either reactive or inactive, and can have a profound effect on the athlete.

Theories of aggression in sport

Frustration-aggression hypothesis happens when people believe they are being stopped from reaching a goal and their frustration at this turns to aggression.

Social learning theory suggests that people watch role models or people they admire being aggressive and being rewarded for it – for example, getting attention from the media – and they copy this behaviour.

OBJECTIVES

The specification requires you to have an awareness of the following:

- Issues of bias in diagnostic systems (e.g. culture and gender)

- Aetiologies of schizophrenia, including physiological and psychological explanations

- Two treatments for schizophrenia (e.g. chemotherapy, behavioural therapies, cognitive therapies, humanistic therapies)

- Aetiologies of unipolar depression, including physiological and psychological explanations

- Two treatments for unipolar depression (e.g. behavioural therapies, cognitive therapies, humanistic therapies).

INTRODUCTION

Abnormal psychology is a division of psychology that attends to unusual patterns of behaviour, emotion and thought which may lead to a mental disorder. The Diagnostic and Statistical Manual of Mental Disorders (DSM) is published by the American Psychiatric Association; this reference book provides a list of disorders and their symptoms. This provides guidance for clinical psychologists and psychiatrists on deciding whether someone has a mental illness and which mental illness they have.

Diagnostic systems

Most diseases have certain symptoms that make them recognisable. For example, measles is recognisable by red eyes, sensitivity to light, cold-like symptoms, increased temperature and a red, spotty rash that starts around the back of the ears. For diagnosis of measles it is necessary to identify the symptoms using a scheme of classification. The International Classification of Diseases (ICD) is the standard diagnostic classification system and classifies every disease and all other health problems. The ICD is used by World Health Organization (WHO) to enable the storage and retrieval of diagnostic information throughout the world.

Mental illness is identified in the same way, through the use of the Diagnostic Statistical Manual of Mental Disorders (DSM). The DSM is published by the American Psychiatric Association (APA) and is used in the USA and around the world, because it provides standard criteria for the classification of mental disorders. The classification of mental illness in this way has the advantage of being able to determine how many people have a certain type of illness, and is also useful for assessing how well a person is responding to treatment. There is the further advantage of being helpful for research purposes, in order to develop treatments for disorders.

Figure 18.1 Mental illness is identified in the same way as physical illness

Remember

The DSM is an attempt to list mental illnesses, with symptoms, in a systematic way, so that clinical psychologists and psychiatrists can make a diagnosis.

Issues of bias in diagnostic systems

Cultural issues

There are limitations with classification systems, however. The first limitation is that of labelling someone as mentally ill; once a diagnosis has been made – for example, schizophrenia – there is a social stigma for the person to cope with, on top of their illness. Different cultures have different ways of interpreting behaviour; in some cultures, some types of behaviour may be considered symptoms of illness, while in other cultures they are socially tolerable or even desirable.

The DSM and ICD were developed by US and European mental health professionals and they reflect the US and European view of symptoms. This is a predominantly white, middle-class view. Nazroo (1997) found that in the UK, African Caribbeans are three times more likely to be diagnosed with schizophrenia. This may be due to their genes or culture, or it might be that they are more likely to be diagnosed as having schizophrenia because they are African Caribbean rather than because they are more prone to the symptoms of schizophrenia.

The DSM includes diagnostic information about some disorders that are only found in certain cultures. The inclusion of these culture-bound syndromes, according to Guarnaccia and Rogler (1999), provides the opportunity to develop a research agenda to study them. They argue that it is necessary to understand culture-bound syndromes within their cultural context, as well as needing to analyse the relationship between the syndromes and psychiatric disorders.

Culture-bound syndromes are psychological disorders only found in certain cultures. A syndrome is a collection of behaviours or characteristics. It has been suggested that anorexia nervosa is a western culture-bound syndrome, while ghost sickness, which involves an extreme preoccupation with death and is often associated with nightmares, fear, anxiety, hallucinations and feelings of suffocation, may be a Native American culture-bound syndrome, as it is only found in certain Native American people. Amok involves short-lived outbursts of aggressive behaviour, where the individual attempts to kill or maim, and can only be found among males living in Southeast Asia.

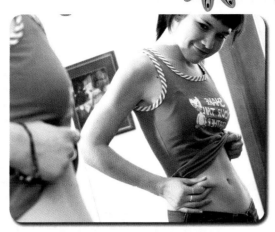

Figure 18.2 Culture-bound syndromes are psychological disorders only found in certain cultures

Gender issues

There are differences in diagnosis between males and females. For example, more males are likely to be diagnosed with antisocial personality disorder and more females are likely to be diagnosed with histrionic personality disorder. Antisocial personality disorder symptoms include aggression, impulsiveness, deceit, irresponsibility, manipulative behaviour, disregard for others and a lack of shame or remorse. Histrionic personality disorder has symptoms of over-dramatisation, vanity, over-exaggerated emotions, crying, uncontrollability, the need for reassurance and constant approval.

> ### Remember
> Kaplan (1983) suggested that this imbalance in diagnoses could be because the diagnostic criteria for these disorders display traditional stereotypes of men and women.

Evaluation of cultural/gender issues

- The two classification systems, DSM and ICD, have been developed in the west by white, middle-class males, and some researchers claim that the symptoms of mental disorders are only seen as mental disorders because they differ from what is normal in white, middle-class, male, western culture.

- Conditions such as amok and ghost sickness have sufficient characteristics to allow diagnosis, but they do not appear to fit the symptoms of other disorders, and therefore give weight to the idea that there are disorders that are found only in certain cultures.

- There is also little evidence to suggest that culture-bound syndromes respond to drug treatments, so they are probably not biological in origin.

- The diagnosis of culture-bound syndromes may be racist, because it suggests that the cultural beliefs of people from different cultures are disorders that need treatment.

> ### Key term
> Aetiology – the cause of a disease or condition, so when we are looking at the aetiology of schizophrenia we are considering the possible causes.

Evaluation

Issues of bias in diagnostic systems

There are many issues with the diagnosis of psychiatric disorders. Rosenhan (1973) demonstrated how subjective the diagnosis was in his research. He used eight people with no signs of psychiatric disorder and they presented themselves at hospitals complaining of hearing voices. Most of them were diagnosed as suffering from schizophrenia. Once they were admitted to hospital, they behaved normally, but this was interpreted by the staff as abnormal. For example, pacing the corridor because they were bored was seen as 'anxiety'. In one case it took 52 days for the staff to become convinced that the pseudo patient was well enough to be discharged.

Rosenhan concluded from this that the task of distinguishing normal from abnormal behaviour is defective. The study made a very powerful statement about the dangers of labelling someone with a psychiatric disorder because, once labelled, it is very difficult to overcome the label.

There is some controversy when it comes to defining schizophrenia as the symptoms described in the DSM and ICD are different. The DSM has five sub-types of schizophrenia and the ICD has seven. This means that psychiatrists may use different systems to diagnose the illness and misdiagnosis is possible. The differences in symptoms between the ICD and DSM mean the definition of schizophrenia is unreliable and this invalidates the classification of the illness.

In addition to this is the fact that the criteria for describing schizophrenia as an illness has changed considerably since it was first diagnosed. The illness described today bears little resemblance to the illness described in the early parts of the twentieth century. Therefore any meta-analysis carried out on studies of schizophrenia may be using data gathered on different criteria and would be invalid.

Afro-Caribbean men in the UK are seven times more likely to be diagnosed with schizophrenia than if they were living in a country predominantly populated by black people. This again points to issues of diagnosis as the statistics would be similar in all cultures if the classification and diagnosis were correct.

Aetiologies of schizophrenia

There are a number of reasons put forward to explain the cause of schizophrenia, so it is a matter for some debate.

The biological explanation

Biological explanations view schizophrenia as being caused by physiological processes. These can include genetics, biochemical factors and neurological factors. Frith *et al.* (1995) found that there may be abnormal functional connectivity between the frontal and temporal cortex.

Genetic factors

Many studies have attempted to establish the role of genetics in schizophrenia using family, twin and adoption studies. There is evidence to suggest that schizophrenia may be inherited, as there is a greater risk of being diagnosed with schizophrenia if a person has relatives with the disorder. Gottesman (1991) found that the closer a person is to a relative who has the disorder, the more likely they are to be diagnosed with schizophrenia themselves. Therefore, an individual with an identical twin who has been diagnosed with schizophrenia has a 48 per cent chance of being diagnosed with it too; this drops to 17 per cent for fraternal twins. If they have grandparents with schizophrenia, they have a 5 per cent risk of developing it.

Adoption studies compare adults diagnosed with schizophrenia with their biological parents and their adoptive parents. As these people were adopted when they were infants, they were raised apart from their biological parents and would not have shared the same environment, so any similarities would indicate a genetic influence, while any similarity to their adoptive parents would indicate an environmental influence. Kety (1988) found that out of 5,500 adults who were adopted in early childhood, 33 were diagnosed with schizophrenia and 14 per cent of those had biological relatives who also had schizophrenia. This compares with only 2.7 per cent of their adoptive relatives.

Biochemical factors: The dopamine hypothesis

Schizophrenia is associated with too much dopamine (a neurotransmitter) in the brain. It is unclear whether the excess dopamine is a cause of the schizophrenia or whether it is another symptom. The excess dopamine causes the neurons that use dopamine to fire too often and produces many of the symptoms of schizophrenia. Amphetamines increase the amounts of dopamine, and people with no history of psychological disorder show behaviour similar to paranoid schizophrenia when they are given amphetamines in large doses. This points to a connection between dopamine levels and schizophrenia. Further evidence comes from the antipsychotic drugs that are used to treat schizophrenia, as these work to block dopamine receptors which prevent the dopamine neurons from firing.

Figure 18.3 The causes of schizophrenia are a matter for debate

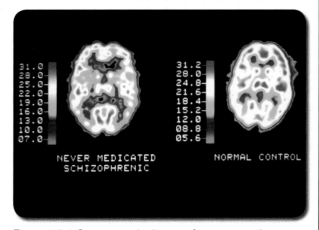

Figure 18.4 Comparing the brains of a person with schizophrenia and a person without the disorder

Evidence for the dopamine hypothesis is mixed, as it would be difficult to measure the exact amounts of dopamine in the brain of live patients. However, Lindström *et al.* (1999) used PET scans to assess the level of dopamine in the brain of schizophrenic patients who had not received treatment and found that there was more dopamine than normal being produced in these patients. There is empirical support to show that dopamine plays an important role in schizophrenia – for example, drugs that block dopamine reduce the symptoms of schizophrenia – but there is some debate about whether dopamine causes schizophrenia or is a symptom of the disease.

Neurological factors

In the early 1900s schizophrenia was thought to be linked to structural changes in the brain. During the 1970s new technology was developed that could give accurate, detailed brain scans, and through these it was found that 25 per cent of people with schizophrenia had enlarged ventricles in the brain.

In the late 1990s, studies found that people with schizophrenia have smaller frontal lobes, with reduced blood flow in their brains, and smaller amounts of cortical grey matter. CAT scans have revealed that the ventricles in the brains of people with schizophrenia tend to be larger than normal. PET scans show

a difference between the brains of those with type 1 schizophrenia, who have negative symptoms, and those with type 2 schizophrenia, who show positive symptoms. The scans show an abnormally low activity rate in the frontal lobe of those with type 2 schizophrenia, while those with type 1 show abnormalities of the limbic system and temporal lobes of the brain. This indicates that there are two distinct types of schizophrenia, which are caused by different brain abnormalities.

Crow (1985) suggested two types of schizophrenia: type 1 is genetically inherited, associated with dopamine and characterised by positive symptoms; type 2 is a neuro-developmental disorder shown in the brain structure and is characterised by negative symptoms.

Psychological theories of schizophrenia

Out of all the psychological explanations for schizophrenia, the two that are subscribed to most are the cognitive approach and the psychodynamic approach. The cognitive approach is the most popular explanation used in Britain and USA, while the psychodynamic approach is used and researched in Europe.

The cognitive approach

People diagnosed with schizophrenia have difficulty processing information and research has shown that they are easily distracted. The cognitive approach explains the behaviour and experiences of people with schizophrenia as problems with information processing. People with schizophrenia have been found to have problems with the ability to reflect on thoughts, behaviour and experience. Frith suggests that individuals with schizophrenia with positive symptoms have a deficit in the central monitoring system, which is the cognitive process in charge of labelling actions and thoughts. This produces problems with the person knowing what the difference is between self and others. Frith and Corcoran (1996) found that patients with positive symptoms of schizophrenia had difficulty inferring the mental states of other people.

Patients with negative symptoms of schizophrenia were found by Frith and Done (1983) to have problems producing spontaneous responses to a design task. In a verbal fluency task – for example, 'Name as many types of fruit as you can', Frith and Done (1986) found that schizophrenic patients with negative symptoms could not produce many words and either did nothing or repeated their previous response.

Evaluation of the cognitive approach

- The cognitive approach attempts to explain specific symptoms of schizophrenia, which avoids the issue of discrepancies between the symptoms experienced by different patients.

- The cognitive approach can explain how faulty mechanisms lead to faulty thoughts and behaviours.

- Hypotheses can be formed about patients' responses, and measured using experiments which allow for a degree of objectivity to be added to patients' descriptions of their experiences.

- There may be a problem with conducting experiments on patients with schizophrenia, as it may not always be possible to tell whether the results are due to cognitive functions or antipsychotic medication.

Psychodynamic explanations of schizophrenia

This theory suggests that family life may influence the onset of schizophrenia. In particular, a dysfunctional family – that is, a family that does not function properly – may cause schizophrenia in its members.

The schizophrenogenic mother is a one who is domineering and insensitive to the needs of her family. This type of mother is overprotective and at the same time rejecting, and her actions are often contradictory – for example, she may say 'yes', but her actions would portray 'no'. This type of mother has a faulty communication system with her child and Fromm-Reichman (1948) suggested that this can lead to the onset of schizophrenia in the child. It was based on the accounts her patients had given her of their childhood that Fromm-Reichmann proposed the idea of a schizophrenogenic mother. What Fromm-Reichmann meant by this was that it is the mother that causes schizophrenia by having a cold and domineering attitude. However, Davidson and Neale (1998) investigated this and found little evidence to support the theory.

Freud suggested that schizophrenia was caused by regression to the oral stage, which is the first stage of psychosexual development. The id is self-indulgent and concerned with the satisfaction of its own needs. The need to satisfy the impulses of the id and the experience of the world result in conflict, and the schizophrenic person's ego is not strong enough to cope with the id impulses. This can lead to self-indulgence and delusions of grandeur, or even delusions of hearing voices which the person attributes to God.

Evaluation of the psychodynamic approach

- There is evidence to suggest that poor family dynamics increase the risk of schizophrenia, but this may be due to genetics.

- Schizophrenia is not treatable by psychoanalysis because the schizophrenic patient has given up attachment to the outside world; this would prevent them from being able to relate to the therapist.

Evaluation

Aetiologies of schizophrenia

There are cases of schizophrenia in all parts of the world and men and women are affected equally. All ethnic groups around the world have similar rates, and symptoms, such as hallucinations and delusions, usually start between the ages of 16 and 30. Men tend to experience symptoms earlier than women and it is rare for someone over the age of 45 to get schizophrenia. However, more black men are diagnosed with the illness in Britain and the USA than black women and white men and women.

It is likely that multiple genes play a part in creating a predisposition to develop schizophrenia, yet it is not yet understood how the genetic predisposition is conveyed and nor is it possible to predict whether an individual will develop the disorder. Factors such as prenatal complications, intrauterine starvation or viral infections appear to influence the development of schizophrenia.

Neuro-imaging has found abnormalities in the brain structure such as enlargement of the fluid-filled cavities, called ventricles, in the interior of the brain and decreased size of some brain regions in individuals with schizophrenia. However, these abnormalities are not found in all people with schizophrenia and they are sometimes found in people that do not have schizophrenia. Neurotransmitters such as dopamine and glutamate have been found to be involved in those with schizophrenia but it is not clear whether the excess of dopamine is due to the development of schizophrenia or its cause.

Studies of brain tissue after death have also shown small changes in distribution of brain cells. Some of these changes may occur before the individual becomes ill and schizophrenia may be a disorder in brain development.

At this present moment there is no known single cause of schizophrenia. Many diseases result from an interaction of genetic and environmental factors and this may be the case for schizophrenia too. Research is still being carried out to find its cause.

Key term

Diathesis-stress – While there is evidence for biological and genetic causes of schizophrenia, it may be that this makes people vulnerable to environmental factors. The environment, therefore, may act as a trigger to schizophrenia in those people who have a genetic and biological predisposition. The environment includes culture and social and family relationships, any of which factors may encourage or discourage the onset of schizophrenia in those people who have the predisposition.

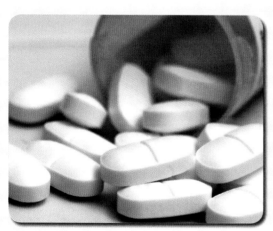

Figure 18.5 The main treatment for schizophrenia is antipsychotic drugs

Treatments of schizophrenia

The main treatment for schizophrenia is antipsychotic drugs, which were first developed in the 1940s. Antipsychotic drugs are given to patients with schizophrenia to help normalise the biochemical imbalances. There are two major types of antipsychotic medications: traditional and new antipsychotics. Traditional antipsychotics, such as haloperidol, chlorpromazine and fluphenazine, help to control delusions, hallucinations and confusion, and have been available since the mid 1950s. These drugs block dopamine receptors and are used to treat the positive symptoms of schizophrenia.

The newer antipsychotic drugs, such as seroquel, risperdal, zypexa and clozaril, have been available since the 1990s. These drugs work on both the dopamine and serotonin receptors, and treat both the positive and the negative symptoms of schizophrenia. In the 1990s, antipsychotic drugs came into use for the acute, most intense and distressing phase of schizophrenia. At other times they may be used when the patient feels unwell or stressed, or even to prevent further episodes. While antipsychotics may eliminate some symptoms, they do not help everyone. Elsesser *et al.* (1996) suggest that the traditional antipsychotics help 65 per cent of those treated, while the new antipsychotics help 85 per cent.

There are other newer antipsychotics, referred to as atypical antipsychotics, which may be more effective in treating a broad range of symptoms of schizophrenia. They still have side effects, although these are different to those experienced with traditional drugs.

Cognitive treatment of schizophrenia

The basic principle of cognitive therapy is that beliefs, expectations and assessments of self and the world affect how we perceive ourselves and others. Schizophrenia has symptoms of disorganised thinking, and distorted perceptions of the self and the world.

The treatment goal for the cognitive therapist is to improve the patient's ability to manage life problems so they can function independently, and to be free from extreme distress and other psychological symptoms. In order to do this, the therapist has to accept the patient's perception of reality and use this to assist the patient to manage the problems he or she may have in life. The aim is to help the patient to use information from the world to make adaptive coping decisions.

Research conducted by Chadwick *et al.* (2000) showed that patients involved in cognitive behavioural therapy (CBT) experienced a significant reduction in negative beliefs about the power of the voices and how much they were controlled by them. This shows that CBT is effective in dealing with the cognitive aspects of schizophrenia, which, in turn, has a positive effect on the individual's quality of life.

Token economy

Another treatment that has been tried for schizophrenia is the token economy. A token economy is the application of operant conditioning and was introduced in the USA in hospitals for the treatment of psychological disorders in the 1960s. Paul and Lentz (1977) reported on a six-year study that used operant conditioning on patients in psychiatric wards suffering from schizophrenia. These individuals were long-stay patients, who in some cases had become mute and withdrawn, while others repeatedly screamed, smeared faeces on the walls, assaulted staff and other patients and buried their faces in their food. The token economy was introduced to one group of patients and was compared to patients who did not take part in the token economy programme. The social, self-care skills of the token economy group improved significantly and their symptoms were reduced.

At the beginning of the programme, 90 per cent of the patients were receiving antipsychotic drugs. Four and a half years into the study, those in the token economy group were so improved that only 11 per cent of the patients were taking the drugs. Of those on the token economy programme, more than 97 per cent of the patients who had been considered ineligible for community living were able to be discharged, with significantly fewer medications and with positive community outcomes.

Combination of treatments

The National Health Service uses a combination of antipsychotic drugs and cognitive behavioural therapy to treat schizophrenia. The results of research has shown that out of 100 people with schizophrenia:

Remember

It is difficult to establish cause and effect because many participants have suffered from schizophrenia for a while and have been undergoing treatment which may have altered or masked anything that may have significance.

- 20 people will never have another acute episode of schizophrenia
- 50 people will have a relapse of symptoms within two years
- 30 people will never be free of symptoms, but the severity of symptoms may fluctuate over time
- 20 people will stay resistant to treatment and will require continuous support and supervision.

Key Example

Rosenhan, (1973): On being sane in insane places (*Science*, 79 (70), 250–8)

Aim: This research aimed to show that psychiatrists cannot reliably distinguish between those with a mental disorder and those who do not have a mental disorder.

Method: A field experiment in which participants (pseudo patients), eight sane people (a psychology graduate student in his 20s, three psychologists, a paediatrician, a psychiatrist, a painter and a housewife), presented themselves to hospital outpatient units complaining of hearing voices saying 'hollow, empty, thud'. These voices were the only symptom and were chosen because they were not similar to any known abnormality mentioned in the health manuals. All pseudo patients were admitted to hospital and upon admission they immediately stopped simulating any symptoms of abnormality.

All information they gave to the hospital about their past medical history and home life, apart from their identity and job, which they changed to protect their future health and employment records, was correct.

They were understandably nervous, which may have been due to a fear of being exposed as a fraud. Apart from this, they took part in ward activities acting as they would normally and when asked by staff how they were feeling, they said they were fine and no longer had any symptoms.

All pseudo patients disliked the experience and wanted to be discharged immediately, but they had to convince the hospital staff they were sane before they could be released.

They spent their time writing about their experiences and observing the behaviour of staff towards patients. At first this was done covertly, but after a while, as no one appeared bothered, they took notes openly.

Findings: None of the pseudo patients were detected and all but one were admitted with a diagnosis of schizophrenia. The diagnosis was made without any clear symptom of the disorder. The length of time it took for them to be discharged from hospital varied from seven to 52 days (an average of 19 days). Although the staff did not suspect them, 35 out of the 118 patients expressed their suspicions, saying things like 'You're not crazy. You're a journalist or a professor. You're checking up on the hospital.'

The medical staff reported the pseudo patients' normal behaviours as features of their supposed illness. For example, writing notes was recorded as 'Patient engaged in writing behaviour', arriving early for lunch was noted as 'oral acquisitive syndrome'. In other words, the medical staff looked for, and found, evidence for an abnormality where none was present.

The pseudo patients were given a total of 2,100 tablets which they flushed down the toilet.

They were all discharged from hospital with the diagnosis of 'schizophrenia in remission'.

Conclusions: Rosenhan concluded that it is clear that the sane cannot be distinguished from the insane in psychiatric hospitals and meanings of behaviour are often misunderstood to fit in with the diagnosis of the patient.

Over to you

If someone presents to a hospital and you were the doctor, would you expect them to be telling you the truth about their symptoms? Did the doctors in Rosenhan's research have any choice apart from admitting them? Was it a mistake to label them as having schizophrenia until further investigations were completed?

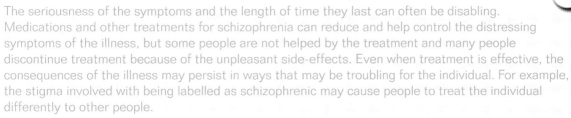

Evaluation

Treatments of schizophrenia

The seriousness of the symptoms and the length of time they last can often be disabling. Medications and other treatments for schizophrenia can reduce and help control the distressing symptoms of the illness, but some people are not helped by the treatment and many people discontinue treatment because of the unpleasant side-effects. Even when treatment is effective, the consequences of the illness may persist in ways that may be troubling for the individual. For example, the stigma involved with being labelled as schizophrenic may cause people to treat the individual differently to other people.

Sometimes it is difficult to tell the type of disorder a person has. For example, some people with schizophrenia symptoms have periods of extreme elation or extreme depression and it is important to determine whether these patients actually have schizophrenia or bipolar disorder.

Aetiologies of unipolar depression

Key term

Unipolar depression – one of the most frequently occurring psychopathologies. It is a disturbance in mood characterised by sadness, disappointment, loneliness, self-doubt, guilt and hopelessness. Depression is so prevalent that it has been called the common cold of mental illness.

Biological explanations of depression

Biological explanations of depression look to twin studies to discern whether there is a genetic link. If genes are a factor in depression, we would expect identical (MZ) twins to have a high concordance rate, as they share almost 100 per cent of their genes. Non-identical (DZ) twins share 50 per cent of their genes. McGuffin *et al.* (1996) found that out of a sample of nearly 200 sets of twins, if one of the MZ twins was diagnosed with depression, there was a 46 per cent chance that the other twin would be also diagnosed with depression; this was reduced to 20 per cent with the DZ twins. These findings would suggest a moderate genetic influence.

Adoptive studies are a good way of looking at genetic factors because most twins share the same environment, but people who have been adopted at an

early age are brought up in a different environment to the rest of their biological family. Since they were raised apart from their biological relatives, this means that similarities with those relatives would indicate a genetic link. Harrington *et al.* (1993) found that biological relatives are more likely than adoptive relatives to have a diagnosis of depression. The concordance rate with biological relatives was 20 per cent, while adoptive relatives had a 5–10 per cent concordance rate.

A twin study which examined the role of both genes and life events was conducted by Silberg *et al.* (1999). This study found that there may not be a gene for depression, but that some people may be particularly vulnerable to depression when unpleasant things happen to them.

> ## Remember
>
> It is possible that more than one gene is involved, as there appear to be a number of neurochemical and neurological factors associated with depression.

Biochemical and neurological factors

There is a great deal of evidence to suggest that depression is the result of neurotransmitter abnormalities. These abnormalities may be the result of inherited factors or other medical conditions, such as hypothyroidism, AIDS or cerebral infarction. Dopamine, noradrenaline and serotonin, the monoamine neurotransmitters, are present in lower levels in people with depression than in people without depression.

Cognitive theories

According to the cognitive view, people become depressed because of the way they think. They have a negative view of themselves and the situation they are in. Brown and Harris (1978) found evidence to support this view in their study 'The Social Origins of Depression', which was based on interviews with women living in Camberwell in London. They found that there was a link between depression and divorce or job loss, which are stressful life events. Some of the women were receiving treatment for depression and some were from the general population. The women who were receiving treatment for depression had suffered far more stressful events in the previous six months than those who were not.

Figure 18.6 Stressful events increase the likelihood of depression

> ## Remember
>
> Diathesis-stress suggests that it is a combination of biological factors and stressful life events that leads to depression. If a person has a biological predisposition to depression, but is able to cope with life events because they are not too stressful, they will probably avoid becoming depressed. However, if there are too many stressful events happening at the same time, the predisposition will trigger the mechanism for depression.

Brown and Harris identified a number of social vulnerability factors which increased the impact of stressful events and the likelihood of depression. Increased risks included such things as having three or more children under the age of 14 years at home; the loss of the individual's own mother before the age of 11; the lack of a social network allowing the individual to confide in others. This led Brown and Harris to conclude that a combination of vulnerability factors and stressful life events often lead to depression, because they lower a person's self-esteem and their psychological coping resources.

Evaluation

Aetiologies of unipolar depression

Recent research evidence supports earlier studies showing a genetic link for depression. So, for example, if one monozygotic twin suffers from depression, the other twin has a 70 per cent chance of also having the illness. Adoptive studies also support this finding as they have found that depressive illnesses among adoptive family members had little effect on the adopted child's risk of depression. However, children whose biological parents suffered from depression were three times more likely to suffer from depression.

There is also research that shows that people suffering from depression have an imbalance of neurotransmitters. Two such transmitters are serotonin and norepinephrine and there is evidence to show that a deficiency in serotonin may cause sleep problems, irritability and anxiety that are associated with depression. Norepinephrine regulates alertness and arousal and a decreased amount of this may contribute to the fatigue and depressed mood. It is unclear whether the imbalances in these cause the illness or if the disease causes the imbalance.

There are environmental situations, such as the stress of a break-up of a marriage, which may contribute to the cause of depression, especially in a vulnerable person.

Continuing research is helping us to understand the part played by genetics and environmental factors in depressed people.

Treatment of unipolar depression

Biological treatment

Antidepressant drugs are used to help elevate mood. The first antidepressant drugs discovered in the 1950s were monoamine oxidase inhibitors (MAOIs) and tricyclics. MAOIs were effective and immediately reduced the symptoms of depression, but, unfortunately, when taken with certain foods, such as cheese, they may increase blood pressure, which puts the patient in great danger. This means that people who take MAOIs must avoid a long list of foods in order to avoid increasing their blood pressure. Tricyclics are effective in tackling depression, but have problematic side effects such as drowsiness, constipation and dry mouth.

In the 1990s, selective serotonin reuptake inhibitor (SSRI) drugs were introduced. These increase the level of serotonin in the brain and therefore improve mood. They appear to have fewer side effects than the older antidepressants, although there are still some side effects, such as heartburn, drowsiness and difficulty having an orgasm.

Evaluation of biological treatment

- There is usually an improvement in psychological symptoms when using antidepressants, but they do take some time to work (up to a month, in some cases).

- Antidepressants may cause side effects and some drugs may be addictive, but this is less likely with modern antidepressants.

Cognitive treatment

At the heart of cognitive therapy is the assumption that irrational and negative thoughts and beliefs lead to psychological problems, especially depression. People with depression do tend to have a negative view of the self, overgeneralise negative events and have a pessimistic outlook on life, as they have a tendency to focus on problems and failures.

Cognitive therapy is used to help people with depression to identify and understand how these cognitive distortions may be affecting their lives. Beck *et al.* (1979) developed a therapy that challenges and reverses dysfunctional beliefs and attitudes; this therapy is called cognitive restructuring. Beck suggested that automatic thoughts are like a running dialogue we have with ourselves; individuals are taught to monitor these thoughts as the first step in identifying dysfunctional beliefs. The therapist then teaches the individual to challenge their beliefs by using evidence from their own life and personal experiences.

Evaluation of cognitive therapy

- A meta-analysis was carried out by Butler and Beck (2000), comparing studies across a range of disorders and therapies. They found that cognitive therapy had a relapse rate of 29.9 per cent and was more effective than antidepressant medication, which had a relapse rate of 60 per cent.

- There are no side effects with cognitive therapy.

- Some people suggest it is presumptuous of the therapist to decide what is rational and irrational for another person, without knowing their full circumstances.

Evaluation

Treatment of unipolar depression

Antidepressants are currently among the most prescribed drugs but surprisingly little research has been conducted on the effectiveness of the different treatments for depression. The way that therapy is evaluated to assess its effectiveness is in a controlled clinical trial in which patients are randomly assigned to treatment and control groups. A double-blind procedure is where the patient and the investigator are kept unaware of whether the patient is in the treatment or the control group. The control group usually receives a placebo and the clinical trial waits to see which group does better.

Antidepressant medicines are not always needed in mild or moderate depression. A large number of people with depression get better within six months without medication. Exercise without medication has been shown to be beneficial in some patients, especially those with mild depression.

The herb St John's wort is a complementary medicine with the active ingredient hypericum extract, thought to work in similar ways to antidepressant medicines by affecting the level of serotonin in the brain. The way it does this though is not clear. Some research has suggested that St John's wort is as effective as SSRIs in treating mild to moderate depression but other studies have failed to confirm this. Some people think that because St John's wort is a herb it has to be totally safe, but this is not always true as it contains chemicals which can cause problems in some people. St John's wort is known, for example, to react with some medications including the contraceptive pill.

In less severely depressed patients, placebo therapy is as effective as antidepressant drug therapy and as effective as weekly visits to a psychologist or psychiatrist for psychotherapy. With severely depressed patients, interpersonal therapy is moderately effective but the most effective treatment is antidepressant drug therapy. Cognitive therapy for severely depressed patients is no better than a placebo.

Summary

Issues of bias in diagnostic systems

Although there are standards in diagnostic methods, cultural and gender bias can be present and affect the diagnosis of psychological disorders.

Aetiologies of schizophrenia

There are biological and psychological explanations for schizophrenic behaviour. Physical evidence includes brain abnormality and chemical imbalance. Psychological approaches are divided into cognitive and psychodynamic.

Two treatments for schizophrenia

Biological therapy of antipsychotic drugs and cognitive behavioural therapy in various combinations have been used to treat schizophrenia successfully.

Abnormal psychology

Aetiologies of unipolar depression

A combination of biological factors and stressful life events lead to depression. Depression is a prevalent problem. According to the cognitive view, people become depressed because of the negative way they think.

Two treatments for unipolar depression

Antidepressant drugs are used to help elevate mood. Cognitive therapy is used to help individuals with depression to identify and understand how irrational and negative thoughts and beliefs may be affecting their lives.

Exam focus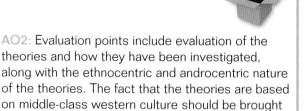

Exam structure: Chapters 14–18

Chapters 14 to 18 relate to section C on the PY 4 exam paper.

Candidates are expected to answer at least one question from this section.

Candidates are expected to be able to describe and evaluate, as appropriate, theories/explanations, research methods, findings, conclusions, usefulness and impact on society.

The question is marked out of 25: AO1 = 10, AO2 = 15.

AO1: **Knowledge and understanding of science and how science works**

AO2: **Application of knowledge and understanding of science and how science works**

Basically, AO1 is describing theories and/or research, while AO2 is evaluating any theories and/or research by referring to research evidence. The question is clearly weighted more towards AO2, evaluating said theories and/or studies, so candidates should not spend too long describing studies and/or research; the bulk of the essay should be evaluating these applications.

Example questions

AO1: **Knowledge and understanding – 10 marks**
AO2: **Evaluation – 15 marks**

Example question: Discuss lifespan theories of development.

AO1: You could receive credit for the description of whole lifespan models, such as those of Erikson or Levinson, explanations of theories of adolescence, such as those of Blos and Marcia, or even theories of bereavement and death. AO1 could be covered in depth by two or three of the theories, or you could take a broad view and mention all of them in less depth.

AO2: Evaluation points include evaluation of the theories and how they have been investigated, along with the ethnocentric and androcentric nature of the theories. The fact that the theories are based on middle-class western culture should be brought into the argument.

Example question: Describe and evaluate theories of profiling

AO1: You could receive credit for a description of the FBI approach, with its database of offenders, and of the UK forensic approach, which is more scientific.

AO2: Evaluation points include evaluation of profiling, how useful it has been (or not) and how the scientific basis of most profiling is weak. Use the research of Snook (2008) to show the value of profiling, and the research of Kocsis (2003) to demonstrate that profilers are able to give more information about a crime scene.

Example question: Describe and evaluate treatment for unipolar depression.

AO1: You could receive credit for description of biologically based treatments, such as antidepressants and electroconvulsive therapy, cognitive-based therapies, psychodynamic therapies and the use of physical exercise.

AO2: Evaluation points include comparing treatments and their effectiveness, cultural variations in treatments, and the strengths and weaknesses of the treatments.

Exam tips

1 Read the question carefully.
2 Clearly describe and evaluate the application.
3 Refer to evidence that supports the application – analyse and criticise this evidence.
4 Watch the time – spend about 40 minutes on each question.

References

Abbey, A., Andrews, F.M., Halman, L.J. (1994) Infertility and parenthood: Does becoming a parent increase well-being? *Journal of Consultant Clinical Psychology*, 62(2), 398–403.

Ackerman, A.M., McMahon, P.M. and Fehr, L.A. (1984) Defendant characteristics and judgment behaviours of adolescent mock jurors. *Journal of Youth and Adolescence*, 13(2), 123–30.

Adam, K. and Oswald, I. (1983) Protein synthesis, bodily renewal and the sleep-wake cycle. *Clinical Science*, 65(6), 561–7.

Ainsworth, M.D.S. and Bell, S.M. (1970) Attachment, exploration and separation: Illustrated by the behaviour of one-year-olds in a strange situation. *Child Development*, 41, 49–65.

Allcock, S.J. and Hulme, J.A. (2010) Learning styles in the classroom: Educational benefit or planning exercise? *Psychology Teaching Review*, 16(2), 67–77.

Andrews-Zwilling, Y., Bien-Ly, N., Xu, Q., Li, G., Bernardo, A., Yoon, S.Y., Zwilling, D., Yan, T.X., Chen, L. and Huang, Y. (2010) Apolipoprotein E4 causes age- and Tau-dependent impairment of GABAergic interneurons, leading to learning and memory deficits in mice. *Journal of Neuroscience*, 30(41), 13707–17.

Asch, S.E. (1951) Effects of group pressure upon the modification and distortion of judgment. In Guetzkow, H. (ed.). *Groups, Leadership and Men* (Carnegie Press, Pittsburgh, PA), pp. 177–90.

Asch, S.E. (1956) Studies of independence and conformity: A minority of one against a unanimous majority. *Psychological Monographs*, 70 (whole no. 416).

Ashton, H. and Golding, J.F. (1989) Smoking: Motivation and models. In Ney, T. and Gale, A. (eds.). *Smoking and Human Behaviour* (Wiley, Chichester).

Atkinson, R.C. and Shiffrin, R.M. (1968) Human memory: A proposed system and its control processes. In Spence, K.W. and Spence, J.T. (eds). *The Psychology of Learning and Motivation* (Academic Press, New York), vol. II, pp. 89–195.

Baddeley, A.D. (1966) The influence of acoustic and semantic similarities on long-term memory for word sequences. *Quarterly Journal of Experimental Psychology*, 18, 302–9.

Baddeley, A.D. and Hitch, G.J.L (1974) Working memory. In Bower, G.A. (ed.). *The Psychology of Learning and Motivation: Advances in Research and Theory* (Academic Press, New York), vol. VIII, pp. 47–89.

Bahrick, H.P., Bahrick, P.O. and Wittinger, R.P. (1975) Fifty years of memory for names and faces: A cross-sectional approach. *Journal of Experimental Psychology: General*, 104, 54–75.

Bandura, A. (1977) Self-efficacy: Toward a unifying theory of behavioural change. *Psychological Review*, 84, 191–215.

Bandura, A., Ross, D. and Ross, S.A. (1961) Transmission of aggression through imitation of aggressive models. *Journal of Abnormal and Social Psychology*, 63, 575–82.

Bass, B.M. (1990) *Bass and Stogdill's Handbook of Leadership* (The Free Press, New York).

Bateson, P. (1986) When to experiment on animals. *New Scientist*, 109, 30–2.

Beck, A.T., Rush, A.J., Shaw, B.F. and Emery, G. (1979) *Cognitive Therapy of Depression* (Guilford Press, New York).

Bergeron, C.E. and Mckelvie, S.J. (2004) Effects of defendant age on severity of punishment for different crimes. *Journal of Social Psychology*, 144(1), 75–90.

Berkowitz, L. (1993) *Aggression: Its Causes, Consequences, and Control* (Temple University Press, Philadelphia).

Berry, J. (1969) On cross-cultural comparability. *International Journal of Psychology*, 4, 119–28.

Berscheid, E., Dion, K., Walster, E. and Walster, G.W. (1971) Physical attractiveness and dating choice: A test of the matching hypothesis. *Journal of Experimental Social Psychology*, 7(2), 173–89.

Berthoud, R. (2000) *Family Formation in Multicultural Britain: Three Patterns of Diversity*. Institute for Social and Economic Research, Working Paper 2000-34.

Blos, P. (1967) The Second Individuation Process of Adolescence. *The Psychoanalytic Study of the Child*, 22, 162–186.

Bouchard, T.J. and McGue, M. (1981) Familial studies of intelligence: A review. *Science*, 212(4498), 1055–9.

Bowlby, J. (1944) Forty-four thieves: Their characters and home life. *International Journal of Psycho-analysis*, 25, 19–52 and 107–27.

Bowlby, J. (1951) *Maternal Care and Mental Health* (World Health Organization, Geneva).

Brady, J.V. (1958) Ulcers in executive monkeys. *Scientific American*, 199, 95–100.

Brawley, L.R., Carron, A.V. and Widmeyer, W.N. (1987) Assessing the cohesion of teams: Validity of the Group Environment Questionnaire. *Journal of Sport Psychology*, 9(3), 275–94.

Britton, P. (1992) *Review of Offender Profiling* (Home Office, London).

Brown, G.W. and Harris, T.O. (1978) *Social Origins of Depression: A Study of Psychiatric Disorder in Women* (Tavistock Publications, London).

Brown, R. and Kulik, J. (1977) Flashbulb memories. *Cognition*, 5(1), 73–99.

Burman, B. and Margolin, G. (1992) Analysis of the association between marital relationships and health problems: An interactional perspective. *Psychological Bulletin*, 112, 39–63.

Buss, D.M. (1990) International preferences in selecting mates: A study of 37 cultures. *Journal of Cross-Cultural Psychology*, 21(1), 5–47.

Butler, A.C. and Beck, J.S. (2000) Cognitive therapy outcomes: A review of meta-analyses. *Journal of the Norwegian Psychological Association*, 37, 1–9.

Cardwell, M. (2003) *The Complete A–Z Psychology Handbook* (Hodder and Stoughton, London).

Cardwell, M., Clark, L. and Meldrum, C. (1999) *Psychology for A Level* (Collins, London).

Cardwell, M., Clark, L. and Meldrum, C. (2001) *Psychology for AS Level* (Collins, London).

Castellow, W.A., Wuensch, K.L. and Moore, C.H. (1990) Effects of physical attractiveness of the plaintiff and defendant in sexual harassment judgments. *Journal of Social Behavior and Personality*, 5, 547–62.

Clifford, B.R. and Scott, J. (1978) Individual and situational factors in eyewitness testimony. *Journal of Applied Psychology*, 63(3), 352–9.

Cloninger, C.R. (1986) A unified biosocial theory of personality and its role in the development of anxiety states. *Psychiatric Developments*, 4(3), 167–226.

Cohen, C.E. (1981) Person categories and social perception: Testing some boundary conditions of the processing effects of prior knowledge. *Journal of Personality and Social Psychology*, 40, 441–52.

Cole, M. and Cole, S.R. (1993) *The Development of Children* (W.H. Freeman and Company, New York).

Conrad, R. (1964) Acoustic confusions in immediate memory. *British Journal of Psychology*, 55, 75–84.

Craik, F.I.M. and Lockhart, R.S. (1972) Levels of processing: A framework for memory research. *Journal of Verbal Learning and Verbal Behavior*, 11, 671–84.

Craik, F.I.M. and Tulving, E. (1975) Depth of processing and the retention of words in episodic memory. *Journal of Experimental Psychology: General*, 104(3), 268–94.

Crow, T.J. (1985) The two syndrome concept: Origins and current status. *Schizophrenia Bulletin*, 11(3), 471–86.

Curtiss, S. (1977) *Genie: A Psycholinguistic Study of a Modern-day 'Wild Child'* (Academic Press, London).

Curtiss, S. (1989) The independence and task-specificity of language. In Bornstein, M.H. and Bruner, J.S. (eds.). *Interaction in Human Development* (Lawrence Erlbaum Associates, Inc., Hillsdale, NJ), pp. 105–37.

Daley, A. and O'Gara, A. (1998) Age, gender and motivation for participation in extracurricular physical activities in secondary school adolescents. *European Physical Education Review*, 4(1), 47–53.

Davies, G.M. (1996) Mistaken identification: Where law meets psychology head on. *The Howard Journal of Criminal Justice*, 35, 232–41.

Davison, G.C. and Neale, J.M. (1998) *Abnormal Psychology*, 7th edn (Wiley, New York).

Deutsch, M. and Gerard, H.B. (1955) A study of normative and informational social influences upon individual judgment. *Journal of Abnormal and Social Psychology*, 51(3), 629–36.

Devlin Report (1976) Report of the Committee on Evidence of Identification in Criminal Cases. Command Paper 338 134/135, 42.

Dobbs, L.W. and Sears, R.R. (1939) Factors determining substitute behavior and the overt expression of aggression. *Journal of Abnormal and Social Psychology*, 34, 293–313.

Dollard, J., Doob, L., Miller, N., Mowrer, O. and Sears, R. (1939) *Frustration and Aggression* (Yale University Press, New Haven, CT).

Duck, S.W. (1982) *Personal Relationships 4: Dissolving Personal Relationships* (Academic Press, London and New York).

Eich, E. (1995) Searching for mood dependent memory. *Psychological Science*, 6(2), 67–75.

Erikson, E.H. (1968) *Identity: Youth and Crisis* (Norton, New York).

Escobar, J.I. and Vega, W.A. (2006) Cultural issues and psychiatric diagnosis: Providing a general background for considering substance use diagnoses. *Addiction*, 101, Suppl. 1, 40–7.

Eysenck, H. (1964) *Crime and Personality* (Routledge and Kegan Paul, London).

Eysenck, M.W. (2005) *Psychology for A2 Level* (Psychology Press, Hove).

Eysenck, M.W. (2005) *Psychology for AS Level* (Psychology Press, Hove).

Farrington, D.P. (2002) Developmental criminology and risk-focussed prevention. In Maguire, M., Morgan, R. and Reiner, R. (eds.). *The Oxford Handbook of Criminology*, 3rd edn (Oxford University Press), pp. 657–701.

Folkard, S., Hume, K.I., Minors, D.S., Waterhouse, J.M. and Watson, F.L. (1985) Independence of the circadian rhythm in alertness from the sleep/wake cycle. *Nature*, 313(6004), 678–9.

Freud, S. (1912–13) *Totem und Tabu. Einige Übereinstimmungen im Seelenleben der Wilden und der Neurotiker* (Hugo Heller, Leipzig and Vienna). Appeared with the title *Über einige Übereinstimmungen im Seelenleben der Wilden und der Neurotiker* as a series of four essays in *Imago* ('Die Inzestscheu', I, 1 (1912), 17–33; 'Das Tabu und die Ambivalenz der Gefühlsregungen', I, 3 (1912), 213–27, I, 4, 301–33; 'Animismus, Magie und Allmacht der Gedanken', II, 1 (1913), 1–21; 'Die infantile Widerkehr des Totemismus', II, 4 (1913), 357–408). English translation (1990) *Totem and Taboo*. Standard Edition (W.W. Norton & Co., Inc., New York).

Freud, S. (1933) *New Introductory Lectures in Psychoanalysis* (Norton, New York).

Freud, S. (1971) *The Psychopathology of Everyday Life*, trans. A. Tyson (W.W. Norton & Co., Inc., New York).

Friedman, C.P. and Stritter, F.T. (1976). An empirical inventory comparing instructional preferences of medical and other professional students. Research in Medical Education Proceedings 15th Annual Conference (San Francisco, CA), pp. 63–8.

Friedman, M. and Rosenman, R.H. (1974) *Type A Behaviour and Your Heart* (Knopf, New York).

Frith, C.D. and Corcoran, R. (1996) Exploring 'theory of mind' in people with schizophrenia. *Psychological Medicine*, 26, 521–30.

Frith, C.D. and Done, D.J. (1983) Stereotyped responding by schizophrenic patients on a two-choice guessing task. *Psychological Medicine*, 13, 779–86.

Frith, C.D. and Done, D.J. (1986) Routes to action in reaction time tasks. *Psychological Research*, 48, 169–77.

Frith, C.D., Friston, K.J., Herold, S., Silbersweig, D., Fletcher, P., Cahill, C., Dolan, R.J., Frackowiak, R.S. and Liddle, P.F. (1995) Regional brain activity in chronic schizophrenic patients during the performance of a verbal fluency task. *British Journal of Psychiatry*, 167, 343–49.

Fromm-Reichmann, F. (1948) Schizophrenia: The critical review of recent adoption, twin and family studies of schizophrenia – behavioral genetics perspectives. *Schizophrenia Bulletin*, 2, 360–98.

Fullin, C. and Mills, B.D. (1995) *Attribution Theory in Sport: Problems and Solutions* (Education Resources Information Center).

Gall, T., Evans, L., David, R. and Howard, J. (1997) The retirement adjustment process: Changes in the well-being of male retirees across time. *Journal of Gerontology B: Psychological Sciences and Social Sciences*, 52B(3), 110–17.

Ghodsian, M. and Lambert, L. (1978) Mum and Dad are not so bad. Sixteen year olds' views of how they get on with their parents. *AEP Journal*, 4(7), 27–33.

Ghuman, P.A.S. (1994) *Coping with Two Cultures: A Study of British Asians and Indo-Canadian Adolescents* (Multilingual Matters, Clevedon).

Godden, D.R. and Baddeley, A.D. (1975) Context-dependent memory in two natural environments: On land and underwater. *British Journal of Psychology*, 66(3), 325–31.

Gold, D.R., Rogacz, S., Bock, N., Tosteson, T.D., Baum, T.H., Speizer, F.E. and Czeisler, C.A. (1992) Rotating shift work, sleep, and accidents related to sleepiness in hospital nurses. *American Journal of Public Health*, 82(7), 1011–14.

Goldstein, A.R., Glick, B., Irwin, M.J., McCartney, C. and Rubama, I. (1989) *Reducing Delinquency: Intervention in the Community* (Pergamon, New York).

Gottesman, I.I. (1993) Origins of schizophrenia: Past as prologue. In Plomin, R. and McClearn, G.E. (eds). *Nature, Nurture and Psychology* (American Psychological Association, Washington, DC), pp. 231–44.

Gottman, J.M. and Levenson, R.W. (1985) A valid procedure for obtaining self-report of affect in marital interaction. *Journal of Consulting and Clinical Psychology*, 53, 151–60.

Gottman, J.M., Levenson, R.W., Swanson, C., Swanson, K., Tyson, R. and Yoshimoto, D. (2003) Observing gay, lesbian and heterosexual couples' relationships: Mathematical modeling of conflict interactions. *Journal of Homosexuality*, 45(1), 65–91.

Gottsman, I.I. (1991) *Schizophrenia Genesis* (Freeman, New York).

Gross, R.D. (1995) *Themes, Issues and Debates in Psychology* (Hodder and Stoughton, London).

Grove, M.W., Eckert, E.D., Heston, L., Bouchard, T.J., Segal, N. and Lykken, D.T. (1990) Heritability of substance abuse and antisocial behaviour: A study of monozygotic twins reared apart. *Biological Psychiatry*, 59, 48–57.

Guarnaccia, P.J. and Rogler, L.H. (1999) Research on culture-bound syndromes: New directions. *American Journal of Psychiatry*, 156(9), 1322–7.

Gupta, U. and Singh, P. (1982) An exploratory study of love and liking and type of marriage. *Indian Journal of Applied Psychology*, 19, 92–7.

Han, C., Mcgue, M.K., Iacono, W.G. (1999) Lifetime tobacco, alcohol and other substance use in adolescent Minnesota twins: Univariate and multi-variate behavioral genetic analyses. *Addiction*, 94(7), 981–93.

Harlow, H.F. (1959) Love in infant monkeys. *Scientific American*, 200, 68–74.

Harrington, L., Affleck, G., Urrows, S., Tennen, H., Higgins, P. and Zautra, A. (1993) Temporal covariation of soluble interleukin-2 receptor levels, daily stress, and disease activity in rheumatoid arthritis. *Arthritis and Rheumatism*, 36(2), 199–203.

Haste, H. (2005) Joined-up texting: The role of mobile phones in young people's lives. *Nestlé Social Research Programme, Report 3*, February. Fieldwork conducted by MORI.

Hebb, D.O. (1949) *The Organization of Behavior* (Wiley & Sons, New York).

Heimlich, J.E. and Norland, E. (2002) Teaching style: Where are we now? *New Directions for Adult and Continuing Education*, 93, 17–25.

Hilgard, E.R. (1986) *Divided Consciousness: Multiple Controls in Human Thought and Action* (Wiley, New York).

Hill, C.T., Rubin, Z. and Peplau, L.A. (1976) Breakups before marriage: The end of 103 affairs. *Journal of Social Issues*, 32(1), 147–68.

Hofling, K.C., Brotzman, E., Dalrymple, S., Graves, N. and Pierce, C.M. (1966) An experimental study in the nurse–physician relationship. *Journal of Nervous and Mental Disorders*, 143, 171–80.

Hofstede, G. (1980) *Culture's Consequences: International Differences in Work-related Values* (Sage, Beverly Hills, CA).

Holland, A.J., Sicotte, N. and Treasure, J. (1988) Anorexia nervosa: Evidence for a genetic basis. *Journal of Psychosomatic Research*, 32, 561–72.

House, J.S., Landis, K.R. and Umberson, D. (1988) Social relationships and health. *Science*, 241(4865), 540–5.

Hui, C.H and Triandis, H.C. (1986) A study of cross-cultural researchers, *Journal of Cross-Cultural Psychology*, 17(2), 225–48.

Ingoldsby, B.B. (1995) Poverty and patriarchy in Latin America. In Ingoldsby,

B.B. and Smith, S. (eds). *Families in Multicultural Perspective* (Guilford Press, New York), pp. 335–51.

Jacobs, P.A., Brunton, M., Melville, M., Brittain, R.P. and McClemont, W.F. (1965) Aggressive behaviour, mental sub-normality and the XYY male. *Nature*, 208(5017), 1351–2.

Jensen, A.R. (1969) How much can we boost IQ and scholastic achievement? *Harvard Educational Review*, 39, 1–123.

Jensen, A.R. (1980) *Bias in Mental Testing* (Methuen, London).

Kalven, II. Jr. and Zeisel, H. (1966) *The American Jury* (Little, Brown, & Co., Boston, MA).

Kaplan, M.F. and Miller, C.E. (1987) Group decision making and normative versus informational influence: Effects of type of issue and assigned decision rule. *Journal of Personality and Social Psychology*, 53(2), 306–13.

Kety, S.S. (1988) Schizophrenic illness in the families of schizophrenic adoptees: Findings from the Danish national sample. *Schizophrenia Bulletin*, 14, 217–22.

Kiecolt-Glaser, J.K. and Glaser, R. (1986) Psychological influences on immunity. *Psychosomatics*, 27, 621–4.

Klein, R. and Armitage, R. (1979) Rhythms in human performance: 2-hour oscillations in cognitive style. *Science*, 204, 1326–8.

Kleitman, N.J. (1963) *Sleep and Wakefulness* (University of Chicago Press).

Kocsis, R.N. (2003) An empirical assessment of content in criminal psychological profiles. *International Journal of Offender Therapy and Comparative Criminology*, 47(1), 37–46.

Kohlberg, L. (1958) The development of modes of thinking and choices in years 10 to 16. PhD dissertation (University of Chicago).

Kohlberg, L. (1969) *Stages in the Development of Moral Thoughts and Action* (Holt, New York).

Kohlberg, L. (1976) Moral stages and moralization: The cognitive-developmental approach to socialization. In Lickona, J., *Moral Development Behavior: Theory, Research, and Social Issues* (Harper & Row, New York).

Koka, A. and Hein, V. (2003) Perceptions of teacher's feedback and learning environment as predictors of intrinsic motivation in physical education. *Psychology of Sport and Exercise*, 4(4), 333–46.

Kolb, D.A. (1976) *The Learning Style Inventory: Technical Manual* (McBer, Boston, MA).

Koob, G.F. and Le Moal, M. (1997) Drug abuse: Hedonic homeostatic dysregulation. *Science*, 278(5335), 52–8.

Kuhn, T.S. (1970) *The Structure of Scientific Revolutions*, 2nd edn (University of Chicago Press).

LaBerge, S. (1985) *Lucid Dreaming* (J.P. Tarcher, Los Angeles).

Lagnado, D.A. and Harvey, N. (2008) The impact of discredited evidence. *Psychonomic Bulletin & Review*, 15, 1166–73.

Landers, D.M. and Petruzzello, S.J. (1994) Physical activity, fitness and anxiety. In Bouchard, C., Shepard, R.J. and Stephens, T. (eds.). *Physical Activity, Fitness and Health* (Human Kinetics, Champaign, IL), pp. 868–82.

Landis, C. (1924) *Studies of Emotional Reactions: General Behavior and Facial Expression* (Williams & Wilkins, Baltimore, MD).

LeBlanc, A., Liu, H., Goodyer, C., Bergeron, C. and Hammond, J. (1999) Caspase-6: Role in apoptosis of human neurons, amyloidogenesis, and Alzheimer's disease. *Journal of Biological Chemistry*, 274, 23426–36.

Lee, L. (1984) Sequences in separation: A framework for investigating endings of the personal (romantic) relationship. *Journal of Social and Personal Relationships*, 1(1), 49–73.

Levinger, G. and Clark, J. (1961) Emotional factors in the forgetting of word associations. *Journal of Abnormal and Social Psychology*, 62, 99–105.

Lindström, L.H., Gefvert, O., Hagberg, G., Lundberg, T., Bergström, M., Hartvig, P. and Långström, B. (1999). Increased dopamine synthesis rate in medial prefrontal cortex and striatum in schizophrenia indicated by L-(β-^{11}C) DOPA and PET. *Biological Psychiatry*, 46, 681–8.

Loftus, E.F. and Palmer, J.C. (1974) Reconstruction of automobile destruction: An example of the interaction between language and memory. *Journal of Verbal Learning and Verbal Behavior*, 13, 585–9.

Lombroso, C. (1876) *L'Uomo Delinquente* (Hoepli, Milan).

McAllister, L.W., Stachowiak, J.G., Baer, D.M. and Conderman, L. (1969) The application of operant conditioning techniques in a secondary school classroom. *Journal of Applied Behavior Analysis*, 2(4), 277–85.

McClintock, M.K. (1971) Menstrual synchrony and suppression. *Nature*, 229(5282), 244–5.

McDougall, R.M., Barnett, R.M., Ashurst, B. and Willis, B. (1987) Anger control. In McGurk, B., Thornton, D. and Williams, M. (eds.). *Applying Psychology to Imprisonment* (HMSO, London), pp. 303–13.

McGeogh, J.A. and McDonald, W.T. (1931) Meaningful relation and retroactive inhibition. *American Journal of Psychology*, 43, 579–88.

McGuffin, P., Katz, R., Watkins, S. and Rutherford, J. (1996) A hospital-based twin register of the heritability of DSM-IV unipolar depression. *Archives of General Psychiatry*, 53, 129–36.

Mackintosh, N.J. and Mascie-Taylor, C.G.N. (1985) The I.Q. question. In *Education for All* (Chairman Lord Swann). The Report of the Committee of Inquiry into the Education of Children from Ethnic Minority Groups (HMSO, London), pp. 126–63.

MacLeod, C. Mathews, A. and Tata, P. (1986) Attentional bias in emotional disorders. *Journal of Abnormal Psychology*, 95(1), 15–20.

Mein, G., Martikainen, P., Hemingway, H., Stansfeld, S. and Marmot, M. (2003) Is retirement good or bad for mental and physical health functioning? Whitehall II longitudinal study of civil servants. *Journal of Epidemiology and Community Health*, 57, 46–9 (doi:10.1136/jech.57.1.46).

Michaels, J.W., Blommel, J.M., Brocato, R.M., Linkous, R.A. and Rowe, J.S. (1982) Social facilitation and inhibition in a natural setting. *Replications in Social Psychology*, 2, 21–4.

Miles, L.E., Raynal, D.M. and Wilson, M.A. (1977) Blind man living in normal society has circadian rhythms of 24.9 hours. *Science*, 198, 421–3.

Milgram, S. (1963) Behavioural study of obedience. *Journal of Abnormal and Social Psychology*, 67, 371–8.

Miller, N.E., Sears, R.R., Mowrer, O.H., Doob, L.W. and Dollard, J. (1941) The frustration–aggression hypothesis. *Psychology Review*, 48, 337–42.

Montemayor, R. (1983) Parents and adolescents in conflict: All families some of the time and some families most of the time. *Journal of Early Adolescence*, 3, 83–103.

Moscovici, S. (1980) Towards a theory of conversion behaviour. In Berkowitz, L. (ed.). *Advances in Experimental Social Psychology*, vol. XIII (Academic Press, New York), pp. 209–39.

Mugny, G. and Papastamou, S. (1980) When rigidity does not fail: Individualization and psychologization as resistances to the diffusion of minority innovations. *European Journal of Social Psychology*, 10, 43–61.

Nazroo, J.Y. (1997) *The Health of Britain's Ethnic Minorities: Findings From a National Survey* (Policy Studies Institute, London).

Neisser, U. and Harsch, N. (1992) Phantom flashbulbs: False recollections of hearing the news about *Challenger*. In Winograd, E. and Neisser, U. (eds.). *Affect and Accuracy in Recall: Studies of 'Flashbulb' Memories* (Cambridge University Press, New York), pp. 9–31.

Nemeth, C. (1977) Interactions between jurors as a function of majority vs. unanimity decision rules. *Journal of Applied Social Psychology*, 7, 38–56.

Nicholson, P. (1995) The menstrual cycle, science and femininity: Assumptions underlying menstrual cycle research. *Social Science & Medicine*, 41, 779–84.

Nosek, B., Smyth, F., Sriram, N., Lindner, N., Devos, T., Ayala, A., Bar-Anan, Y., Bergh, R., Cai, H., Gonsalkorale, K., Kesebir, S., Maliszewski, N., Neto, F., Olli, E., Park, J., Schnabel, K., Shiomura, K., Tulbure, B., Wiers, R., Somogyi, M., Akrami, N., Ekehammar, B., Vianello, M., Banaji, M. and Greenwald, A. (2009) National differences in gender: Science stereotypes predict national sex differences in science and math achievement. *Proceedings of the National Academy of Sciences*, 106 (26), 10593–7.

Novak, R.D., Smolensky, M.H., Fairchild, E.J. and Reves, R.R. (1990) Shiftwork and industrial injuries at a chemical plant in southeast Texas. *Chronobiology International*, 7(2), 155–64.

Oakland, T., Black, J.L., Stanford, G., Nussbaum, N.L. and Balise, R.R. (1998)

An evaluation of the dyslexia training program: A multisensory method for promoting reading in students with reading disabilities. *Journal of Learning Disabilities*, 31(2), 140–7.

Odinot, G., Wolters, G. and van Koppen, P.J. (2009) Eyewitness memory of a supermarket robbery: A case study of accuracy and confidence after three months. *Law and Human Behavior*, 33, 506–14.

O'Neill, S.T. and Parrott, A.C. (1992) Stress and arousal in sedative and stimulant cigarette smokers. *Psychopharmacology*, 107, 442–6.

Paul, G.L. and Lentz, R.J. (1977) *Psychosocial Treatment of Chronic Mental Patients: Milieu Versus Social-Learning Programs* (Harvard University Press, Cambridge, MA).

Pavlov, I.P. (1927) *Conditioned Reflexes* (Oxford University Press).

Penedo, F.J. and Dahn, J.R. (2005) Exercise and well-being: A review of mental and physical health benefits associated with physical activity. *Current Opinion in Psychiatry*, 18(2), 189–93.

Pennington, N. and Hastie, R. (1986) Evidence evaluation in complex decision making. *Journal of Personality and Social Psychology*, 51(2), 242–58.

Peterson, L.R. and Peterson, M.J. (1959) Short-term retention of individual verbal items. *Journal of Experimental Psychology*, 59(58), 193–8.

Pointer, S.C. and Bond, N.W. (1998) Context-dependent memory: Colour versus odour. *Chemical Senses*, 23, 359–62.

Popper, K. (1959) *The Logic of Scientific Discovery* (Basic Books, New York).

Pozzulo, J., Dempsey, D., Maeder, E. and Allen, L. (2010) The effects of victim gender, defendant gender, and defendant age on juror decision making. *Criminal Justice and Behavior*, 37(1), 47–63.

Raine, A., Buchsbaum, M. and LaCasse, L. (1997). Brain abnormalities in murderers indicated by positron emission tomography. *Biological Psychiatry*, 42(6), 495–508.

Rees, T., Ingledew, D.K. and Hardy, L. (2005) Attribution in sport psychology: Seeking congruence between theory, research and practice. *Psychology of Sport and Exercise*, 6(2), 189–204.

Regoli, R. and Hewitt, J. (1994) *Delinquency in Society*, 2nd edn (McGraw Hill, Boston, MA).

Riechmann, S.W. and Grasha, A.F. (1974) A rational approach to developing and assessing the construct validity of a student learning styles scales instrument. *Journal of Psychology*, 87, 213–23.

Rezler, A.G. and Rezmovich, V. (1981) The learning preference inventory. *Journal of Allied Health*, 10, 28–34.

Rhawn, J. (1999) Environmental influences on neural plasticity, the limbic system, emotional development and attachment. *Child Psychiatry and Human Development*, 29, 187–203.

Roddenberry, C. and Burton, R.M. (2000) Testing the impact of biased jurors on the efficiency of the story model of jury deliberation process. CASOS conference (Carnegie Mellon University, Pittsburgh, PA).

Rose Review (2009) *Identifying and Teaching Children and Young People with Dyslexia and Literacy Difficulties* (DCSF, Nottingham) (also available at www.teachernet.gov.uk/publications).

Rosenthal, R. and Jacobson, L. (1968) *Pygmalion in the Classroom* (Holt, Rinehart & Winston, New York).

Rusbult, C. (1983) A longitudinal test of the investment model: The development (and deterioration) of satisfaction and commitment in heterosexual involvements. *Journal of Personality and Social Psychology*, 45, 172–86.

Rutter, M., Tizard, J., Yule, W., Graham, P. and Whitmore, K. (1976) Isle of Wight studies, 1964–74. *Psychological Medicine*, 6, 313–32.

Sarbin, T.R. and Slagle, R.W. (1979) Hypnosis and psychosociological outcomes. In Fromm, E. and Shor, R. (eds.). *Hypnosis: Developments in Research and New Perspectives* (Aldine, New York), pp. 81–103.

Scarr, S. and Weinberg, R.A. (1983) The Minnesota adoption studies: Genetic differences and malleability. *Child Development*, 54, 260–7.

Schiffer, A.A., Pedersen, S.S., Widdershoven, J.W., Hendriks, E.H., Winter, J.B. and Denollet, J. (2005) The distressed (type D) personality is independently associated with impaired health status and increased depressive symptoms in chronic heart failure. *European Journal of Cardiovascular Prevention and Rehabilitation*, 12(4), 341–6.

Schwartz, B. and Barsky, S.F. (1977) The home advantage. *Social Forces*, 55, 641–61.

Segraves, R.T. (1985) *Medical Aspects of Human Sexuality* (Hospital Publications, Inc.).

Seligman, M.E.P. (1974) Depression and learned helplessness. In Friedman, R.J. and Katz, M.M. (eds.). *The Psychology of Depression: Contemporary Theory and Research* (Winston Wiley, Washington, DC).

Selye, H. (1936) A syndrome produced by diverse nocuous agents. *Nature*, 138, 32.

Sheldon, W. (1940) *The Varieties of Human Physique: An Introduction to Constitutional Psychology* (Harper, New York).

Sherif, M. (1935) A study of some factors in perception. *Archives of Psychology*, 27, 187.

Shields, J. (1962) *Monozygotic Twins* (Oxford University Press).

Shmeck, R.R., Ribich, F.D. and Ramania, H. (1977) Development of a self-report inventory for assessment of individual differences in learning processes. *Applied Psychological Measurement*, 46, 753–60.

Sigall, H. and Ostrove, N. (1975) Beautiful but dangerous: Effects of offender attractiveness and nature of the crime on juridic judgment. *Journal of Personality and Social Psychology*, 31, 410–14.

Silberg, J., Pickles, A., Rutter, M., Hewitt, J., Simonoff, E., Maes, H., Carbonneau, R., Murrelle, L., Foley, D. and Eaves, L. (1999) The influence of genetic factors and life stress on depression among adolescent girls. *Archives of General Psychiatry*, 56, 225–32.

Silverman, I. (1977) *The Human Subject in the Psychological Laboratory* (Pergamon, Oxford).

Skinner, B.F. (1938) *The Behaviour of Organisms* (Appleton-Century-Crofts, New York).

Smith, P. and Bond, M.H. (1993) *Social Psychology Across Cultures: Analysis and Perspectives* (Harvester Wheatsheaf, New York).

Snook, B. (2008) What's behind the smoke and mirrors? *Criminal Justice and Behavior*, 35(10), 1257–76.

Spanos, N.P. (1986) Hypnotic behavior: A social-psychological interpretation of amnesia, analgesia, and 'trance logic'. *Behavioral and Brain Sciences*, 9, 449–67.

Squire, C. and Newhouse, J. (2003) Racial effects in sentencing: The influence of facial features and skin tone. *UW-L Journal of Undergraduate Research*, VI, 1–5.

Steinberg, L. (1981) Transformations in family relations at puberty. *Developmental Psychology*, 17(6), 833–40.

Steinberg, L. (1990) Autonomy, conflict, and harmony in the family relationship. In Feldman, S.S. and Elliott. G.R. (eds.). *At the Threshold: The Developing Adolescent* (Harvard University Press, Cambridge, MA), pp. 255–76.

Stephens, T. (1988) Physical activity and mental health in the United States and Canada: Evidence from four population surveys. *Preventive Medicine*, 17(1), 35–47.

Stewart, J.E. (1985) The attraction–leniency effect in the courtroom. *Journal of Social Psychology*, 125(3), 373–8.

Stubbe, J.H., de Moora, M.H.M., Boomsmaa, D.I. and de Geus, E.J.C. (2007) The association between exercise participation and well-being: A co-twin study. *Preventive Medicine*, 44(2), 148–52.

Suler, J.R. (2004) The psychology of text relationships. In Kraus, R., Zack, J. and Striker, G. (eds). *Hypotheses about Online Text Relationships in Online Counselling: A Manual for Mental Health Professionals* (Elsevier Academic Press, London).

Tamir, P. and Cohen, S. (1980) Factors that correlate with cognitive preferences of medical school teachers. *Journal of Educational Research*, 74, 67–74.

Thibaut, J.W. and Kelley, H.H. (1959) *The Social Psychology of Groups* (Wiley, New York).

Twining, K. (1998) *Success in Psychology* (John Murray, London).

Underwood, B.J. and Postman, L. (1960) Extra experimental sources of interference in forgetting. *Psychology Review*, 67, 73–95.

Valentine, E.R. (1982) *Conceptual Issues in Psychology* (Routledge, London).

Walster, E., Aronson, V., Abrahams, D. and Rottmann, L. (1966) Importance of physical attractiveness in dating behavior. *Journal of Personality and Social Psychology*, 4, 508–16.

Watson, J.B. and Raynor, R. (1920) Conditioned emotional reactions. *Journal of Experimental Psychology*, 3(1), 1–14.

Waugh, N.C. and Norman, D.A. (1965) Primary memory. *Psychological Review*, 72(2), 89–104.

Webb, W.B. and Agnew, H.W., Jr (1971) Stage 4 sleep: Influence of time course variables. *Science*, 174(4016), 1354–6.

Weinberg and Hunt (1976) The relationship between anxiety, motor performance and electromyography. *Journal of Motor Behaviour*, 8(3), 219–24.

Wells, G.L., Liepe, M.R. and Outroin, T.M. (1979) Guidelines for empirically assessing the fairness of a lineup. *Law and Human Behaviour*, 3(4), 285–93.

Wells, G.L., Lindsay, R.C.L. and Tousignant, J.P. (1980) Effects of expert psychological advice on human performance in judging the validity of eyewitness testimony. *Law and Human Behavior*, 4(4), 275–85.

West, R. and Zhou, X. (2007) Is nicotine replacement therapy for smoking cessation effective in the 'real world'? Findings from a prospective multinational cohort study. *Thorax*, 62(11), 998–1002.

Westcott, M.R. (1982) Quantitative and qualitative aspects of experienced freedom. *Journal of Mind and Behaviour*, 3, 99–126.

Woods, B. (1998) *Applying Psychology to Sport* (Hodder and Stoughton, London).

Worrell, J. and Remer, P. (1992) *Feminist Perspectives in Therapy* (Wiley, Chichester).

Zajonc, R.B. (1965) Social facilitation. *Science*, 149, 269–74.

Zimbardo, P.G. (1973) On the ethics of intervention in human psychological research: With special reference to the Stanford prison experiment. *Cognition*, 2, 243–56.

Index